FEEDING THE BEAST

FEEDING THE BEAST

The White House Versus the Press

KENNETH T. WALSH

Random House
New York

Library of Congress Cataloging-in-Publication Data
Walsh, Kenneth T.
Feeding the beast: the White House versus the press/Kenneth T.
Walsh
p.   cm.
Includes index.
ISBN 0-679-44290-1
1. Presidents—United States. 2. Press and politics—United
States. I. Title
E176.1.W28   1996   071'.3—dc20   95-41555

Printed in the United States of America on acid-free paper
98765432
First Edition
Book design by JoAnne Metsch

For Barclay,
Gloria and Tom,
Jean and Chris

Acknowledgments

T his book was conceived as a combination of history, journalism, and personal memoir, all based on a decade of covering the White House for *U.S. News & World Report.*

I am grateful to Merrill McLoughlin and Mike Ruby, the co-editors of the magazine, and John Walcott, the magazine's national editor, for giving me the opportunity and the time to undertake this project.

I also want to thank my friends and colleagues in the Washington journalism community for their ideas and support. They include Richard Benedetto, Wolf Blitzer, Matt Cooper, Jack Farrell, Gene Gibbons, Brit Hume, Terry Hunt, Brian Lamb, Jessica Lee, Carl Leubsdorf, John Mashek, Ann McFeatters, Larry McQuillan, Andrea Mitchell, Bill Plante, Stewart Powell, Andy Plattner, Lee Rainie, Tim Russert, Helen Thomas, and others who were so generous with their time and suggestions, and those reporters who requested anonymity but answered my survey of White House correspondents.

I also must thank a large group of White House staffers and advisers to Ronald Reagan, George Bush, and Bill Clinton over the last decade, including Roger Ailes, the late Lee Atwater, Don Baer, Gary Bauer, David Beckwith, Paul Begala, Sandy Berger, Mike Berman, Bob Boorstin, Lisa Caputo, Torie Clarke, B. Jay Cooper, David Demarest, David Dreyer, Ken Duberstein, Marlin Fitzwater, Al From, Craig Fuller, Bob Gates, Mark Gearan, David Gergen, Mary Ellen Glynn, Stan Greenberg, Frank Greer, Tom Griscom, Walter Kansteiner, Bill Kristol, Jim Lake, Tony Lake, Evelyn Leiberman, Mike McCurry, Mack McLarty, Elaine Mintzler, Dee Dee Myers, Roy Neel, Leon Panetta, Anna Perez, Jim Pinkerton, John Podesta, Roman Popadiuk, Jody Powell, Tom Ross, Brent Scowcroft, Gene Sperling, George Stephanopoulos, Tara Sunnenshine, Sheila Tate, Dennis Thomas, Barry Toiv, Dick Wirthlin, and Natalie Wozniak. To preserve their confidentiality, I cannot name many of the others, but their help was crucial.

Thanks also to Joe Spieler, my agent, and my editors at Random House for their wise counsel along the way.

I owe an enormous debt to my wife, Barclay, for her rigorous research and loving support in this project. She is simply the best.

KENNETH T. WALSH
Bethesda, Maryland
December 1995

Contents

FEEDING THE BEAST

White House Horrors

Maureen Dowd was shell-shocked. The normally glib and irreverent *New York Times* correspondent could barely manage a coherent sentence as she sat forlornly on a folding metal chair. Her eyes were swollen with fatigue, and she rested her chin awkwardly on the palm of her hand.

Dowd was among sixteen reporters and eight White House staffers who were stranded in Cambridge, England, on President Bill Clinton's June 1994 trip to commemorate the fiftieth anniversary of D day. White House logistics had broken down completely. The helicopter that was to have transported the group a hundred miles to Portsmouth, England, could not fly because of bad weather. Worse, the buses that were supposed to serve as backups were out of service; the drivers had already been on the job for ten hours—the maximum workday, according to their contracts—and they refused to make the long drive to the coast. The increasingly frantic reporters had no idea what kind of news Clinton was making in Portsmouth, where he was scheduled to meet the queen of England that evening. They could be missing one of the biggest stories of the trip.

Dowd begged Jeremy Gaines, a peach-fuzzed White House aide who found himself in charge, to get a message to her bureau chief, R. W. "Johnny" Apple: She doubted that she could file a story before her deadline, because she would miss the meeting with the queen and whatever else was going on in Portsmouth. "Johnny," Dowd moaned, "is gonna be pissed."

It was one of the low points on the most badly organized trip I had ever seen in nearly a decade of covering the presidency. As is customary, the White House had agreed to provide transportation, at media expense, for the small army of reporters, editors, and photographers. No one, however, had made adequate contingency plans for bad weather, even though storms are common in Britain and Normandy every June, as anyone familiar with the D day landing would have known.

In the end, a rump group of half a dozen radio correspondents, fed up with White House incompetency, took a British Rail line to London and connected to a train to Portsmouth. They arrived twelve hours late. Most of us in the "Cambridge 24" waited it out and finally boarded a bus driven by a chap hastily recruited by the local transportation company. We rolled into Portsmouth eleven hours behind schedule, just after a fireworks display to commemorate D day that caused a horrendous traffic jam. At a standstill, our weary group decided to file off the bus, toting our carry-on bags and laptop computers, in an attempt to make our way to the media center where we could file our stories. At various points as we trudged along the seawall in the dark, young Jeremy would flash his White House identification pin to puzzled tourists and ask them how to get to the media center. No one knew, so we kept shuffling toward some lights in the distance.

After two miles, we reached a chain-link fence where a kindly guard took pity on us and let us through the gate. More than twelve hours late, we had finally arrived at the Portsmouth filing center, long after Clinton had gone to bed. Everyone was fuming.

This episode was only a skirmish in the war between the press corps and the White House, but it gave reporters more evidence that either the Clintonites didn't respect journalists enough to treat them decently or that they weren't competent enough to make their own helicopters and buses run on time. Even the big media stars were treated with surprising ineptitude. Army helicopters transporting network television hotshots—Tom Brokaw of NBC, Sam Donaldson of ABC, and Harry Smith of CBS—got lost trying to find the USS *George Washington,* the aircraft carrier on which President Clinton was to spend the night.

Maureen Dowd, for one, got her revenge in a piece for *The New York Times Magazine* on June 19. "With the exception of the First Lady, a tidy traveler, the presidential operation has the smell of a dormitory about it, with everyone crashing for exams," Dowd wrote. "Each White House reflects the personality of its leader, and this President, immune to punctuality and discipline, will always have a Pigpen cloud of chaos around him."

There was a final insult. A few days after the trip, the executive officer of the aircraft carrier billed the White House $562 for sixty-eight towels and sixteen bathrobes that had disappeared from the staterooms being used by forty White House staffers and twenty-three journalists. White House press secretary Dee Dee Myers was quick to point fingers at the reporters, even though we journalists didn't have any bathrobes in our rooms and our towels were of the threadbare white institutional variety that no one would want to take home. It was the White House staffers who had fluffy blue robes and towels bearing the insignia of the USS *George Washington.* The President made matters worse on June 24 when he exploded in anger during an interview with KMOX Radio in St. Louis. Not only did Clinton suggest that "press people" stole those robes and towels, but he went on to deliver a diatribe against the mainstream media, the Christian conservative movement, and right-wing radio pundits such as Rush Limbaugh. All of them, the President complained, were out to get him.

Even Clinton's critics were embarrassed by his foolishness. Sheila Tate, the former press secretary for First Lady Nancy Reagan and later for presidential candidate George Bush, saw the trouble that the President and his staff were causing for themselves. "You can't have that kind of belligerent, in-your-face message all the time," Tate said. "The press corps is writing about you every day. If you treat them like garbage collectors, they will reflect it in their coverage. They're human beings." A senior Clinton adviser, who was appalled at the growing animosity between the two sides, put it more succinctly. "It goes to show you," he said. "When the White House treats the media like shit, the media will treat the White House like shit."

Too often, this is exactly what happens.

THE SAD FACT is that the White House and the news media have entered an era in which neither side trusts or understands the other, and the American public is getting shortchanged in the process. Whoever wins the 1996 presidential election will have to cope with this harmful legacy.

First, some misconceptions about the White House and the Clinton administration need clearing up. There has never been any media conspiracy to destroy Bill and Hillary Rodham Clinton, as many Democrats around the country and people in the Clinton White House have believed. Nor was there a media conspiracy to protect and promote them, as Republicans have charged. The two thousand members of the accredited White House press corps—and certainly the sixty or seventy reporters who are full-time White House regulars—are too competitive, independent, and frazzled by deadline pressures for any of that.

Yet, conspiracy theories aside, there is ample reason for concern about the relationship between the presidency and the news media. Logistics have improved in the Clinton administration since the June 1994 trip, but there is still an unprecedented mutual cynicism between the two institutions.

Many veteran reporters say the worst relationship between a President and a White House press corps occurred during Richard Nixon's administration. Nixon kept an "enemies list" that included a variety of journalists, he had a deep hatred of the Washington media, and he authorized his Vice-President, Spiro Agnew, to repeatedly berate the fourth estate for unfairness and vindictiveness.

But what has happened in recent years is in some ways worse. Today, in late 1995, it is not solely Republicans who have contempt for the media; now the Democrats agree with them, and a significant portion of the public is heading in that direction. Virtually all Washington politicians say that the mainstream media are too eager to expose the character flaws of the nation's leaders and the failures of public policy rather than to inform the country about the positive side of government and the people who run it.

To some extent, as this book will show, the politicians are correct. We in the news media are too cynical and have lost touch in some important ways with our readers, viewers, and listeners. Part of the reason is cultural. At the upper levels of the media establishment in Washington, journalists don't live like ordinary middle-class Americans. They make far more money than average citizens and operate in a world that is dominated by politics and government. Too often Washington journalists—including members of the White House press corps—think that by talking to one another they are really talking to America. Of course they aren't.

One fundamental fact affecting the relationship between the media and the presidency is that both institutions are changing so drastically that we will hardly recognize either of them within a generation. The media are more competitive than ever, and reporters are trying to set themselves apart by adding opinion or "edge"— often in the form of a derisive tone or smart-ass attitude—to their stories or by rushing to judgment about the people and events they cover. Adding to the problem is that today's news cycle never ends. The traditional morning- and afternoon-edition newspaper and evening-news-show deadlines have been supplanted by round-the-clock televised news capability and coverage: Anything that happens around the world can be shown on America's television screens instantaneously, at any time of day or night. This means the mainstream media are constantly groping for ways to move a breaking story forward rather than cover it in depth, and too often the result is sensational, superficial, or negative coverage. Just as important, television has greatly accelerated the velocity of White House decision-making and increased the difficulty of governing.

The presidency has always been what political scientist Thomas Cronin calls "a very elastic institution," able to accommodate great change. But for good or ill, the presidency has been diminished as one of the central institutions in our national life—and, with it, the White House press corps. Yet the news media and the White House are behaving as if the notion of the magisterial executive branch were still in full bloom. Neither the Clinton administration nor the news media has come to terms with what is gradually becoming a marginalized presidency.

For six decades, Americans looked to the White House for their national salvation—first from the Great Depression and then from the evils of fascism during World War II. During the Cold War, the country—indeed much of the world—looked to the President of the United States as the ultimate protector against what Ronald Reagan so dramatically called "the Evil Empire" of Communism. Every President during that period had the fate of the world in his hands, and a misstep could have resulted in a nuclear holocaust. Under such conditions, it was natural that the White House became the most important, most glamorous, and most exciting beat in the world. Over the years, the best reporters in the business made it their career objective to reach 1600 Pennsylvania Avenue. Once these journalists reached the pinnacle, they could count on a steady diet of stories virtually guaranteed to lead the nightly news or page one. When the Cold War ended, however, the presidency deflated like a red, white, and blue balloon.

Another factor in the marginalization of the presidency and the White House press corps was cynicism about Washington and centralized political power. The desire to devolve power to the states and municipalities was an underlying theme in the midterm elections of 1994, in which Bill Clinton and big-government Democrats were repudiated as the Republicans took over Congress for the first time in a generation. It is clear that the days of increasing power in Washington are over, at least for the foreseeable future.

For their part, the Clintonites made some basic errors as they ascended to power—errors that amount to case studies in how not to handle the press. They neglected to forge relationships with the journalists covering them. Instead, they started off by treating the mainstream media with distrust, condescension, and disrespect, and tried—with pathetic results—to go over the heads of the press corps via "new media" techniques such as television and radio talk shows, electronic mail, local cable stations, town meetings, and satellite interviews with local reporters. The Clintonites made little or no effort to understand the folkways of the fourth estate, let alone the needs and personalities of individual journalists. They also started out with no senior official who had any substantial recent journalistic experience. The situation improved with the addition of David Gergen, now departed, as senior counselor to the President, but the culture of the White House during Clinton's first two years was too anti-media to allow for big changes. As of this writing, improvements have been made, partly at the behest of press secretary Mike McCurry, Myers's successor, but it remains to be seen whether the early damage can be repaired as Clinton begins his re-election campaign for 1996.

One of the Clintonites' biggest problems was their failure to "feed the beast," as the media are called by Washington insiders. The White House would have been well advised to listen to Jack DeVore, the longtime press secretary to former senator and Treasury secretary Lloyd Bentsen, who said that a press secretary's job was to manufacture a constant supply of doggie biscuits for the press. Reporters would gleefully lick the hand that fed them, but if you ran out of treats or news, DeVore said, the press would devour your arm and try for more.

Complaints from the press corps were unusually intense and bitter. Not only were logistics a mess, suggesting a broader pattern of incompetence in the administration, but the Clinton White House seemed to disdain journalism as a profession and journalists as individuals. Phone calls were not returned by the press staff. Appointments were made and not kept by nearly everyone from press secretary Myers to communications director George Stephanopoulos. "They've been contemptuous of the way we do things," fumed Gene Gibbons, chief White House correspondent for the Reuters news agency. This view was widely shared in the press corps during President Clinton's first two years. "On the simple, really ordinary stuff," said Bill Plante, who covers the White House for CBS News, "they paid very little attention to filing time and deadline concerns at first, because they thought they didn't have to. 'You don't have time to file? Well, too bad. Make the best of it. We have to leave at six.' Stupid stuff like that, where it's not worth the antagonism that it causes you. . . . They not only didn't get it right, but they often seemed not to care that they didn't get it right."

Day after day, the press corps felt humiliated and frustrated. A report by Freedom Forum Media Studies Center at Columbia University summarized the problem in late 1994 by suggesting that

White House reporters suffered from a painful conflict: "At the pinnacle of their craft, working some of the highest profile and most prestigious jobs in journalism, their day-to-day job is excruciatingly dull and demeaning. And now they are assigned to cover a President who seems to dislike them, would prefer not to have to deal with them and has available to him a variety of alternate means for getting his message out to the public without enduring the media filter."

STAN GREENBERG, A White House pollster, admits that there was never any press strategy at the beginning of the Clinton administration. That was the first mistake. It was always assumed that the effective campaign plan of going around the mainstream national media would simply continue once the candidate was in the White House. Further aggravating this blunder, the Clintonites had no qualms about boasting of their intentions publicly, which seemed to be an insult to mainstream journalists.

A key misstep was naming Stephanopoulos to be Clinton's chief spokesman in the first place. Stephanopoulos was a policy specialist and congressional strategist, not a press expert. He had no real philosophy for dealing with the media other than acting as if the White House press corps were irrelevant and as if he had no obligation to convey information. The atmosphere at Stephanopoulos's press conferences was angry and confrontational. He lorded over journalists his intent to keep secrets from them, and refused to tell them even the smallest details about Clinton's activities at the White House, as if his number-one mission was to show the press corps how inconsequential and powerless it was.

The White House staff, and the Clintons in private, began whining about their press coverage instead of doing something to improve it. Bill Clinton always thought of himself as a political empath, telling Americans, "I feel your pain." Yet the voters increasingly saw him as precisely the reverse, a public figure on whom Americans would project their fears, angers, doubts, and concerns. America didn't know him. He never explained what he stood for, and the media never knew what to believe about him. In large part because he would not reveal himself to the country or the press corps, Clinton became a caricature—an overeating, inde-cisive, womanizing, waffling adolescent-as-commander-in-chief. Many of his current image problems can be traced to those early days in the White House.

MY VANTAGE POINT in observing the interaction between the two sides is unusual. I have been White House correspondent for *U.S. News & World Report* since mid-1986, and in July 1994, I began serving a one-year term as president of the White House Corre-spondents' Association, the organization that represents the several hundred journalists who cover the presidency on a periodic basis and the sixty to seventy correspondents who cover the White House full-time. In that capacity, I have been intimately involved with both the press corps and the administration and have repre-sented the media on many questions of coverage, access, ethics, and logistics.

There is plenty of blame to go around: Bill and Hillary Rodham Clinton took office with enormous bitterness toward journalists, and consequently missed a terrific opportunity to get the Wash-ington press corps in their corner. Many members of the national media were waiting to be courted and willing to give the First Cou-ple a fresh start. But the White House staff was still swept up in a campaign-style us-against-them approach in which every major issue needed a "war room"—literally, a suite in the Old Executive Office Building next door to the White House—to coordinate strategy. This meant that Clinton's senior strategists were always on the lookout for enemies to wage war against, and the media be-came a convenient target.

When Clinton could not meet the expectations he had raised about new, bold leadership, the media and the voters turned on him. As he broke some of his key campaign promises—to grant a mid-dle-class tax cut, to revolutionize government in his first one hun-dred days, to reverse George Bush's foreign policy in Haiti, Cuba, and China—he was derided in the press as a phony. At that point—less than six months into his presidency—Clinton had gen-erated so little goodwill among journalists that he had few allies willing to defend him.

Clinton has also had to deal with a relatively new dynamic in the mainstream media: A President's character has become, for both the press and the public, the single most important measure of his fitness for office. After a string of lies, deceits, and betrayals that included the Vietnam War and the Watergate scandal, reporters were no longer willing to give a President the benefit of the doubt, and many were always ready to assume the worst.

"As many people have observed," says ABC White House correspondent Brit Hume, "it grew out of Vietnam and Watergate, because of two lessons coming out of those two stories. One of them was that the government could and would lie, and that extraordinarily crummy and dishonorable things were engaged in at a higher level than we might once have thought possible. The second thing was that those times when these things were happening may have been difficult times for the country, but they were absolutely wonderful times to be a journalist in Washington, particularly one who had a piece of the story. It helped to promote a certain romance about the news media and its role in American life, and it also enhanced the prestige of the news media generally, and made news media personalities, print and broadcast alike, into much bigger players on the national scene than they had ever previously been. And there was a tendency then by everybody from the generals down to the buck privates in our trade to fight that last war over and over again, and to look for entry points into what might be the great new scandals of the day."

As a group, White House reporters are the most privileged and prosperous journalists covering any beat in the nation and are among the most hard-working, self-disciplined, and careful in the world. Yet they often work under humiliating and exhausting conditions. They are lied to and dismissed as untrustworthy or ignorant. They are cooped up in an area of tiny work spaces and cubicles, penned behind rope lines, or herded about in large groups—conditions that would make most American workers chafe. No wonder these reporters often get cantankerous, rude, and angry.

More troubling are the profound changes affecting the news business as a whole. Recent surveys indicate that journalists are distrusted by increasing numbers of Americans, who consider the national news media isolated, out of touch, and arrogant—and often inaccurate. It has not helped the media that the distinction is so often blurred between real journalists, politicians, commentators, lobbyists, and public-relations specialists, all of whom appear regularly on the same television talk shows. Even the nightly network news shows often feature journalists and beat reporters as "experts" giving their opinions willy-nilly. Increasingly, local and cable news shows imitate the national shows.

As a result of all this, journalism's credibility is in tatters.

2

The Way It Was

From the beginning of the Republic, Presidents have complained about the press. In fact, many of the current frictions between the White House and the media have always existed. Presidents as a rule are secretive and obsessed with ensuring favorable coverage; whenever possible, they prefer to circumvent the press and speak directly to the public. On the other hand, the media tend to be critical, sensationalistic, and fascinated more by a President's personal life and character than by his policies. The tension between the two sides is enduring and inescapable. The wonder is that Presidents, including Bill Clinton, have so rarely learned from the past.

THE PROPAGANDA PRESS

WHEN THE NATION was born, there was no such thing as an impartial newspaper; the concept of objectivity would not emerge until the twentieth century. Presidents had stables of favorable newspapers, often run directly by political allies, and opposition factions had their own journals. George Washington often flew into private fits of rage at the opposition papers, which labeled him treacherous, inefficient, and hypocritical. He was particularly offended by the *National Gazette,* which accused him of behaving like a hereditary monarch and allowing himself to be manipulated by his advisers.

In 1792, Washington protested that some gazettes were filled with "malignancy" that could result in "rendering the Union asunder." He feared that the press would make governing impossible and taint America's reputation abroad. "From the complexion of some of our newspapers," Washington wrote Gouverneur Morris in Paris, "foreigners would be led to believe that inveterate political dissensions existed among us, and that we are on the very verge of disunion; but the fact is otherwise."

After he delivered his farewell address upon leaving the presidency, Washington was excoriated by the *Aurora,* an anti-Federalist newspaper in Philadelphia: "If ever a nation was debauched by a man, the American nation has been debauched by Washington. If ever a nation has suffered from the improper influence of a man, the American nation has suffered from the influence of Washington. If ever a nation was deceived by a man, the American nation has been deceived by Washington. Let his conduct then be an example to future ages. Let it serve to be a warning that no man may be an idol."

Strong words. Yet, in the end, the attacks from the press had little impact on public opinion. Washington was revered until his death in 1799 and remains an American icon today. So much for the awesome power of journalism.

John Adams, a Federalist who succeeded Washington, did not follow the first President's wise policy of avoiding public feuds with the press. Quite the contrary. Adams became one of the worst media-bashers in history. Even though he had been a prolific writer who regularly attacked the British prior to the Revolution, Adams supported the Alien and Sedition acts passed by Congress in 1798, one of the most flagrant attempts to control the press in U.S. history. Those laws authorized fines of up to $5,000 and prison terms of up to five years for anyone found guilty of "printing, writing or speaking in a scandalous or malicious way against the government of the United States, either house of Congress, or the President with the purpose of bringing them into contempt, stirring up sedition or aiding and abetting a foreign nation in hostile designs against the United States."

Today we would regard such restrictions as a clear infringement on the First Amendment, but Adams defended the acts on national-security grounds. He believed that French subversives were agitating around the country and that war with France could be imminent. Adams also supported the acts because opposition newspapers had embarrassed his administration by publishing secret government documents such as correspondence between American diplomats and the French government. But he overreached, as Presidents so often do in dealing with the fourth estate. Public opposition to the Alien and Sedition acts was an important reason for Adams's defeat in the election of 1800.

Thomas Jefferson, his successor, started out as a vigorous defender of freedom of the press. His most famous declaration was his letter to Edward Carrington in January 16, 1787, in which he said if it "were left to me to decide whether we should have a government without newspapers or newspapers without a government, I should not hesitate to prefer the latter." Yet his experiences with the press would embitter him over the years.

One of his worst came when J. T. Callender, editor of the Richmond *Examiner* and a former Jefferson supporter, promulgated the rumor that the new President had fathered a child with Sally Hemmings, one of his slaves. Opponents of Jefferson argued publicly that this alleged extramarital liaison rendered him unfit for the presidency. It was the first time the "character issue" was used against a President, and it would not be the last.

Jefferson tried to dictate his image as much as possible. He maintained control of his own newspaper, the *National Intelligencer*, into which he funneled news and information favorable to his administration. But the opposition press drove him to distraction. By 1807, he wrote, "The man who never looks into a newspaper is better informed than he who reads them, inasmuch as he who knows nothing is nearer the truth than he whose mind is filled with falsehoods and errors." By 1819, Jefferson was even more of a media-basher; "Advertisements," he said, "contain the only truths to be relied on in a newspaper."

Andrew Jackson did much more than criticize; he took management of the news to a crass new level. The crusty old hero of the War of 1812 felt that news management was a matter of political survival because the number of newspapers had grown from 359 in 1810 to 852 in 1828, the year he was elected President. He would sit with his favorite editor, Francis Blair of the Washington *Globe,* and together they would write laudatory stories about the administration and the President. The *Globe* itself was financed in part through profitable government printing contracts ordered by the President. At one time, Jackson had fifty-seven reporters and editors on his payroll, and three journalists, including Blair, were in his "kitchen cabinet." He appointed another editor, Amos Kendall of Kentucky, postmaster general and allowed him to seize anti-slavery publications to limit the spread of abolitionist sentiment. "No President ever had a supporting press more vociferously loyal, or more intolerant," say historians John Tebbel and Sarah Miles Watts. "Even such a respected figure as William Cullen Bryant, who had been editing the New York *Evening Post* with a decorum not seen since its founding in 1801, went so far as to cane a [Henry] Clay supporter as he walked along Broadway. Jackson's influence was so pervasive that, when it reached its peak in the election of 1832, one Republican editor wrote that he had 'no heart to publish election returns.' "

THE ERA OF GROWING MEDIA INDEPENDENCE

JACKSON'S DOMINATION OF the media may have been envied by his successors, but it was short-lived. From the mid-1830s to the 1850s, newspapers began a dramatic rise in influence, circulation, and independence from political parties and the White House. By the time of Abraham Lincoln's election in 1860, the whole dynamic between the presidency and the press had changed. Breaking with custom, Lincoln refused to authorize any newspaper to serve as his mouthpiece, because he felt that the partisan press had become "impotent." But he understood that favorable coverage in the mass-circulation newspapers was more important than ever in shaping public opinion.

Lincoln sought favor with critical newspapers, such as Horace Greeley's *New York Tribune,* by flattering the editors and by giving them exclusive information from time to time. But amid the furies of the Civil War, such techniques rarely worked. In fact, newspapers that opposed Lincoln's war policies, even those in the North, were as vitriolic in attacking the President as any in American history, often in the most personal terms. He was called an ape, a "half-witted usurper," and "head ghoul." He was accused of taking his salary in gold while giving Union soldiers their pay in depreciated currency.

Lincoln occasionally criticized the press, but generally he suffered in silence. The exceptions came when he believed that newspapers were jeopardizing his war aims, and his subsequent actions represented some of the worst examples of presidential excess in history. Not only did he impose strict (if only sporadically effective) censorship on war-related news, but his administration suspended publication of some newspapers and jailed their editors when Lincoln felt their coverage revealed military secrets or damaged Northern morale. "From the press point of view, actions and threats against reporters during this period were more threatening to the freedom of the press than even the actions carried out under the Alien and Sedition Acts," writes media historian Carolyn Smith.

Yet Lincoln showed a rare gift for public relations. In order to enhance public support for the war, he wisely allowed the press to romanticize some of his generals, including the insufferable George McClellan, even when the adulation came at Lincoln's expense. When he issued the Emancipation Proclamation just after the Union victory at Antietam, Lincoln elevated the federal cause to a higher moral plane and forestalled any intervention by Britain on the rebel side. "He had an excellent sense of timing," says historian James E. Pollard. "He had a gift that amounted almost to genius for keeping his finger on the pulse of public opinion. Where patience was called for he knew how to exercise it. Where tact was needed he employed it, and where plain speaking was in order no man was more of a master at it. . . . As with other Chief Executives, the more formal relations with the newspapers had to await a later day. . . . At the same time he dealt on a far wider scale with individual newspapers and newspapermen than any of his predecessors."

THE CULT OF PERSONALITY AND YELLOW JOURNALISM

ULYSSES S. GRANT was an archetype of American history—a "man on horseback" whose image of military heroism was irresistible to the press and the public. His misfortune was that, unlike other military leaders who became President (such as Washington, Jackson, and Dwight Eisenhower), he had no talent for government.

During the 1868 campaign, newspapers described Grant as the Man of the Hour, the national savior who had conquered the Confederacy as commander of the Union armies and who would heal the nation as President. He got an important boost from *Harper's Weekly* cartoonist Thomas Nast, whose pro-Grant illustrations were widely distributed and added to his heroic image.

But when he was President, Grant's incompetence and the corruption he tolerated around him became easy targets for the press. He accepted gifts, including three homes, from wealthy admirers. He allowed speculators Jay Gould and Jim Fisk to attempt to corner the gold market, resulting in life-shattering financial losses for thousands of people and a decline in public confidence in the administration. Grant's failures quickly antagonized Charles A. Dana, editor of the powerful New York *Sun,* who had been a Grant supporter. The *Sun* attacked the President as a tool of "charlatans and adventurers" and for his "frightful blunderings and flounderings."

Despite the opposition of the *Sun* and most other leading newspapers, Grant won reelection in 1872. His opponent, New York *Tribune* editor Horace Greeley, was considered even more out of step with the times, and Grant remained a hero to many voters, who managed to ignore the press criticism. His second term was, if anything, worse than his first, and the New York *World* began calling Grant "Kaiser Ulysses." Articles in Dana's *Sun* and cartoons in *Harper's Weekly* revived the image of him as a drunkard.

All this hostility made it impossible for a real relationship to develop between the President and the press, and Grant had little contact with journalists during his eight years in the White House. This made his press relations worse than they otherwise would have been. "Without substantial or extensive press connections, uncommunicative by nature, surrounded by a secretariat inexperienced in such matters, Grant suffered from a bad press during most of his eight years in the White House," historian Pollard writes. "His own hasty and ill-advised acts often cost him the support or at least the silence of elements of the press which at first were disposed to be favorable or to give him the benefit of the doubt."

GROVER CLEVELAND, LIKE other Presidents before and after him, was almost ruined by the "character issue." His problems in some ways foreshadowed those of Bill Clinton.

In Cleveland's 1884 presidential campaign, the Buffalo *Evening Telegraph* reported that the Democratic political reformer had fathered an illegitimate child in his youth by a widow named Maria Crofts Halpin. Although his parternity was in doubt, Cleveland had supported the boy, Oscar Folsom Halpin, for years. The press pressured Cleveland into admitting both his liaison with Maria Halpin and the possibility that he had fathered young Oscar, prompting his Republican opponents to march in the streets chanting, "Ma! Ma! Where's my pa? Gone to the White House, ha! ha! ha!"

Cleveland also was criticized for not serving in the Civil War. In fact, he had hired a substitute to replace him in the military draft for $300 so he could support his family, a perfectly legal—if ethically questionable—practice at the time. (Some of the sting was taken from the charge, however, when it turned out that his Republican opponent, James G. Blaine, had avoided service in the Civil War, too.)

Lacking any riveting national issues, the campaign was fought largely in the gutter. The newspapers made much of Cleveland's alleged adultery, but they also portrayed Blaine as a corrupt and venal man and contrasted his image with Cleveland's reputation for honesty as a public official. In the end, many newspapers sided with Cleveland, especially those in the East. Blaine also made a key mistake that alienated many Catholic and working-class voters when he refused to immediately repudiate the inflammatory statements of a Protestant clergyman, Samuel Burchard, who introduced the candidate at a New York rally by condemning the Democrats as the party of "Rum, Romanism, and Rebellion." Blaine's campaign also was hurt when Joseph Pulitzer's New York *World*, leading a trend toward coverage of scandal and corruption, published a front-page cartoon by Walt McDougall entitled "Belshazzar's Feast" depicting Blaine cavorting with his millionaire friends at a banquet he attended at Delmonico's restaurant. When the Democrats reproduced the cartoon and circulated it across the depression-wracked country, it devastated Blaine.

Cleveland brought an innovation to the White House by hiring George F. Parker, a newspaperman, as the first presidential press secretary, but he shared most Presidents' disdain toward the press and held reporters at a distance. "I don't think that there ever was a time when newspaper lying was so general and mean as at present and there never was a country under the sun where it flourished as it does in this," Cleveland wrote. "The falsehoods daily spread before the people in our newspapers, while they are proofs of the mental ingenuity of those engaged in newspaper work, are insults to the American love for decency and fair play...."

One episode that contributed to the President's scorn came early during his first term. (Cleveland is the only President to have served two nonconsecutive terms. He lost his bid for reelection in 1888 to Benjamin Harrison, but won a second term in 1892.) The forty-nine-year-old bachelor took as his bride twenty-one-year-old Frances Folsom, the daughter of one of his former law partners. Cleveland was infuriated by the resulting press behavior and coverage. Indeed, no President's privacy had ever been invaded quite so egregiously before. The mass-circulation press sent a platoon of reporters and photographers to camp almost on the doorstep of the President and his bride at their honeymoon cottage in Deer Park, Maryland. The coverage was both sensationalistic and voluminous, and Cleveland never forgave the press. He made an argument that many of his successors would repeat: Every chief executive is entitled to a certain measure of privacy. The media, of course, have never conceded the point.

THE BULLY PULPIT

POLITICAL SCIENTIST MICHAEL Nelson points out that until the late nineteenth century, most Presidents saw their main role as "executing the will of Congress rather than stepping out front with policies and proposals. Washington reporters focused their attention on congressional debates and reported the activities of senators and representatives far more extensively than those of Presidents. In addition, few Presidents did much either to assert themselves as leaders of the people or to woo reporters." But as newspapers became more eager to expand circulation by emphasizing personality coverage and the sensational side of American life, the focus on the President intensified.

Like no President before him, Theodore Roosevelt pioneered the use of the press to promote himself and his causes. He called the presidency his bully pulpit, and he mastered the art of creating news that was favorable to his administration. As John F. Kennedy would do sixty years later, Roosevelt wooed reporters and treated them with respect. He added a press room to the White House complex—in effect, encouraging the formation of a permanent White House press corps—hired a press secretary, as Cleveland had done, and served up a variety of off-the-record comments and salty remarks to delight and amuse journalists and make them feel like insiders. Teddy would invite half a dozen White House correspondents to watch his 1 P.M. shave every afternoon, and would regale them with arguments and anecdotes. He saw other reporters on an individual basis once or twice a week, and would call still others into his office for impromptu briefings on a regular basis.

Reporters, fed more information than they could use, loved the President's attention, even though it was media manipulation of the most intense sort. Few reporters could ever get a word, or a question, in edgewise. Yet their reports were overwhelmingly favorable to the President, even if their newspapers' editorials were sharply critical of his progressive ideas. Roosevelt knew that public opinion was shaped by the news columns, not editorials, and his public-relations strategy was a big success.

Like Ronald Reagan, who would master television, Roosevelt understood the dominant medium of his day, newspapers, and their increasing desire to serve as a watchdog for the public in dealing with business, government, and anyone who possessed power, so he fed the papers with criticisms of the "robber barons" and other ogres of the period. He realized that Sunday was a slow news day, so he made sure to issue press releases on Sunday nights, guaranteeing them good play in the Monday papers. Roosevelt also is credited with inventing the trial balloon—the leaking of possible policy pronouncements to test public and congressional reaction.

But Teddy was extremely harsh in dealing with newspapers whose stories he found offensive. He once banned a reporter from the White House when the journalist wrote an article noting that the Roosevelt children had teased Thanksgiving turkeys on the White House grounds. He sometimes complained to offending reporters' bosses about critical articles and demanded that they be fired. And he ordered criminal libel suits brought against the New York *World* and the Indianapolis *News* when they speculated about a possible scandal relating to the route for the Panama Canal, the President's pet project. The cases were eventually dismissed.

Perhaps Roosevelt's most important contribution to the press-presidency relationship was the degree of his engagement with the press. After his administration, no President could avoid direct and regular contact with the press, because dealing directly with the media had become an essential part of running the government.

WOODROW WILSON WAS the first President to hold formal, regular news conferences, meeting with reporters at least once a week for two and a half years. He gave all accredited reporters an opportunity to ask him whatever they wanted, although journalists were required to submit questions in writing in advance. He felt it was his duty to communicate with the country and, at least in the beginning, thought the media might be a suitable conduit for his views.

Eventually, however, the brittle and arrogant Wilson came to detest the need to communicate through the press. One early incident set the tone. While Wilson was relaxing at his summer home in Sea Girt, New Jersey, as he awaited word on whether he had won the Democratic presidential nomination, a reporter casually asked him how he would deal with the huge volume of mail he was getting. Wilson said the difficulty of replying to the letters made him feel like a frog that had fallen into a well and "every time he jumped up one foot, he fell back two." With considerable whimsy, a New York newspaper headlined the story the next morning as "Wilson Feels Like a Frog." The future President was not amused.

At his first presidential press conference, Wilson was suspicious and resentful, and the newspapermen who attended were angered by his disdain. "They came out of that conference almost cursing, indignant," said a reporter who was friendly to Wilson. A former President of Princeton University, Wilson behaved as if reporters were dullards who were incapable of recognizing the brilliance of his academic style and policies.

After the Germans sank the *Lusitania,* Wilson held no press conferences for a full year, claiming that national security demanded it. Privately, however, he was telling aides that press conferences had become a waste of time because reporters were not interested in policy, only "the trivial and the personal." These remarks could just as easily have been made by Bill Clinton and most other Presidents. Wilson told a friend in 1913 that he did not believe anything he read in the papers because "their lying is shameless and colossal." During his second term, he held only three press conferences.

Wilson's hostility to the press became so intense that he refused to work with reporters to sell his League of Nations to the country, and at least partly as a result, the League was defeated in the Senate. His neglect of and subsequent antagonism toward the press cost him dearly in his public image.

At the end of his presidency, Wilson's health deteriorated dramatically; he suffered at least one incapacitating stroke that left him partially paralyzed. His wife headed a small group of advisers who dealt with the outside world. As usual, the White House's policy of secrecy backfired. Although the President was at times near death, Wilson's aides tried to cover up the nature of his illness, telling the press he was suffering from nervous exhaustion and would be back at work after some rest. Yet week after week, the President did not appear. Rumors spread that he was insane, in a coma, dead; the White House policy of secrecy had led to just the kind of harmful speculation in the press that Wilson wanted to avoid. Four months after Wilson's stroke, his family and friends finally announced the truth. Wilson tried to govern again despite his condition, but his presidency was discredited.

IN 1920, TWO newspaper publishers ran for President for the first time. One was three-term Democratic governor James M. Cox of Ohio, publisher of the Dayton *News* and the Canton *News*. The other was Warren G. Harding, former lieutenant governor and senator from Ohio and publisher of the Marion *Star*. With Wilson's Democratic policies in disrepute, Republican Harding won almost by default.

Since Harding was a publisher, the press expected more positive relations than it had experienced under Wilson, and Harding tried his best to achieve harmony. He resumed Wilson's early custom of holding White House press conferences once or twice a week, and appeared to enjoy the give-and-take. (After committing a gaffe in discussing the diplomatic status of Japan, however, he adopted Wilson's rule that all questions had to be submitted in writing in advance.) The newspapers felt the President trusted them, and gave him generally favorable coverage. He even met with newspaper correspondents during midnight walks around the White House grounds. On one such occasion, he confided that he might not be the most talented President in history, but he wanted to be the best-loved.

Harding turned out to be an innovator in press relations. Not only did he establish permanent and regular press conferences, but he took reporters into his confidence and established clear rules of engagement, including the concept that the President was not to be quoted directly except with specific permission, a version of the modern rule of talking "on background."

Yet too many scandals were developing in the Harding administration, including the infamous Teapot Dome, for the flattering coverage to continue. Harding died suddenly of an apparent stroke on August 2, 1923, in San Francisco while a political furor was gathering around him. "As one shocking disclosure after another was bared in the months following the death of Harding, the press as a whole dealt kindly and considerately with his memory," Pollard writes. "This was not only because he could no longer defend himself but also because newspapermen generally still remembered him with affection if with less respect than formerly. On the whole they were convinced that he was never personally a party to the corruption and the scandals that so quickly honeycombed his administration of barely twenty-nine months."

HERBERT HOOVER STARTED out by holding regularly scheduled press conferences and enjoyed good relations with the press. He even said he wanted reporters to quote him directly in some cases, an unprecedented step toward openness. "Hoover's rise coincided with an immense expansion in the mass media, particularly newspapers and radio," writes historian James David Barber. "Hoover was a genuine hero; his remarkable effectiveness in European relief activities [after World War I] cannot be seriously challenged. . . . He was the subject, not the instigator, of a vast public relations build-up largely due to increasing media demands for news and to the drama and success of his works. But Hoover in the White House 'transmuted all adventure into business.' He detested the office's demands for dramatization." This was something he shared with many other Presidents, including, in recent years, George Bush.

But collegial relations with the media dissolved when the stock market crashed seven months after Hoover took office. He said the Depression was such a massive crisis that reporters should censor themselves and limit what they wrote about it. He even made the ludicrous suggestion that stories about the nation's economic troubles be submitted to the White House for approval in advance. He asked publishers to fire or transfer reporters he found offensive or who broke his rules.

Even under such crisis conditions, Hoover derided the kind of "showmanship" displayed by Theodore Roosevelt, and as a result he seemed callous toward the suffering around him. Perhaps nothing could have saved Hoover from political ignominy as the man who was President when the stock market crashed and the Depression began, but more attention to public relations might have limited the damage to his reputation.

His successor would not make that mistake.

3

World Crisis and
Presidential Dominance

Franklin Delano Roosevelt changed everything. As he broadened executive-branch power to combat the Depression and wage World War II, the White House became the premier assignment in journalism. Reporters were grateful to be close to the center of power, and generally they treated the President with respect and deference.

For his part, FDR adopted Theodore Roosevelt's techniques of getting to know reporters personally and revealing himself as a human being. Even though he believed that White House reporters were often told what to write by their publishers, he got along superbly with the press corps and began an era of unprecedented openness. He accepted direct, off-the-cuff questions at his many press conferences; he and his press aide, Steve Early, seemed to enjoy the company of reporters; and he experienced the longest media honeymoon of any President in history. It seemed natural for reporters to defer to the President in those days of economic crisis and, later, world war.

When he was upset by critical articles, Roosevelt did not hesitate to shame the offenders, sometimes by scornfully reading their stories aloud in front of the entire press corps. At the start of one press conference in the Oval Office, FDR ordered a journalist to stand in a corner wearing a dunce cap—and the reporter did so. By and large, the reporters liked him, even if he sometimes acted as if they lacked the education to write intelligently about his presidency.

It was the newspaper publishers, columnists, and radio commentators whom Roosevelt detested. He was constantly angry at the editorial criticism he endured, and he let it show. Like all Presidents, he preferred his words and ideas to be transmitted directly to the American public, unfiltered by the media, and he quickly found a way to accomplish this through his "Fireside Chats" broadcast on the radio.

Journalist Hedrick Smith says, "FDR used radio vividly to evoke the miseries of the 'little people' and to offer them hope amidst the economic holocaust of the Depression. His Fireside Chats deliberately eschewed silver oratory. They were compassionate conversations with a mass audience, FDR's easy, confident voice an immediate presence to millions of plain people. His folksy anecdotes invited listeners to conjure reality in the theater of the mind. Like [Ronald] Reagan, Franklin Roosevelt was a master at simplifying, at brushing aside the complexity of the nation's problems. He exulted in his own dramatic talents, once telling Orson Welles, 'There are only two great actors in America—you are the other one.' "

FDR ushered in a new era, lasting from the early 1930s to the mid-1960s, when relations between the press and the presidency were characterized by a genteel old-boys'-club atmosphere.

THROUGH THE ADMINISTRATIONS of Harry Truman and Dwight Eisenhower, most journalists and Washington officials saw themselves as part of a governing team, especially on matters of foreign policy, where keeping secrets and preventing embarrassment for the United States were considered patriotic. James Reston, former Washington correspondent for *The New York Times,* recalled visiting secretary of state Cordell Hull every morning during World War II for an off-the-record chat. Sometimes Hull would show Reston a few overnight cables from American ambassadors and ask his reaction.

"The relationship between press and government was relaxed enough in those days that Reston understood it was all off the record, not for direct use, and he would hand back the cables after reading them, without stealing secrets," says Hedrick Smith. "Henry Brandon, for decades the London *Times*'s correspondent in Washington, recalled traveling with a small White House press corps to Key West, where President Truman relaxed. Truman, who normally wore a corset to tuck in his tummy, would hold bare-chested press conferences in swimming trunks. Even though this exposed a pear-shaped profile, Truman did not flinch at informal snapshot taking. On such trips, the U.S. Navy not only provided billets for reporters but arranged deep-sea fishing excursions for their amusement. Brandon, thinking of the angry confrontation between press and government since Vietnam and Watergate and everyone's sensitivity to buying influence with favors, chuckled quietly and asked, 'Can you imagine either side putting up with that kind of arrangement these days?' "

Don Oberdorfer, a retired reporter for *The Washington Post,* recalls: "Today the attitude of the press corps is starkly different from what I found when I arrived in Washington as a young reporter in 1958. Then the vast majority of journalists covering national affairs in the capital were trusting and uncritical of the ways of government. There was a certain coziness, a degree of intimacy and civility, between most of the press corps and the people they covered. Thirty-five years later, many reporters have gone to the other extreme, assuming that nearly every official statement is a lie or half-truth until proven otherwise. There is a pervasive sense of being manipulated by official spokesmen, a sense that is intensified by the widened physical distance between reporters and officials."

In the late 1950s, the press room at the White House was just off the main lobby in the West Wing. Visitors would come and go, and the reporters would wait in the lobby to interview them without the staff "escorts" required today for reporters to move around the White House—and absent the theatrical atmosphere generated by television cameras at every public event. Jim Hagerty, President Eisenhower's press secretary, would summon the media regulars to his office when he had something to say, and the correspondents would stand around his desk taking notes with pad and pencil. It was all very chummy.

If anything, the men's-club atmosphere intensified under John F. Kennedy. As journalist Richard Reeves points out, JFK transferred much of his own aura of glamour and style to the press corps, especially through his news conferences:

"It was Kennedy's show. He was the man in the arena—charming, informed, caring, and witty—gracefully drawing reporters into his cape or even pricking them with his sword on occasion. His dominance in that arena changed the journalism of Washington and, to a large extent, that changed the Presidency and government itself. When Kennedy took office, there had been only a few dozen men and women regularly covering the White House full-time. There were hundreds now as 1962 began. One after another, news organizations shifted their men and women to where the action was. Reporters like Peter Lisagor of the *Chicago Daily News* or Sander Vanocur of NBC News had begun covering the Kennedy administration in the traditional way, checking in daily with the big departments; but within the year, they were covering only Kennedy. The President was gaining more and more control over information going out of the government, information that used to be distributed by Cabinet secretaries, appointees, and civil servants with their own agendas. Reporters and editors, and Republicans, grumbled periodically about 'news management,' but for the gentlemen and ladies of the press it was fair exchange, a lovely affair. And many White House regulars were becoming celebrities themselves."

Reporters felt that JFK liked them and cared about them. For example, his White House hired stenographers and typists to quickly provide transcripts of the President's speeches and press conferences, facilitating the reporters' work. "He was shameless in exploiting his family and children," Reeves says, "using them to take over the slots newspapers usually reserved for photos of local kids and their puppies. It was all within the context of a rule cited by his friend Senator Smathers: 'If they were for Kennedy, Kennedy was for them.' He democratized the business of news as he concentrated it, allowing more reporters and photographers more access than ever before, but directing their attention away from the edges of government to the very center."

All this care and feeding of the media paid big dividends. Not only did reporters bond with Kennedy and create a mythic image of his presidency as a modern-day Camelot, but journalists overlooked his marital infidelities. In those days, the standard for scandal was whether the behavior, be it adultery or drunkenness, affected a President's conduct of his office. Today, of course, this standard has changed dramatically.

THREE DEVELOPMENTS HAVE fundamentally defined the late-twentieth-century relationship between the media and the presidency: the Vietnam War, Watergate, and, in a different way, television.

The falsehoods and deceptions surrounding Vietnam and Watergate persuaded an entire generation of journalists that no President—indeed, no politician—could be trusted. Government seemed a nest of lies and scandals waiting to be exposed, and journalists considered it their duty to root them out.

Since I was a college student in the late 1960s, Vietnam was more than an abstract issue for me: Once my student deferment ran out, I was very likely to end up in combat. Like most of my peers, I initially believed Lyndon B. Johnson and Richard Nixon when they said that the war was being waged for a noble cause and that it was winnable. But the manipulation of body-count figures, the self-delusion in the White House about the supposed lack of determination of the Viet Cong and the North Vietnamese, and the spying on domestic political opponents made it seem that our leaders were not only fallible but, especially in Nixon's case, evil.

Considering their sins, no amount of scorn seemed excessive. I remember the chant of young people demonstrating against Johnson: "Hey, hey, LBJ, how many kids did you kill today?" Later, Nixon inspired an even more intense antipathy, which would come to permeate much of my college generation and the shapers of mass culture. He seemed to represent all that was wrong with the country: cynicism, manipulativeness, venality, phoniness—and lies.

As the Watergate scandal unfolded in the early 1970s, it became clear that Nixon had betrayed the nation's trust and poisoned the White House's relationship with the news media. Nixon's men hated the press. From the start, they considered the Washington and

New York media to be unredeemably liberal, an enemy to be openly attacked, undermined, and isolated. Briefings with White House officials became combative and vitriolic, and the press corps was moved from its clubby little waiting area off the West Lobby to a larger but more sterile briefing room at another location in the West Wing, more distant from the policymakers.

In addition to becoming a generational symbol for the corrupt politician, Nixon represented to journalists the worst form of media-hater. For one thing, he instructed his press secretary, Ron Ziegler, to give the regular White House reporters as little information as possible. Instead, he communicated with the country mainly through speeches, brief White House announcements, and rare press conferences. It was a throwback to the nineteenth century. He once told David Gergen, at the time a young speechwriter in the White House, that he never wanted any statement he made in the media briefing room to consist of more than a hundred words—and he would count them. If they ran over, he would insist that Gergen and the other speechwriters cut them down. His theory was that a hundred words was about the length of a "sound bite" that the television networks would use, and he didn't want anyone editing his words. Nixon also ordered his speechwriters and media strategists to ask themselves what the "lead" on a story would be if the President read the words presented to him. If they couldn't find a lead, or if it seemed likely to be critical of the President, they were to edit the text. It was excellent training in media manipulation.

But Nixon didn't stop there. In a dramatic break with precedent that every one of his successors would copy to some degree, he created an Office of Communications under former newspaper editor Herbert Klein. Klein's operation was designed to carry Nixon's message directly to the non-Washington media, which the President felt would be more favorably disposed to him than the "liberal" press in the nation's capital. While press secretary Ziegler dealt with the media regulars by stonewalling and obfuscating, Klein went on the offensive. His office sent a wide variety of pro-Nixon propaganda—reports, press releases, speeches, and other documents—to news organizations and civic groups around the country, trying to "sell" Richard Nixon to what the President called "the great silent majority." It amounted to a vast multimillion-dollar propaganda machine. (Over the years, the Communications Office or its equivalent has become extremely sophisticated. Today the White House uses its own television equipment to stage regular "satellite interviews" with the President in which he talks directly to local television and radio personalities and circumvents the White House press corps.)

As James Deakin, former White House reporter for *The St. Louis Post-Dispatch,* points out, the Nixon White House was not content to bypass Washington reporters: "They would persist in writing and broadcasting anyway. The Nixon administration also was determined to draw attention to mistakes and distortions in the news whenever they occurred. By itself, this was an entirely legitimate activity. But the Nixon people were not satisfied with merely correcting the record. They set out to convince the American people that the media were distorting the news *deliberately*. It was a conspiracy. Not just the derelictions but *the conspiracy behind them* must be exposed."

In the end, Nixon would encourage his Vice-President, Spiro Agnew, to undertake one of the most vitriolic assaults on the news media in the country's history. In November 1969, Agnew delivered a speech in Des Moines, Iowa, attacking the national media as "nattering nabobs of negativism." He also condemned opponents of the Vietnam War, including media critics, as "an effete corps of impudent snobs." With his "enemies list," which included journalists he could not abide, Nixon brought the adversarial relationship to a new low.

Two young journalists—Bob Woodward and Carl Bernstein, of *The Washington Post*—were instrumental in forcing Nixon's resignation with their dogged pursuit of the Watergate story. This came after journalists in Vietnam had helped change national policy toward Indochina by reporting that the war was being lost, at horrendous cost to the people of Vietnam and the United States.

Watchdog journalism in the style of Woodward and Bernstein became the ultimate power trip for a generation of reporters. We thought we could do good, represent the public, and wield power at the same time. It seemed so easy; but we were wrong.

AFTER SERVING IN the Army (I was never sent to Vietnam after all),
I began my professional career with the Associated Press in Denver
in 1972. From the start, I wanted to keep government honest, just
as the reporters who had covered Vietnam and Watergate had
done. Investigative reporting had become the hottest job in journalism, and I was part of it. Covering the statehouse in Colorado
for the Associated Press and later for *The Denver Post,* I turned over
rocks at every level of state government, looking into the governor's
Contingency Fund and how it was being used for wining and din-
ing guests at his official mansion, probing the Colorado Athletic
Commission and its repeated violation of the Colorado open-meet-
ings law, exposing lies and deceptions in political campaigns. It was
good journalism and great fun. Other young reporters were practic-
ing the same type of investigative, public-spirited journalism all over
the country. We felt that to do our jobs properly as watchdogs for
the public, we had to be adversaries of all government officials and
never give them the benefit of the doubt.

We overdid it. Cynicism got worse and worse. Positive stories became less and less credible inside the newsrooms of America. The
media watchdog was becoming an attack dog. It got so bad that
just before the 1976 election, Jimmy Carter told *Playboy* magazine:
"The national news media have absolutely no interest in issues at
all. . . . There's nobody in the back of this plane [referring to the
press seats] who would ask an issue question unless he thought he
could trick me into some crazy statement."

After Carter was elected, his relationship with the news media
deteriorated further. Jody Powell, Carter's press secretary at the
White House, says, "I feel to this day that one of Carter's problems
was that there were at least a few folks in journalism who felt like
they had to prove they could be as tough on Jimmy Carter as they
were on Richard Nixon, without regard to whether he ever did anything that bad. But it still has resulted in a downward spiral toward
an ungovernable country, a society where leadership is virtually impossible. . . ."

Powell and Carter make valid points, but the bitterness in the White
House–media relationship was masked by the Carter administra-

tion's incompetence and bad luck. Inflation struck. There were massive oil shortages from the Middle East. America's standing around the world seemed in decline. U.S. hostages were taken in Iran and the President seemed powerless to do anything about it.

By the time Carter left office, Americans had concluded that he was a well-meaning but inept leader and that his presidency had been a failure. In such a climate, the growing cynicism of the news media was far down on everyone's list of concerns. Yet the problem remained very real.

AS JOURNALISTS' CYNICISM deepened, a parallel trend guaranteed that the harsh light of news coverage would focus not only on a President's public-policy decisions but on his personality and, by association, his character. This trend grew with the increasing dominance of television as the most important medium of mass communication in the country, leading it to become the main source of news for most Americans.

The presidency was made-to-order for television. "Television, with its need for a simple way to organize its coverage of the national government, settled on the President and the presidency as its vehicle for doing so," says ABC White House correspondent Brit Hume. ". . . Here you have a protagonist and you have the continuing daily drama of his effort to get across the high wire to the safety of reelection, or the failure that may come if he falls off. And each day we get to make a little progress report on how he did. For the longest time it was a pretty good way to organize your coverage, because it had a legitimacy. The President indubitably was the central actor in the drama. If there was an agenda moving or failing to move through Congress, invariably it was the President's agenda."

Television encouraged Americans to focus more on a President as a person than on anything else in evaluating his suitability for office. "Radio, and then television, drew our attention away from issues and caused us to focus on the more personal qualities of the politician, his ability to speak, and his style of presentation," says political consultant Tony Schwartz. "Today, in judging [politicians], voters do not look for political labels. They look for what they consider to be good character: qualities such as conviction, compassion, steadiness, the willingness to work hard."

John Kennedy came to office before television was the dominant news medium, but he recognized its potential from the start. On December 16, 1962, he took questions from three correspondents from ABC, CBS, and NBC, for ninety-five minutes. The conversation, edited down to an hour, was shown on all three networks the next night and won rave reviews from around the country. Kennedy told a friend in the print media: "Well, I always said that when we don't have to go through you bastards, we can really get our story over to the American people." Presidents have been saying the same thing, in one way or another, ever since.

Television can be a magical tool in the hands of a President who knows how to use it—such as a Kennedy or a Reagan or, occasionally, a Bill Clinton. It enables a leader to show empathy, concern, passion, anger—the widest range of emotion—and to boost his popularity by twenty percentage points in one night.

But television also can damage a President in a single moment—as Gerald Ford learned after his debate with Jimmy Carter in 1976 when his bungled comments about Eastern Europe, magnified on television, made it appear that he didn't understand that Communists dominated the region. On balance, television has crippled the presidency as an institution. The constant scrutiny and continual demand for news generated by television have accelerated the velocity of presidential decision-making. If a President fails to feed the beast, he can look indecisive, evasive, and weak.

THE WASHINGTON POST's David Broder says in summary:

"From 1960, when Eisenhower and Kennedy both had a basically comfortable relationship with reporters, to 1980, at the end of Carter's tenure, the course of White House-press relations had gone downhill. And so had the course of the Presidency. Kennedy was assassinated. Johnson was driven into political exile by Vietnam, Nixon was forced to resign under threat of impeachment, Ford and then Carter were defeated running as incumbents.

"All of these Presidents had attempted to go over the heads of the White House reporters and to establish a direct channel of communication with the voters—via television or personal cam-paigning—that would provide a stable base from which to govern. Each devoted considerable energy and staff effort to managing the day-to-day coverage of his Presidency by the White House corre-spondents—who, of course, both resisted and protested, even while they acknowledged that they were being used.

"It was not good politics or good government or good journal-ism, and it was a pattern that Ronald Reagan and his advisers were determined to change. Change it they did, but . . . not necessarily for the better."

4

Secrets of
the Great Communicator

From the start, Ronald Reagan and his senior staff made it one of their top priorities to manipulate the news media, and their overwhelming emphasis was on television. It amounted to stage-managing an entire presidency. Reagan met periodically with small groups of reporters and columnists for off-the-record chats, and proved to be a genial companion. But he rarely delivered any news, either at such private sessions or in his on-the-record interviews. I found him almost impenetrable. He could tell funny stories with great charm and could make strangers feel at home in an instant, but when asked a question of substance, he would deliver familiar lines from his speeches or remarks that his aides had provided in advance.

As an actor, Reagan had been trained to operate from a script. He preferred to make news under carefully controlled circumstances, mostly in speeches or brief announcements. Even at news conferences, his staff would anticipate virtually all the questions (reporters tend to be very predictable, focusing on whatever is in that day's news), and the President would rehearse his answers carefully. It was the perfect style for television.

No one was more important in helping Reagan exploit the medium than Michael Deaver, a public-relations man from California who was Reagan's first-term media strategist. "I have always believed that impressions are more important than specific acts or issues, especially with the President," Deaver told me over lunch in the fall of 1994. "Ronald Reagan used to tell me, 'The camera doesn't lie.'

"I believe TV is a great boon to us in judging our leaders," Deaver argued. "It lets us see all the dimensions that, in the past, people could only see in person: the body language, the dilation of the eye, the way they perspire. We see them when they are tired, worried, under great crises. If television focuses on somebody every day, it shows all the dimensions." Further, Deaver said, unlike Bill Clinton, President Reagan "was comfortable with himself . . . You felt his feet were on the ground and he knew where he was going."

Bill Plante, who covered the Reagan presidency for CBS, agrees. "Reagan did well because he was comfortable in his own skin to begin with, and utterly certain that what he was saying was right. The only time he was ever uncomfortable was when he was pinned down at a news conference, which wasn't often, on specifics; then he'd say, 'Well, we'll have to have the boys get back to you on that.' As long as he could generalize, he was fine." Just as important, Reagan's sunny disposition came through clearly on TV and gave him a "Teflon" quality so that criticism of his administration didn't stick to him. "Reagan, I believe, was a genuinely nice man, not inclined as are many politicians to be mean or vindictive, and it showed," Plante says. ". . . If there are conflicts, or if you're dodging and weaving, it shows. Or if you're busy trying to weigh the moral relativity of everything, as Clinton does, it shows. Or if you're distracted and think disconnectedly as George Bush did, it shows."

Reagan instinctively understood that even though Americans might disagree with a President's policies, they would respect him if he maintained a sense of dignity and strength during a crisis. After he was shot in 1981, he was barely conscious when he reached the hospital with a bullet in his chest. But when he got out of the car, he insisted on hitching up his pants and buttoning his suit jacket, only to collapse when he shuffled through the door. He didn't want to show any weakness, Deaver says: "He believed it was part of the role of the President of the United States."

Reagan recognized that media scrutiny was part of the life of any President, and he grudgingly conceded that the country was entitled to know virtually everything about its leader, no matter how embarrassing the information might be. Still, disclosure didn't come naturally. Ronald and Nancy Reagan were always unhappy when the news media covered the President's physical ailments in clinical detail. One day a worried Deaver rushed into the Oval Office after hearing that the President wanted to slip out to Bethesda Naval Medical Center, without notifying the press, to let doctors check him for colon and prostate cancer. It was a matter of manhood with Reagan. He didn't want people to know he was having such intimate physical problems.

"Mr. President," Deaver said. "You know you can't do that. Sure, we could slip you into the back of a car with a hat and a raincoat on and get you out of the White House, but in fifteen minutes, word would get out, the stock market would drop, and the Soviets would go on alert" as the world speculated that the President was dying.

Reagan threw his pencil down on his big mahogany desk and exploded: "You want me to go into the press room, drop my pants, and show 'em my pecker!"

Deaver smiled and said this wasn't what he had in mind at all, and Reagan's anger dissipated abruptly. Recognizing that he was now public property, including his most private parts, the President let Deaver notify the press.

Journalist David Broder says Reagan's press policies were based on three principles: limit direct access to the President; make news management a major priority for trusted White House aides and cabinet secretaries; and shut down the flow of information from lower levels of the administration. The goal was to give a handful of media managers total control of the message coming out of the White House each day.

This was done in many ways. Reagan developed a technique of walking to and from his helicopter when its engines were roaring, and letting reporters shout their questions like poorly trained seals. The journalists, of course, looked like hectoring, obnoxious fools, which was fine by the White House. But there was a more important purpose in the gambit. Reagan could pretend not to hear the questions he didn't like but could answer those for which his aides had given him clever one-liners.

During the height of the Iran-contra scandal (involving allegations that Reagan aides had traded arms for hostages and used the profits to help the anti-Communist contra rebels in Nicaragua), a bizarre media scene occurred with great regularity. Reagan would stride across the South Lawn of the White House toward his helicopter, and reporters would be reduced to shouting above the din: "What about Iran-contra?" Reagan would cup his hand to his ear and shrug his shoulders to indicate that he couldn't understand. Then he would snap off a sharp salute to his marine guard, bound up the stairs of the chopper, and vanish. From the White House viewpoint, it was perfect media management. The President didn't appear to be avoiding the questions intentionally, and at the same time he looked accessible and eminently agreeable; it was just those damned helicopter engines that kept him from talking to the media.

When he did take questions from reporters or discuss issues off the cuff, Reagan made so many mistakes that his aides and Nancy Reagan intensified their efforts to script him. David Broder notes that at a June 1986 news conference, he incorrectly summarized a Supreme Court abortion decision, misstated a Warsaw Pact proposal to reduce nuclear arms in Central Europe, and misstated his position on the SALT II nuclear-arms treaty. It was not a heartening performance to Americans who thought their President should be on top of issues. But most people didn't care as long as the economy was doing well and Reagan's staff seemed capable of making up for his disengagement.

For the first time, news management was not merely a matter of periodic discussion but an absolute cornerstone of the White House's everyday operations. Richard Wirthlin, Reagan's pollster and an architect of his political strategy, told me that from the start, the Reaganites developed three principles for media handling:

"The Reagan presidency always recognized the media as our most important single constituency.

"The press was different in outlook and philosophy from Reagan, his advisers, and their supporters.

"Journalists really did seek balance and would work with the White House to develop stories and provide some sense of fairness to the administration."

"We'd spend a lot of time," Wirthlin says, "talking about the media, about how to get stories, about the TV anchors and their constituencies."

That is an understatement. A primary purpose of the daily 8:15 A.M. senior staff meetings was to design events, activities, and presidential statements that would dominate that night's network news programs and, secondarily, the next morning's newspaper headlines. At 9:15, Reagan spokesman Larry Speakes would tell White House reporters what was on the public agenda and provide print reporters with a few choice quotes or one-liners on the theme of the day, to encourage them to do the story the White House wanted. At noon, Speakes would hold another briefing for reporters to reinforce the message and, most of the time, to dodge questions on other topics. By late afternoon, after Reagan had conducted his public events, David Gergen and other White House aides would phone the three broadcast networks to offer help in putting their stories together, and to find out what they were up to. If the stories sounded negative, they would provide information to change the slant or else argue about the pieces in order to alter their direction.

For Deaver, Reagan's chief media adviser, network television became the be-all and end-all in the White House effort to shape public opinion. "If you only get thirty or forty seconds to get your message across on the evening news," Deaver says, "then it's important that you restate that message in as many ways as you can."

In the White House, Deaver argued that the visual was as critical as whatever the President might be saying, so he made sure that Reagan was always placed in interesting, patriotic, or beautiful settings to provide the networks with images they couldn't resist putting on the air.

In dealing with White House reporters, the Reagan staff also emphasized manipulation, but much of it was conducted in a benign way under the guise of adding to the flow of information to the country. Senior Reaganites were remarkably accessible to the major national news media. Whatever anti-media feelings they harbored—and many Reaganites, like Nixon's men before them, believed that the national media were hopelessly liberal—they kept their lines of communication open and treated reporters with respect.

High-ranking officials, including Deaver, chief of staff James Baker, deputy chief of staff Richard Darman, budget director David Stockman, media strategist Gergen, senior adviser Ed Meese, and key officials with the National Security Council met with reporters regularly and were eager to shape news coverage. Even when a reporter criticized the President, the contacts generally continued, and the White House was able to at least get its side of the story into print and on the air.

These staffers regularly used the media to snipe at one another—often with the insistence on being quoted anonymously. But what was most important was that they fleshed out Ronald Reagan's views and put a human face on the Great Communicator's decisions. Over time, Americans believed that they knew their President well.

The Reaganites also understood and catered to the needs of the media, especially television reporters. "The Reagan people knew our deadlines and they played to the cameras," says Andrea Mitchell, who covered Reagan for NBC. When the President was scheduled to give a major speech or make an important announcement, Baker, Gergen, Deaver, and other aides would thoroughly brief the network correspondents early in the day so that by 3 or 4 P.M., each of the big three—ABC, CBS, and NBC—knew exactly what the story would be and could plan their newscasts accordingly.

Mitchell says that when Reagan was to give a speech outside Washington, an advance text was almost always available before 9 A.M. when reporters arrived at Andrews Air Force Base to board the press plane. When the President was scheduled to give a speech at Eureka College unveiling his strategic-arms proposals to limit nuclear weapons, senior White House officials made sure to brief reporters in advance. The network correspondents were then able to call their editors and explain what the sound bite or theme of the day would be. In turn, the networks immediately decided to include the Reagan piece in their prime-time newscasts, so graphics and visuals were prepared and reactions were solicited. The President always stuck to the script, reading his lines exactly as written. Everyone was happy: The networks could plan their broadcasts, and the White House could get its message across. The public was also well served in terms of clarity. "What came out was a much more coherent proposal," Mitchell recalls. No other presidency understood the networks so well or manipulated them so effectively.

Tim Russert, host of NBC's *Meet the Press,* says Reagan's magic derived from his single-mindedness. "Reagan will be remembered for his ideas," Russert says. "He had one central idea—that he was a conservative, and he was going to go to Washington to change things and reduce the size of government. Now, that never happened, but what he did do was to unleash a robust economy, one result of which is these huge deficits, and a lot of people took advantage of it. But his single idea was communicated and projected brilliantly, and every day he reinforced it. He was very pragmatic, but what the viewers saw was someone in charge and in control, principled, steadfast."

Russert argues that Reagan effectively exercised power because he acted so "presidential": "He was a national m.c. in many ways. He was able to move us in and out of funerals and mourning and celebrations and ethos and pathos. He had an uncanny ability to touch us, reach us, move us, inspire us, and motivate us as a nation. I don't think you can teach these things, and you can't blame it on television's being manipulated. He had an ability to do it."

BY THE TIME I arrived on the White House beat in the spring of 1986, Reagan's heyday was over. That summer the Iran-contra scandal began building. Moreover, the imperious Donald Regan, Reagan's first-term Treasury secretary, who had taken over as White House chief of staff after Reagan won reelection in 1984, was alienating more and more people in Washington.

The White House quickly came under siege. The President was just as rigidly controlled and scripted as ever, but the senior staff was no longer as accessible, stopping the flow of explanations about what the White House was up to. Donald Regan loved to say that nothing happened at the White House without his knowledge, but he refused to share much of it with others, especially with the media, which, he felt, only spelled trouble. Instead of trying to learn about journalists, he isolated himself from them, causing hard feelings and adding to the impression that he was a rich, brittle Wall Street broker ill-suited to running the government.

Internally, Regan limited policy discussions to a handful of aides, so few people in the White House had any information to impart. He loved to build on the impression that he was indispensable, and popped up frequently at Reagan's side so he could be photographed at the center of power. At a summit meeting between Reagan and Mikhail Gorbachev, he insinuated himself into the key photo opportunity and was photographed standing between the seated superpower leaders as if it was the White House chief of staff, not the two heads of state, who was the most important individual at the event. Many of President Reagan's other aides, a number of prominent Republicans around Washington and, most important, Nancy Reagan, were aghast. Regan reinforced their impression that he was hurting the septuagenarian President by making it appear that Ronald Reagan could do nothing without his handlers.

Inside the press corps, the competition for sources and information became nasty as the amount of news diminished. The sixty to seventy "regulars" divided more than ever into rival groups or "tongs," banding together to lure sources into interviews, or to lunches and dinners that no reporter could arrange individually.

For most of the press corps, Reagan's trips to his ranch north of Santa Barbara became bizarre quasi-vacations. Reporters rarely saw the President on such occasions. He went to Rancho del Cielo and stayed there without the pretense of doing much work. Meanwhile, the reporters were ensconced miles away in Santa Barbara, either lolling poolside during down time or making frenzied efforts to get someone—anyone—to provide a morsel of news.

On one of my first trips to Santa Barbara, I wandered alone one evening on the noisy streets downtown as cars cruised by and loud music blared from one nightspot after another. No one in the press corps seemed particularly friendly, so I was on my own, looking for a place to have dinner. Suddenly I heard someone call my name. It was David Beckwith, then a White House correspondent for *Time* and one of my competitors. (Two years later, Beckwith would become Vice-President Dan Quayle's press secretary, a job that tested his communication skills and patience to the limit.) He was in a car with NBC White House correspondent Andrea Mitchell, and they asked me to join them for a meal. I gratefully accepted, and we shared a pleasant evening.

But that kind of collegiality was rare in the Reagan press corps, at least during those last two years. More common was a spirit of exclusion laced with paranoia, and this was always at its worst in Santa Barbara. All the reporters desperately feared getting beaten on a story while spending hundreds of dollars every day for posh hotels and meals at their employers' expense. Larry Speakes's briefings became useless. By the time he was about to leave the government for a job with Merrill Lynch in February 1987, he rarely briefed the press corps at all in Santa Barbara; instead, he would issue terse written statements reporting that the President was spending his time chopping wood, clearing brush, and riding horses—hardly earth-shattering developments.

Dennis Thomas, Regan's deputy, who traveled on virtually all the Santa Barbara trips, dutifully met with reporters almost daily, often for dinner. But his boss would not allow him to divulge much information, so his contacts with reporters became an exercise in frustration. Because so little news was generated at these media-financed dinners, members of the press corps nicknamed Thomas "America's Guest."

WHEN, AFTER TWO years covering Congress for *U.S. News & World Report,* I landed the job as the magazine's White House correspondent, I was elated. I felt that at the age of thirty-nine, I was at the height of my talents and energies, and was eager to immerse myself in the exciting, glamorous world of 1600 Pennsylvania Avenue.

Yet when I first walked onto the White House grounds to begin my new job one warm spring morning in 1986, the scene could hardly have been more different than I had imagined.

Jim Hildreth, the *U.S. News* White House correspondent whom

I was replacing, got the necessary clearances for me to go through the entrance at the Northwest Gate. After we walked through the metal detectors in the guards' booth, Hildreth told me that covering the White House was a relatively simple matter. "Who's up? Who's down? Who's in? Who's out?" he said. This seemed to me a myopic view of how to cover the most powerful collection of people in the world, but it turned out to be a common one in the press corps.

The initial impression of a first-time visitor to the press area is how cramped and grungy the place is. The door to the press quarters opens directly into the media briefing room, which consists of a podium and forty-eight coffee-splattered blue fold-up chairs, each bearing a nameplate for a specific news organization. Nothing much was going on that first day, and various photographers and technicians were sprawled in the seats, reading newspapers and chatting. Some were asleep. This scene, I learned, is typical during the many idle hours that those covering the White House are forced to spend waiting for the President and his staff to do or say something newsworthy. So much for instant excitement.

Hildreth introduced me around. First we went down to the basement, where *U.S. News* had a work space along with several other news organizations. My neighbor turned out to be Al Sullivan, correspondent for the U.S. Information Agency. Could this be the same Al Sullivan with whom I'd worked twenty-two years earlier when I was a copyboy at *The Asbury Park Press* in New Jersey the summer I graduated from high school? Al allowed as how, yes, he was the same guy who had covered the state government in Trenton for the *Press* back then.

Even more surprising was that the reporter assigned to the desk directly behind me was Owen Ullmann, then of Knight-Ridder Newspapers, with whom I had attended Rutgers University in the 1960s. I was editor-in-chief of *The Rutgers Daily Targum,* the campus newspaper, in 1967–68, and Owen followed me in the job in 1968–69. Further, Owen was in the assigned seat next to mine in the briefing room, and directly in front of us was Jim Gerstenzang of the *Los Angeles Times,* who had been Ullmann's managing editor on the *Targum* all those years ago.

That Sullivan, Ullmann, Gerstenzang, and I ended up covering the White House together drove home for me a central dictum of life in Washington: Try never to make permanent enemies, because you never know when you'll be dealing with someone again. The fact is that the men and women who work in Washington, whether in journalism or politics, usually do so after a strenuous climb up through a particular meritocracy. After they arrive, few leave voluntarily, so a journalist might show up as your colleague one day and your competitor or source the next. Likewise, a public official or a consultant could be in power one moment but lose his or her influence the next, depending on the results of the last election— only to turn up in another incarnation later.

Washington's incestuous culture requires that in order to thrive you need to cultivate relationships and treat people with decency. This is a lesson that seems fundamental but is often forgotten—as some of the more arrogant officials I've dealt with, ranging from Donald Regan to several influential members of Bill Clinton's team, ultimately came to realize.

IN THOSE FIRST days on the White House beat, Jim Hildreth introduced me to a few senior administration officials and various middle-level members of the White House press staff. But the biggest revelation was the extent to which the White House press corps had deteriorated into factions that were constantly being manipulated by Larry Speakes.

A stocky, sandy-haired former aide to conservative Mississippi senator James Eastland, Speakes had been a deputy to James Brady, Reagan's original presidential press secretary. After Brady was permanently disabled in the assassination attempt on Reagan in 1981, Speakes stepped into the chief spokesman's job (though Brady retained the title of chief spokesman for several years as a courtesy). The power went to Speakes's head. He placed a sign on his desk: "You don't tell us how to stage the news, and we don't tell you how to cover it."

Actually, Speakes and his staff tried hard to do both. His twice-daily briefings for the media became maddening exercises in frustration for reporters. With sarcasm and a smirk, he loved to antagonize journalists and mock their questions as inane or ill-informed. The press often would rise to the bait and argue with him, which only diverted attention from the questions that Speakes did not want to answer. Frustrated again and again, reporters turned rude and petty, asking the same questions over and over in different forms in an effort to trick Speakes or badger him into making a mistake. It rarely happened. I came to feel sorry for the reporters who had to rely on those briefings for their stories, because the sessions were so ludicrously uninformative.

The worst of the briefings had occurred before I arrived on the beat. Back in Reagan's first term, before the economic recovery of the mid-1980s, the atmosphere was particularly poisonous. At one briefing in August 1982, a reporter called Reagan's comments about tax legislation "dribble" and Speakes called the briefing "foolish." When he tried to explain the benefits of a Reagan tax bill, he was interrupted by Texas reporter Sarah McClendon. "Choke it down, Sarah," Speakes said. "I've got a little bit more." Another reporter interjected, "She keeps bubbling up back there." But McClendon persisted in asking for documentation of the economic recovery that Reagan had promised. Speakes dismissed her questions as badgering and, after sparring with other reporters, turned to Lester Kinsolving of the Globe syndicate, who asked about a published report that the government was hiring people regardless of their sexual preference. "Does President Reagan believe that the United States should be represented by all the many kinds of announced sexual preferences or not?" Kinsolving asked.

Speakes: "I haven't heard him advocate a quota system of sexual preferences for government employees."

Kinsolving: "I understand that. Does he believe that you should hire all kinds of sexual preferences? I mean, there is a wide variety."

Another reporter: "How many kinds are there, Lester?"

Kinsolving: "Well, there is necrophilia, bestiality, sodomy . . . I just want to know, where does the President stand on this?"

Speakes: "Is there a serious question anywhere here?"

At another briefing, in February 1983, then-NBC reporter Chris Wallace accused Speakes of lying about whether the White House was conducting an internal investigation of possible improper government contacts with the Environmental Protection Agency.

When Wallace said that Speakes's answers were "misleading," the press secretary replied, "Screw you, then."

Wallace: "I consider it a lie, frankly."

Speakes took offense: "Wait a minute. That's the most serious charge that you can level at me. It was not a lie. It was the word 'investigation' that was used. [White House counsel Fred] Fielding is not doing an investigation. He is not doing anything but receiving reports. Do you want to call that a lie?"

After more sparring, this exchange occurred:

SPEAKES: "You call that a lie?"
WALLACE: "You knew that this had been asked?"
SPEAKES: "Sure."
WALLACE: "Yes, I do."
SPEAKES: "Okay, that's it, then. Good enough."

At the conclusion of the briefing, Wallace walked up to Speakes. "I'm not having anything to do with you, Chris," the White House spokesman said with a glare. "You're out of business as far as I'm concerned."

DURING REAGAN'S FIRST term, Speakes had exercised his power by rearranging the seats in the briefing room according to his own arbitrary standards. His rationale was simple: He assigned the best seats, the ones up front where a reporter had a high chance of being called upon, to those who were most favorable to Ronald Reagan or to the news organizations that were most important in his pecking order. The front row was anchored by the three broadcast networks—ABC, CBS, and NBC—along with the three wire services, Associated Press, Reuters, and United Press International. They were the organizations most important to Speakes's efforts to put a positive spin on the news each day. The second row included *The Washington Post* and *The Wall Street Journal,* two undeniably influential newspapers, but also contained a seat for Agence France Presse because Speakes liked the AFP correspondent at the time. The third row included *The New York Times,* the *Los Angeles Times,* and, because Speakes took a liking to its reporter, Unistar Radio.

My seat in the fourth row placed *U.S. News* squarely in the middle of the pecking order.

Yet I quickly learned that the most valuable information came not from the goings-on in the briefing room but from a series of "background" interviews provided privately to White House reporters by senior and middle-level officials. It was at these sessions that we could ask the questions that Speakes had refused to answer or dodged at his public briefings. For their part, the officials were often more candid while "on background," because their names were not attached to the information; by prior arrangement, they were not to be named. Also, many officials are more comfortable talking one-on-one to a reporter they trust rather than saying something to a group of journalists, some of whom might mangle or distort it.

By 1986 Speakes seemed more willing than ever to take retribution against reporters whom he didn't like or who had written too many negative stories about the White House or himself. One of his techniques was to put an offending reporter "out of business," as he had done with Chris Wallace. This meant that Speakes would not deal with the reporter again, a serious punishment for journalists who were dependent on the press secretary for news. To their credit, few other White House officials ever followed Speakes's lead and isolated a reporter.

I learned all this from personal experience. In October 1986, Reagan traveled to Reykjavík, Iceland, for a summit with Soviet leader Mikhail Gorbachev. At that time, neither Reagan nor anyone else could be sure that Gorbachev was a real reformer, and there was considerable Cold War tension in the air. After all, Reagan had said he regarded the USSR as an "Evil Empire" seeking to dominate the world. But in Reykjavík, Reagan and Gorbachev met privately for several hours and, to everyone's astonishment, came close to agreeing to cut their strategic nuclear arsenals in half.

The deal fell apart at the last minute, partly because Reagan insisted that the United States would still pursue the Strategic Defense Initiative, the futuristic anti-missile system dubbed Star Wars. Reagan's critics were shocked that such a historic treaty could have come so close to fruition on the spur of the moment, especially when the American President seemed to have little understanding of the complexities he was dealing with. Reagan had gone on instinct—

in retrospect, not bad instinct—but his critics immediately began questioning whether he had nearly given away the store.

Speakes immediately recognized that he was facing a public-relations disaster. The night before leaving Reykjavík and on Air Force One en route home to Washington, he and his aides Dan Howard and Roman Popadiuk hatched an elaborate media strategy to put cabinet members, national security advisers, and other U.S. officials on TV and in print—through interviews, speeches, and op-ed essays—to portray the near-agreement as a brilliant attempt to secure a more peaceful world. I decided to write about the episode for *U.S. News,* and scheduled an interview with the press secretary a few days after he returned from Reykjavík.

Speakes began by bragging about how well he understood the White House press corps and how easy it was to manipulate reporters. "It's like starlings on a wire," he said cockily. "When one flies, they all fly." I asked him if I could use a few of his quotes on the record. He laughed, waved his hand, and said, "Use it all on the record." My story (written with colleague Dennis Mullin), however, raised doubts whether Speakes's strategy would succeed in the end. "Sometimes," I wrote in my concluding paragraph, "the starlings just don't fly."

Speakes never gave me a private interview again. In fact, he insisted on playing a petty little game to humiliate me. He allowed his assistant to schedule an appointment with me each week, generally on Thursday afternoon, a busy day for any newsmagazine. I would dutifully show up at his office and wait at his door. And wait. And wait. Finally, his assistant would tell me that Mr. Speakes had called and said he could not see me. This went on for a few weeks until I finally got the message. I asked one of Speakes's aides, Pete Roussel, what was going on, and it was he who told me that I was "out of business."

Fortunately for me, Speakes resigned a few months later to work for Merrill Lynch in New York. But he was forced to leave his Merrill Lynch job after the publication of his White House memoirs, in which he admitted making up quotes for Reagan. (It also didn't help his reputation that his book savaged many people in the press corps.)

As Speakes's replacement, Reagan settled on Vice-President George Bush's press secretary, Marlin Fitzwater, who had been a deputy to Speakes a few years earlier. I remember walking with Marlin along a riverbank in Davenport, Iowa, not long before his promotion. Bush was taking some private time and Fitzwater decided to take a stroll in the bright, warm sunshine to relax. He invited me, one of the few reporters on the road with Bush that day, to come along.

As Fitzwater puffed on his trademark cigar, I told him it seemed to me that he was the natural choice to succeed Speakes. Nah, Marlin replied, he was not a TV type—not glamorous enough, too old, bald, and overweight. But I had talked to some other officials at the White House and knew Reagan was leaning toward the congenial and self-deprecating Marlin, which is what everyone called him. He was, after all, a veteran of the administration; he understood government, politics, and the media, and he was loyal and steady. When Reagan made the announcement, he called Marlin "simply the best." In that assessment, the President was correct.

THE LARGER REALITY—and something that not even Fitzwater could or would try to change—was that contrary to the television images of an accessible Ronald Reagan bantering easily with reporters, the President knew very few of those who covered him by name. Richard Wirthlin, Reagan's pollster, later told me that Reagan never considered the press corps as a monolith but as a group of individuals. This may have been true in the abstract, but he never took the time to get to know us very well, except for a few veterans such as ABC's Sam Donaldson, UPI's Helen Thomas, and *The Washington Post*'s Lou Cannon, who had covered Reagan as governor of California.

The President's lack of familiarity with his press corps sometimes had embarrassing consequences. Reagan was always thoroughly rehearsed before his press conferences at preparatory sessions held in the family theater of the East Wing, the residential quarters of the White House. Reagan aides would pose as reporters and quiz the President in an elaborate ritual. The staff would prepare a three-by-four-foot chart showing exactly where each reporter would be seated, with the photo of each journalist placed above his or her name.

Just before airtime, Reagan would spend a few minutes in the Red Room or the Blue Room at a television monitor. Government cameras would pan the ornate East Room, where the reporters had taken their places assigned by press aide Liz Murphy; Speakes (or, later, Fitzwater) would point out the people that Reagan should call on. Finally, as prime-time television coverage began, the President would stride down a long corridor into the East Room, a solitary figure entering the lion's den with his shoulders squared and a bounce in his step, and stand behind a podium in which a seating chart had been placed with the names of each reporter he would call on underlined or marked in yellow.

The system seemed foolproof, but it wasn't. On one occasion, the staff decided that Reagan should call on Bob Thompson, then bureau chief of Hearst Newspapers in Washington. But the President didn't have time to pre-identify Thompson on the monitor in the anteroom, so during the press conference he looked down at his seating chart, looked up toward Thompson's assigned seat and, pointing and smiling with the delight of intimate familiarity, called on "Bob." When there was no response, the President repeated, "Bob." The press corps began murmuring; the Gipper, many thought, had finally lost it. But Thompson was at home watching the proceedings on television, taking notes on a yellow pad and sipping a glass of wine. He was flabbergasted. "All of a sudden, the President called my name," he recalls, "and I stood up in my living room."

Desperate to impress their bosses by getting "face time" on national television, reporters would do almost anything to draw Reagan's attention. Women reporters eventually realized that the President was attracted to the color red, Nancy's favorite, so they began wearing red dresses. Sure enough, female reporters wearing red were called on at press conferences. The gambit reached an extreme when Johanna Neuman of *USA Today* showed up wearing elbow-length red gloves and, of course, the President called on her.

AS THE IRAN-CONTRA scandal unfolded, Reagan's popularity declined. He insisted throughout that he knew of no wrongdoing, but many voters thought he was lying or was dangerously disengaged from his administration. Meanwhile, Donald Regan's ego and arrogance had alienated Mrs. Reagan and many of the President's core supporters, and the chief of staff was forced out of his job. In the sad finale of his government service, he watched on television in his big West Wing office as Cable News Network reported that he would be asked to resign. When Regan phoned the President to check the report, Reagan would not take the call—in effect confirming that the news was true. Regan angrily walked out, got into his car, and drove home.

Within a few days, the President had announced that former Senate Republican leader Howard Baker of Tennessee, a moderate known for his genial ways and negotiating skills, would be the new chief of staff. Former Reagan congressional liaison Kenneth Duberstein returned to the White House from the lobbying ranks as deputy chief of staff. It was exactly the combination that the President needed, and from the start the new team was far more open and accessible to Reagan's friends, supporters, and the press corps than Regan had ever been. White House relations with the press began to improve and with it, so did Reagan's image.

After a steady decline in his popularity—he had dropped from 60 percent job approval in mid-1986 to only 40 percent by early 1987, largely because of the Iran-contra scandal—the President started an ascent that lasted for almost the remainder of his term. Lacking firm evidence that Reagan had committed any crime, the country wearied of the Iran-contra controversy. The economy was still booming, and the White House's relations with the news media were on the upswing.

THE ARRIVAL OF Baker and Duberstein marked another new phase for the press corps. The two men were veteran schmoozers, and they met regularly with White House reporters.

Yet, by this time the Reagan presidency had run out of gas on domestic issues. Since Reagan was barred by the Constitution from serving a third term, he would be out of office in January 1989, and the lame-duck President began to focus on foreign policy. Soviet leader Gorbachev had finally persuaded Reagan that he was a genuine reformer, and the President saw hope for real progress in superpower relations. We in the press corps took his cue, shifting our attention more and more to East-West issues. To that end, the press corps found itself in closer contact with the staff of the National Security Council, and we reporters were particularly impressed with the deputy to White House national security adviser Frank Carlucci, an articulate Army general named Colin Powell.

With his chest full of ribbons and his imposing military bearing, Powell cut a striking figure. He was even more of a standout because he was one of the few prominent blacks in the Reagan administration. The press corps gradually realized it was dealing with someone special. Powell's press conferences were masterful expositions of complicated national-security issues, and he never seemed to make mistakes. In background interviews, where he followed the White House custom of speaking anonymously, he was equally impressive as a loyal spokesman for administration policies. He also earned the press corps' respect for refusing to snipe privately at other officials, a rare characteristic among Reaganites.

Eventually, Powell became national security adviser after Carlucci resigned to return to private life. During George Bush's presidency, he was promoted to the chairmanship of the Joint Chiefs of Staff, making him the top-ranking officer in the military. By mid-1995, political strategists and journalists were looking at the now-retired general as a possible presidential candidate in 1996, a prospect further enhanced by the September 1995 publication of his memoirs, which received extraordinary media coverage.

Reporters who had covered Powell during his stint in government were regularly asked by their editors to do stories about his background and his views. But he had built up such goodwill in the press corps that few journalists wanted to write or report anything negative about him, so his coverage remained almost totally positive. One reason for the pro-Powell bias was that the mainstream media didn't want to undermine a black man who had become a role model for many African-Americans. But there was another reason: Colin Powell had always played fair with the media, had treated reporters decently, and had tried to be cooperative. He had developed relationships with Washington journalists, and now they were paying off.

Another highly respected Reagan adviser was Ken Duberstein. When Howard Baker left the White House in 1988, he was promoted by Reagan to be chief of staff, and he quickly established himself as a strong manager. Like Powell, he was decent and fair-minded, and he was assiduous in cultivating the media. Duberstein understood the importance of relationships with individual reporters, and he had an intuitive sense of what their needs were, and how far he could go in divulging information without violating confidences inside the administration.

After one summit meeting between Reagan and Gorbachev, I was on deadline and in desperate need of a few anecdotes to fill out my story for *U.S. News*. I phoned Duberstein's office repeatedly that afternoon, and his assistant assured me that he had promised to call before the day was over. This kind of explanation, of course, often means that an official has no intention of getting back to a reporter at all, but sure enough, close to midnight, my phone rang at the office. It was Duberstein, sounding exhausted. He was calling from his car phone on the way home and passed on a few choice morsels, knowing exactly the kind of inside-the-room details I needed. They were all positive from Reagan's point of view, but they were all true, and they helped me build an interesting story. I have always remembered this incident. It showed that cultivating the media is hard work, but it can help both a presidency and a journalist.

ONE OF THE bright spots of the Reagan years was the foreign travel. A septuagenarian accustomed to the good life, the President would make his way around the world in grand style, not only staying in the best hotels but leaving himself (along with his staff and the press corps) plenty of time to relax during his excursions. This set the tone for his trips, and his press staff would generally make sure that the regular White House reporters were given first-class treatment, because they knew that happy reporters who experienced the best amenities were more likely to be favorably disposed to their handlers. It's simple human nature, and certainly it was true in those free-spending days, when media expense accounts were open-ended. As the Clinton White House would later learn to its chagrin, failure to provide creature comforts for the press on the road, or at least to make planes and buses run on time, can cause hard feelings and generate stories about logistical screw-ups and White House incompetence.

In the summer of 1987, Reagan headed for the summit meeting in Venice of the seven biggest industrialized democracies known as the Group of 7. The entire traveling party, press included, arrived a few days early so that the President could rest in advance. The press corps was quartered on the Lido, an island across the lagoon from Venice; our hotel was the Excelsior, an expensive and elegant resort on the beach.

I spent most of my time on the Lido trying to track down White House officials to arrange lunches or dinners at which I could get to know them better, and perhaps extract a few news tidbits. But I was a junior correspondent on the beat and wasn't sure how successful I would be. One night, however, I scored a coup. I arranged a dinner with Duberstein and Tom Griscom, the longtime spokesman and aide-de-camp for chief of staff Baker, who had come with his boss to the White House as communications director. We converged on La Caravella, one of the finest restaurants in Venice, for a two-hour meal along with a handful of other reporters I had invited. While our two anonymous sources delivered only a few bits of news that evening, I felt I had arrived as a White House correspondent and could play the game.

5

The 1988 Campaign

By early 1987, it had become clear that the best approach for a White House correspondent who wanted to stay on the beat was to get to know George Bush. The Vice-President was preparing to run for the 1988 Republican presidential nomination as Reagan's heir, and clearly he would be a contender. The journalistic tradition was that if a reporter covered a successful candidate for President, he or she would follow the winner into the White House. If only because I had a natural perch from which to cover him, Bush was my best bet.

But the Vice-President had been a deferential and low-key number two for seven years. He rarely made news, and few Americans knew much about him. I gradually shifted my attention from the Reagan White House, which was increasingly a caretaker operation, to the Old Executive Office Building next door, where the Bushies were.

I began regular interviews with Craig Fuller, the Vice-President's chief of staff. Fuller was a pleasant, unflappable Californian who was given his job because of his political sensitivities and his connections to the Californians surrounding Reagan, especially

Michael Deaver and Ed Meese. Fuller filled me in on Bush's official activities, which were not very consequential, but he also began my education about George Bush—the man and the politician, his family, his background, his philosophy, and his strategy for winning the White House.

We talked frequently about Bush's belief in duty and honor and about how, out of a sense of loyalty, he refused to break out of Reagan's shadow until he thought the time was right—probably after he had won the GOP nomination. Fuller argued that Bush had always been underestimated in his public life but would prove himself to be a tireless pursuer of his ambition to be President. In the end, Fuller was correct.

As I reported on every aspect of the Vice-President's life, I came away with a more accurate picture of Bush than most of the Washington punditocracy, who tended to dismiss him as a rich aristocrat from Yale who would wilt under pressure once the 1988 campaign heated up. The more I got to know about Bush, the less I thought of that theory.

I began to talk systematically to the Vice-President's friends and advisers to get the fullest possible understanding of the man. I arranged lunch with Nick Brady, an investor and former senator from New Jersey who was an old Bush pal and would become his secretary of the Treasury. Brady told me how Bush was hardly the weakling that his detractors portrayed. Why, George loves to take his cigarette boat out on Cape Maine just after a storm to plow through eight-foot seas, just for the thrill of it. There was, Brady said, a good deal of machismo in the Vice-President. Brady's example, however, failed to connect with me—and with most Americans, I suspected. I wasn't even sure what a cigarette boat was. (I later found out: It's a sleek, high-powered speedboat.) A better example was Bush's wartime heroism. He was an eighteen-year-old Navy aviator, flying a torpedo bomber to attack Japanese positions in the South Pacific. On one such run, he was shot down and spent a harrowing few hours bobbing in the water until he was picked up by a U.S. submarine.

Vic Gold, a longtime Bush media adviser and one of the most pleasantly cantankerous individuals I've ever encountered in politics, provided an insight into Bush's soft side, the facet that the unforgiving Gold never could quite fathom. He told me of how, during Bush's unsuccessful 1980 campaign for the presidency, reporters would write negative stories about him but he would still give interviews to them despite Gold's insistence that they be punished. These folks have jobs to do, Bush insisted; it's nothing personal. Throughout Bush's presidency, I would regularly meet Gold for lunch at a downtown Washington steak house, where he would rail against the "white-sleeve nine-to-five crowd" surrounding his old friend, especially the campaign advisers in 1992 who, Gold believed, weren't tough or hard-working enough and were letting Bush down.

Over time, I also got to know Lee Atwater, a young political adviser who had served in the first-term Reagan White House and who was to become Bush's campaign manager in 1988. Atwater, who died of brain cancer in 1991, was a hard-nosed but charming South Carolinian whose specialty was negative campaigning. As a political consultant, he prided himself on finding an opponent's weaknesses and ruthlessly exploiting them rather than developing a positive message about his own candidate.

Preparing myself to cover Bush in the 1988 race, I began to travel with the Vice-President and spend more and more time with Atwater on the road. As we discussed American culture, he talked about how much he loved rhythm-and-blues music, how he had jammed on the guitar with black musicians around the South, and how he enjoyed slipping off with a few friends to watch what he called "slasher movies," such as the gory teen flick *Halloween*. Atwater also said that he sometimes attended professional wrestling shows and for some reason took special delight in matches involving dwarfs. There definitely was something unique about Lee Atwater.

I never figured out whether Atwater told me all this to shock me or to demonstrate that George Bush had a variety of people on his team. But it quickly became clear that Atwater was the cultural outsider of the Bush campaign, the "bad boy" amid all the strait-laced Brahmins, who offered insights into aspects of American life that the Vice-President could never comprehend.

For Atwater, winning was everything. As he boasted about state and local campaigns he had won, his eyes would grow wide with excitement, he would sway in his chair, and one of his knees would bounce up and down rapidly in a nervous twitch. One of his friends told me that the young campaign manager had once organized a free Election Day beer-and-barbeque party for black voters in South Carolina. Knowing that these voters were sure to vote against his Republican candidate, Atwater carted them off to a remote location where they could party to their hearts' content—and conveniently miss voting.

In 1980, Atwater ran the congressional campaign of Republican Floyd Spence in South Carolina and undermined Democratic candidate Tom Turnipseed. After learning that Turnipseed had once been counseled for depression and had undergone electroshock therapy, Atwater said he couldn't take seriously someone who had been "hooked up to jumper cables." Turnipseed lost the election.

At one point, Atwater and I were not on speaking terms—always a possibility with a senior campaign staffer or government official when a journalist is trying to do his or her job candidly. At the start of the primary and caucus season in 1988, Bush seemed in danger of losing the Republican nomination to Senator Bob Dole of Kansas, so I wrote a story in *U.S. News* about how Atwater planned to use his talents as a negative campaigner to undermine Dole and attack his way out of the political crisis. Atwater took offense, telling friends that I had made it appear he was responsible for everything that had gone wrong in the Bush campaign (he was, after all, the campaign manager), but I always thought the real reason for his pique was that I had spelled out his strategy too clearly. Promoting Bush as Reagan's rightful heir, Atwater had erected a firewall of political support in the South for the Vice-President that would, in effect, deliver him the nomination by providing an insurmountable lead. When the Super Tuesday of Southern primaries arrived that spring, Atwater reasoned, Dole would be a goner, and in the end he was correct.

Still, for weeks after my story appeared, Atwater refused to return my phone calls. At a state Republican convention in Texas, I noticed him walking across a large hall near the media center, and I started to intercept him. As soon as he saw me, he speeded up his pace and raised a hand to wave me off. I got close enough to ask if he had a few minutes for an interview, but he shook his head vigorously and stalked away.

A few weeks later, Atwater called. "That's it," he said. "It's over. Let's move on," and our relationship returned to normal. In the end, he was able to put aside bruised feelings if he thought a critical journalist was not mean-spirited or vindictive. He was a professional and knew he couldn't afford to alienate a reporter he might need in the future.

BUSH FOLLOWED ATWATER'S pattern of avoiding personal animosity with journalists. In fact, he began to cultivate personally the reporters he thought would be covering his 1988 presidential race. His aides later admitted that Bush harbored deep resentments toward the press, which he thought was biased toward the left, but he rarely let them show. Before moving from Bush's chief spokesman to Reagan's press secretary late in Reagan's second term, Marlin Fitzwater was appalled when the Vice-President attacked the press in front of his staff. After one such episode, Fitzwater talked to him privately. "Mr. Vice-President," he said. "We need these people. Don't encourage the staff not to deal with them. We need to talk to them." Marlin understood that the staff of a Vice-President or President will instinctively reflect his views on the media. If the boss lets it be known that he hates reporters, eventually this attitude will seep into every cranny of the White House. (This is exactly what would happen in the Clinton White House when both the President and the First Lady made it clear from the start how much they disliked and distrusted the media. As a result, relations were quickly contaminated.)

Although Bush never lost his private disdain for the press, most of the time he was able to control his displays of anger in front of his staff and in public. That self-control lasted until late in the 1992 campaign, when his frustration with unfavorable coverage boiled over. At rallies he would draw cheers when he held up a bumper sticker that read: "Annoy the media. Reelect Bush."

During the latter part of his vice-presidency, Bush persevered in his media cultivation even when his coverage was overwhelmingly negative. Fitzwater recalls that in 1985 and 1986, Bush did seventy-five one-on-one interviews, and "the stories were almost all bad." Reporters wanted Bush to criticize Ronald Reagan, or at least show independence from him. Bush refused. Journalists also wanted him to provide behind-the-scenes details of White House decision-making, and to leak embarrassing information about colleagues or potential rivals for the presidential nomination. Again he refused. Bush was generally bland and boring in those interviews, and reporters created a storyline following the conventional wisdom that he was blindly following Reagan, had no independent ideas, and, most harmful to his image, was a wimp.

But Bush kept at it. At one meeting, when the staff began sniping at the press, Bush defended the media, saying reporters were only doing their jobs and had every right to cover the issues as they saw fit. When he spotted Fitzwater in a back corner, he gave him a wink, as if to say he really agreed with the critics but would follow his press secretary's advice and pretend otherwise.

Fitzwater also had another bit of advice for Bush, which every politician would be wise to heed: If you judge reporters as professionals you won't be disappointed with their friendship, but if you judge them as friends, you will never be happy with their work. Ever eager to have people like him, Bush, like most Presidents, could never get this distinction straight. He was always distressed that journalists he considered friends would write harshly critical stories about him.

STARTING IN 1987, many of us in the Reagan White House press corps began traveling to Kennebunkport, Maine, where Bush had vacationed since his boyhood, to keep close to him while he was, in his words, "recreating." On one of those occasions, he began a tradition of inviting reporters en masse over to Walker's Point, his mansion by the sea, for burgers, hot dogs, beer, and soft drinks. This allowed us to see Bush and his inner circle at close quarters.

This was where I met Roger Ailes, and immediately took a liking to this gruff bear of a man who enjoyed projecting an atmosphere of menace. Like Atwater, he was very different from Bush, rough-edged and willing to let his anger flare. The son of a factory foreman in Warren, Ohio, Ailes had risen from the working class, as I had, to become one of the leading media consultants in America. (More recently, he has left the political world for private enterprise.) He told me his philosophy was simple: "Other consultants live for their clients. I'll die for mine."

As the campaign of 1988 proceeded, Ailes was demonized as a stop-at-nothing exponent of all that was wrong with American politics—too negative, too willing to tear down an opponent on flimsy charges, too mean. He openly derided Massachusetts governor Michael Dukakis, the Democratic nominee, as "Shorty," and was blamed, along with Atwater, for unfairly portraying the governor as unpatriotic, too liberal and weak. But I always liked Ailes; he was passionate about his beliefs and loyal to George Bush, and I admired this.

I also got to know Barbara Bush, and realized that she was not the self-effacing, endlessly patient grandmother that the media made her out to be. With her plump figure, wrinkled face, and silver hair, she certainly looked the part, but she had a spiky side.

During one media barbecue at Walker's Point, a wind suddenly came up and the Vice-President considerately offered his guests an armful of varsity jackets that he had been given by colleges and universities around the country. As each of us took one to ward off the chill, I grabbed a jacket and offered it to Mrs. Bush. Noting that I was presenting her with an extra-large size, she squinted, looked at me disdainfully, and said, "Do you think I'm fat?" I was taken aback, which of course was her purpose. She wanted the press to know that she was not to be taken lightly. At succeeding gatherings at Walker's Point, I noticed how "Bar," as her husband called her, would be friendly and outgoing for about an hour. Then she would retreat to the periphery of the main house and stay away from the media pack while George shook every hand, held every baby, and fetched soft drinks for his inquisitors. "Bar" barely tolerated us.

Whether it was genuine or feigned, Bush was unfailingly gracious. Once at Kennebunkport, he took me and my wife, Barclay, out for a trip on *Fidelity*, his cigarette boat. With the Vice-President at the wheel and a Secret Service man aboard, along with Atwater, we eased out of the dock at Walker's Point and proceeded toward the open sea. "Hold on," Atwater whispered to us. Suddenly, Bush gunned the engines and *Fidelity* took off with a tremendous lurch. The seas were calm, but the boat bounced off the waves like a Ping-Pong ball. I learned later that Bush had once taken television correspondent Tom Petit of NBC out on *Fidelity,* raced over some huge swells, and sent Petit sprawling. The newsman later learned that he had fractured a vertebra. Maybe Nick Brady had a point about Bush's macho instincts after all.

Those afternoons at Walker's Point also gave us an insight into Bush's constant mangling of the English language, which was to become the target of endless jokes. Once he invited some of the press regulars into his backyard to play horseshoes, and I asked him to explain some of the terminology. He launched eagerly into a description of the terms he and his family used. A "good shoe" meant a ringer or a good throw. "Ugly pit" meant that a throw had gone off course into the sand pit. "So those are the two main terms?" I asked politely.

"Yeah," Bush replied. "Good poo and ugly shit." Then, realizing he had inadvertently transposed the words, he reddened and shrugged his shoulders.

One of my discoveries at Kennebunkport was Jim Pinkerton. I noticed this gangly, six-foot-nine, rail-thin fellow standing around Atwater and asked who he was. No one in the press corps seemed to know, so I introduced myself, and Pinkerton and I became friends. Later I introduced him to other reporters over a lobster dinner at a Kennebunkport eatery. He was brilliant and helpful, and over the years has become a valued source on conservative thinking and strategy. At the time, he was a twentysomething researcher of the opposition, and one of Atwater's acolytes. It was Pinkerton who discovered Willie Horton for the Bush campaign. In poring over transcripts of debates, speeches, and interviews involving Bush's opponents, he ran across a question posed by Tennessee senator Al Gore to Dukakis during a debate in the New York primary campaign. Gore had asked whether the governor should have allowed his state to grant parole to a convicted murderer named Willie Horton, who had been sentenced to life in prison without parole. After he was freed, Horton raped a woman and savagely beat her fiancé. In the spring of 1988, as Dukakis rolled up one primary victory after another, Pinkerton mentioned the issue to Atwater, and they resolved to use it against Dukakis that fall. In the end, the Willie Horton issue proved devastating against Dukakis, making him seem weak on crime and a soft-headed liberal.

The Democrats and much of the media claimed that since Horton was black, the issue was a racist ploy designed to scare whites into voting Republican. Pinkerton denied this, but the criticism burned him deeply. After entering the Bush White House as a domestic-policy adviser, he spent much of the next four years trying to escape his reputation as a slash-and-burn operative. He finally did so, and is now a respected conservative thinker and author.

I BEGAN TO travel more frequently with Bush. While his campaign was generally well organized and efficient, there were glitches. On one memorable cross-country trip, our press plane was to follow the candidate from Billings, Montana, to Seattle. The Vice-President's jet left on schedule, but the press plane was delayed. We finally taxied down the runway, gained speed, but then abruptly slowed down amid loud popping noises from the engines. We tried again, and again there were popping noises and an abrupt deceleration. Finally, the pilot announced that the high winds sweeping across the runway were preventing the engines from drawing in the proper amount of air, causing him to abort the two takeoff attempts.

Pandemonium erupted. Some reporters shouted that no campaign was worth losing your life over; they wanted to stay in Montana for the night and pick up the Bush campaign in the morning. Other reporters argued just as vociferously that we should take off because it was our job to follow the candidate wherever he went. Alixe Glen, a young press aide for the Bush campaign, suggested that we take a vote. More pandemonium. Alixe tried again. How many reporters want to take off? Many hands went up. How many want to stay? More hands went up. Alixe said she would inform the crew of our decision to remain on the ground and try to arrange a place for us to spend the night.

Suddenly, the doors opened and reporters began gathering up their luggage and personal effects preparing to depart. Bob Schieffer of CBS quickly donned his coat, picked up his carry-on bags, and walked off the aircraft. An instant later the pilot's voice came over the intercom. He knew we had voted, the pilot said, but he was in charge, and now the winds had died down, so he was ignoring our decision and would try to take off once again. Immediately, the doors were closed and the plane began rolling. The last thing I saw through my window was a forlorn Bob Schieffer, standing alone on the windswept tarmac with his carry-on bags, watching as the presidential campaign of 1988 went on to Seattle without him.

ONE OF THE biggest stories of the 1988 campaign was the rise and fall of Colorado senator Gary Hart. As *The Denver Post*'s chief political writer, I had covered Hart's first winning campaign for the Senate in 1974 and had followed his career closely since then, both for *The Denver Post* and for *U.S. News & World Report*. In fact, only weeks after I arrived at the magazine in 1984, Hart won the New Hampshire primary in a dramatic upset that catapulted him into contention for the Democratic nomination. Suddenly, I became *U.S. News*'s expert on Hart. Drawing on my experience in covering him for the previous ten years, I wrote about how difficult it was to know him, how intent he was on keeping his private life to himself, and how ambitious he was. Hart lost the 1984 nomination to Vice-President Walter Mondale, but he had proved himself a strong candidate with powerful appeal. As the 1988 campaign began, he was the favorite not only for the nomination but to win the presidency itself.

Hart's big problem quickly became "the character issue," particularly the question of whether his personal life and rumors of adultery had any place in public discourse. I had heard many rumors about Hart over the years but had never gained enough information to publish anything. Yet there was a subtext to the Gary Hart story that the news media, myself included, found intriguing. Was he too enigmatic and self-absorbed to be President? Why had he changed his name (from Hartpence), his age (subtracting a year in his official biography), and his signature (becoming more flamboyant over time)? Why did he never want to talk about his personal life and his upbringing in the ultrastrict Church of the Nazarene? Was he really the Gary Hart who had managed George McGovern's liberal campaign for the presidency in 1972, or was he the Gary Hart who in 1988 pledged to find new ways of solving the country's problems? Was he a Colorado conservative, complete with cowboy boots and an aw-shucks laugh, or was he out of the cultural mainstream, influenced too much by Hollywood friends like Warren Beatty and Julie Christie? Was he really the candidate of new ideas and a new generation, or was he an old-fashioned advocate of big government trying to brighten his image?

Though in historical terms the character issue was nothing new—Thomas Jefferson, Grover Cleveland, and other Presidents had endured controversies about their character—the news media were unsure how far to go as the 1988 campaign began. Hart would force the issue, prompting changes in the way the media treated a presidential candidate's privacy. "The changes were not dissimilar from the ones that had taken place throughout our society in the discussion of supposedly taboo subjects," wrote columnists Jules Witcover and Jack Germond. "In 1960, there was an unspoken understanding that personal privacy was to be respected. Newspapers were considered daring if they referred to a politician who was a heavy drinker as having a reputation for 'conviviality' or, in the case of a notorious lush, 'excessive conviviality.' Elected officials who were conspicuous womanizers were described then as possessing 'an eye for a well-turned ankle.' But by 1988, many newspapers felt free to describe oral sex techniques, and in political reporting, too, there was a new 'freedom'—for the press, not for the candidates.

"The old guideline, seldom discussed, was that if personal conduct didn't affect the candidate's performance on the stump and wasn't a detriment to his conduct of the office he was seeking, it was his business. Now everything, in the view of a new generation of reporters schooled during or after a dark period of betrayal by politicians at the highest levels, was fair game. . . . The dominant issue had now become whether the candidate had the moral fiber, on and off stage, to be President."

One reason the press corps focused so intently on the adultery issue was that increasing numbers of women were covering the campaign. In many conversations with women reporters, I found an intensity to their focus on the character issue that men didn't have. More than one of my female colleagues found resonance in the notion that if Hart couldn't be true to his wife, then he couldn't be true to his country.

In my own work, I have developed three rules for assessing the character issue: Is the questionable behavior real—that is, is the story true? Is the behavior relevant to the person's conduct of office? Do the voters care? In Hart's case, and in Clinton's four years later, I became convinced that at least some of the adultery allegations met all three tests, and voters were entitled to know the charges so they could make up their own minds about how to assess them.

Deciding to do a story on adultery allegations is only half of the problem, however. Just as important is how a news organization handles the story—whether it is played on page one or leads a newscast, whether it gets five inches or sixty seconds, or whether it is mentioned only in passing or is sensationalized. The media are not monolithic, and each organization will handle these decisions in its own way.

In the end, of course, Hart's campaign was shattered by the character issue when he was caught by *The Miami Herald* in a Washington townhouse with a twenty-nine-year-old part-time actress and model named Donna Rice. Despite Hart's claims that there had been no philandering, incriminating information mounted that he had been up to monkey business and had lied about it. Not only was his credibility ruined, but he also showed bad judgment in cavorting with a woman young enough to be his daughter in the middle of his presidential campaign after he had challenged reporters to follow him to see if he was a womanizer. Gary Hart seemed to have a political death wish—not the most comforting trait in a potential President.

During the initial wave of publicity, Rice admitted that after running into Hart on at least two occasions, she had given him her phone number, that he had called her apartment to invite her on a boat trip, and that she had accepted. The part-time model and the would-be President joined another couple on a cruise to Bimini on a chartered yacht called *Monkey Business*. Subsequently *The National Enquirer* would publish on June 2 a photo of Rice holding a cocktail glass and sitting seductively on Hart's lap at a pier. The grinning senator was wearing a T-shirt that said MONKEY BUSI-NESS CREW. His presidential dreams were over.

MY MAIN GOAL in late 1987 and 1988 was to continue developing an understanding of George Bush. It became apparent that the Vice-President was not likely to self-destruct or immolate himself in the manner of Hart; he seemed to be in the race for the long haul.

I remember vividly one of my early interviews with Bush. When I walked into his spacious suite on the second floor of the Old Ex-ecutive Office Building, he bounded up to shake my hand and in-vited me to sit down. He was gracious and engaging. Over time, he and I would talk every few months, and I became impressed. Ad-mittedly, he had flaws. He was a terrible communicator on televi-sion, he didn't have much of a domestic or foreign agenda, and he was easily caricatured as a pampered elitist from Andover and Yale. But he was much smarter and stronger than the conventional wisdom granted him, he had assembled an impressive staff, and, most important, he had a relentless desire to be elected President. He promised to work harder than anyone else to achieve this goal, and he was developing an effective strategy to win the nomination.

Bush clearly understood that his wimpy image was a problem—he knew his stature had been diminished by seven years in the vice-presidency—even though he wasn't sure what to do about it. In one memorable interview, he told me, "I have people say to me as I walk into a room, 'Hey, I thought you were a short guy.' I've been six-foot-two since I was sixteen. Why do they say that? There's some-thing distorted."

IN THE GENERAL election campaign, Bush's fundamental strategy would be an overwhelmingly negative one, based on the ideas of Lee Atwater. First, he would stay away from the news media by avoiding press conferences and troubling questions about the Iran-contra arms-for-hostages scandal, or such basic points as exactly what he had been doing for the previous eight years. Instead his han-dlers would try to keep Dukakis on the defensive every hour of every day with a series of charges and allegations about him, many having little substance. The goal would be not to build Bush up but to tear Dukakis down.

The GOP left little to chance. It used polls and focus groups (small groups of citizens convened to answer questions in depth) to find the weaknesses in Dukakis and the Democratic party. Then the Republican team used television ads, interviews given to carefully selected reporters, and speeches by the candidate to raise doubts about Dukakis.

This attack-dog style of campaigning would become still another reason for the negativity of the news media that has persisted and grown ever since. Journalists are always drawn to stories of conflict, but in 1988 they were trapped in a perpetual cycle of attack and response, and felt badly manipulated. Under Atwater's cynical tutelage—which became widely admired in the political-consulting business because it was so effective—the way to overcome a candidate's negatives was simply to raise the negative perceptions of his or her opponent, and in 1988 the Bush campaign set a new standard for pitbull politics.

In many cases the unrelenting Republican attacks against the Democratic nominee were unfair. The Republican platform bashed Dukakis with a promise: "We must never allow the Presidency and the Department of Justice to fall in the hands of those who coddle hardened criminals and turn killers and rapists loose on the public." Bush and his minions went on to attack the Democratic nominee for being soft on national defense, for being a tax-and-spend liberal, and for a multitude of other alleged sins. Even Dukakis's patriotism was impugned because he was a member of the American Civil Liberties Union, which had for years aggressively defended unpopular civil liberties cases across the country. The Massachusetts governor didn't believe that voters would buy the Bush campaign's distortions, and didn't bother to answer the charges until the damage had been done. As it turned out, many voters *did* believe the attacks.

One of the most absurd examples of Bush's obsession with the patriotism issue was his attempt to capture the symbol of the American flag as his own. Everywhere he went, he surrounded himself with the Stars and Stripes as he attacked Dukakis's patriotism. At one point his aides had him campaign at a flag factory in northern New Jersey, and the media decided they had been manipulated long enough. "The coverage that night could only be described as withering and ridiculing," recalls ABC White House correspondent Brit Hume, "and it was the last flag event Mr. Bush did. . . . Despite all the lovely pictures of Mr. Bush with the flags, it was a bad day for the Bush campaign. . . . The opening line of my piece was something like this: 'There is an old saying about politicians wrapping themselves in the flag, but today George Bush came close to physically doing it.' Then I went back to a series of flag-waving, chest-thumping speeches he had started the week before. We showed sound and clips . . . The piece was just scathing."

Still, in his own mind George Bush believed that personally he had remained above the dark side of his campaign. He approved the fundamentals but left the nastier details to Atwater, Ailes, and campaign chairman James Baker. Sometimes even Ronald Reagan did the dirty work. At one point, rumors were flying that Dukakis had undergone psychiatric counseling for depression, a tale that turned out to be false. The Bush campaign didn't want to touch the issue directly, fearing that it would seem to be a cheap trick, but wanted to keep the rumor alive. The media were reluctant to treat the idea seriously because there was no solid evidence that Dukakis had undergone such counseling.

Reagan solved the problem at a news conference. When a reporter asked about the rumor, Reagan broke into a smile and said he didn't want to discuss the matter because he didn't want to take advantage of an "invalid." Here was the news peg legitimizing the story for the press, and virtually every news organization covered the episode. When Reagan left the podium, he saw chief of staff Ken Duberstein and national security adviser Colin Powell and said sheepishly, "I don't think I should have said that." Duberstein immediately called Kirk O'Donnell, a Dukakis adviser, and apologized, but the damage was done, and the media placed the story in the public consciousness.

All in all, the 1988 campaign caused the press to sink even deeper into cynicism. Once again voters rewarded the campaign that took the low road. Another lesson of 1988 was that no matter how much reporters tried to put matters in perspective—and many stories were published and broadcast that attempted to distinguish truth from falsehood—the professional political managers had the know-how and resources, largely through paid television advertising, to override any news critiques with their own message.

6

The Bush Years

Of the three Presidents I have covered, George Bush was the one I liked best. He was unfailingly decent and considerate, and whatever resentment he harbored toward the press corps, he mostly kept it to himself. But the world changed during Bush's watch as the Communist empire collapsed and the economic boom of the 1980s gave way to a bitter recession. By 1992 Americans decided that George Bush was no longer the man they wanted as President, and in the end he was powerless to do much about it.

Bush's presidency was one of the greatest lost opportunities in American history. It could have been a time when the best minds in America, led by the White House and reinvigorated by the dissolution of the Soviet empire, devoted themselves to solving the nation's immense social and economic problems. It could have been a time when the President, his popularity at an unprecedented level after an overwhelming military victory in the Persian Gulf War against Iraq, used his political capital to address domestic concerns such as the economic insecurity of the middle class, the country's fear of crime, and the need for sensible reforms in the health-care system.

Instead, Bush squandered his presidency. He defined himself as a transition figure, a man of the moment who preferred to preside over the nation rather than to lead it, a man of few clear objectives who frittered away his personal popularity by choosing inertia over action. Most damaging, in 1990 he broke the central promise of his presidency—his campaign pledge "Read my lips— no new taxes." This infuriated the Republican party's hard-line conservatives, who had never trusted him to begin with, and destroyed his credibility with the American public. It also deepened the cynicism of the media about whether any President could be trusted.

Bush established the limits of his administration early on. During a series of meetings with key advisers after he was elected in November 1988, he made clear that he did not have a real agenda. As press secretary, Marlin Fitzwater asked him what kind of media operation he had in mind, and the new President outlined a minimalist approach. He didn't want the country to think that he or the federal government had an opinion on every issue or a solution for every problem. People simply want to live their own lives, he said, and they don't want Washington or their President to meddle. During the winter of 1989, when his writers gave him drafts of speeches, he would often excise the soaring rhetoric and write in the margins with a felt-tip pen, "That's not me." Eventually, the speechwriters got the point and homogenized his words. Bush insisted on keeping everything low-key and understated; there would be no crusades or grand visions during his regime. His mother, the new President explained to aides, had always warned him against "the great 'I Am.' "

In one strategy session after another, Bush explained that he wanted only to take the country in a generally conservative direction and implement a milder form of Reaganism based on less government and a strong military. Beyond that, he talked vaguely about tinkering with what his pollster Robert Teeter called "change at the margins"—focusing more on the environment, education, and only a handful of social issues, including child care and assisting disabled Americans. To their chagrin, aides learned that Bush believed, as Richard Nixon had, that a President's main responsibility is to run foreign policy; domestic life would take care of itself. This was a passive, Panglossian approach to leadership that would cost him a second term.

In March 1989, less than two months after Bush took office, Fitzwater went public with this minimalist approach. "There are not enough stories out of the White House to keep one honest person doing an honest day's work," Fitzwater told the National Press Club. "What's happened is this: An exaggerated preoccupation with the White House has forced stories to come from the President that should be coming from the secretary of State, the secretary of Defense, or any one of the other cabinet officials who help run the government. And so one of my pieces of advice to those who really want to improve the quality of White House journalism is [to] back off! Let real people do real work."

Bush was taking a big risk by diminishing his own presidency—especially given that, as the Cold War ended, the office was already declining as a central force in American life. "It often seemed that some presidential scholar somewhere was releasing new findings each month showing that Bush was getting less network airtime than previous Presidents," wrote journalists Michael Duffy and Dan Goodgame. "The numbers were dramatic: in his first 22 months in office Bush made the evening news a third as often as his predecessor. One survey by the Center for Media and Public Affairs announced that his dog, Millie, grabbed 'more airtime than three cabinet secretaries.' National news coverage ceased to matter—a sentiment that drove network TV producers berserk. The problem was no less acute for print reporters, who found themselves no longer leading the newspapers every day but instead chasing quotes and doing legwork for their colleagues."

Nor would Bush cooperate with his media managers in constructing an appealing public persona. He rebelled against Reagan-style "handlers"—he hated the term—and refused to be scripted. But this admirable independence led him in a hundred different directions at once, and since he had no top priorities that he was passionate about, he bounced from one issue to another without giving adequate attention to any of them. He seemed aimless, confusing motion with progress. He was unable to give definition or what he dismissively called "the vision thing" to his presidency.

While Reagan had allowed his senior aides to offer reporters and the nation a "narrative" or storyline for his administration, as well as innumerable anecdotes to flesh out the President as a man, Bush preferred to be his own spin doctor. He held more than 250 press conferences, most of them in the afternoon in the briefing room. He knew us by name and would take our questions, often working his way to the last row, until we had nothing left to ask. Not that *he* had much to say. That was his problem: He rarely made news, because there wasn't much his administration was doing, at least on domestic issues. But with the collapse of the Communist empire and the end of the Persian Gulf War, the country was turning inward and wasn't much interested in foreign affairs.

On *Air Force One,* Bush would make a habit of stepping into the press cabin to say hello, sometimes a few times a day. He would allow the TV cameras to roll, and sometimes he could be seen talking about some faraway crisis on the evening news, his hair mussed and with a goofy expression on his face, as he tried to keep his balance while *Air Force One* rumbled down the runway. At the last possible moment, he would rush off to the forward cabin to strap himself into his seat for takeoff.

Once I asked Fitzwater if Bush would be interested in giving me an interview about his experiences hunting quail, which he did every year over the New Year holiday at Beeville, Texas. *U.S. News* was planning a cover story on hunting, and I thought a sidebar on the "First Hunter" would be a readable piece. Fitzwater said he would find out. The next morning at 6:55, my phone rang at home. As I reached groggily for the receiver, I thought to myself, Could it be the President? Nah. But it was. As the adrenaline pumped into my bloodstream, I heard the White House operator say, "Mr. Walsh? President Bush is on the line." I groped for a pen and pad and scribbled madly as he talked about his joy in hunting and nature and the excitement that took over when a covey of birds burst into the air and he had to react in a split second to aim and shoot. Actually, the interview worked out well and I had a nice sidebar, but the circumstances were a shock to my nervous system.

The next time I asked for a telephone interview with the President, I was ready. We were doing a cover story on Barbara Bush, and I asked Marlin if Bush would call me. Again Fitzwater said he would find out. The next morning, just before seven, the President rang me at home again, but this time I was up early and ready with pen, notebook, and tape recorder.

IN MARCH 1990, I had lunch with Sheila Tate, a public-relations consultant who had been Bush's traveling press secretary during the 1988 campaign. I told her that things were pretty slow at the White House and asked if she had heard any news. Glancing down at her plate of unfinished broccoli, Tate asked me if I knew that the new President had banned broccoli on *Air Force One.*

No, I said, I hadn't heard that; tell me more.

Tate said that during the campaign Bush had frequently expressed his distaste for the vegetable, but never took action. Now that he was President, he had told the staff on *Air Force One* that he never wanted to see it again. Word had spread to the White House household staff, and broccoli was now, in effect, banned. (Tate was a good source on these matters because in addition to having served as Bush's campaign press secretary in 1988, she had been Nancy Reagan's press secretary and was well acquainted with the staff at the presidential residence.)

It seemed like a funny story, but I held it that week while I did some futher sleuthing. Everything checked out, and my light-hearted piece ran in *U.S. News* on March 26. "After eight years of swallowing his pride," I wrote, "George Bush is enjoying a taste of victory. The President has banned broccoli on *Air Force One.* As Vice-President, Bush often complained that he did not enjoy eating broccoli, that he had never enjoyed eating broccoli, and that he never would enjoy eating broccoli. Yet for all his protestations, the chewy green vegetable kept showing up on his menu, perhaps because of Barbara Bush's frequently overheard admonitions: 'Now, George, eat your vegetables.' But a few months ago, when broccoli made still another airborne appearance, Bush could stomach it no longer. He then made it perfectly clear he would no longer tolerate broccoli on the Presidential plate. This time the order stuck, leaving aides to wonder which veggie would be the next to feel the wrath of George. Confesses one source familiar with the President's dietary prejudice: 'He hates vegetables. Maybe he'll tolerate a lettuce leaf on his plate, but that's about it.' To which Bob Carey of the

Produce Marketing Association responds: 'The President is sending the wrong message to the kids of America. What will parents
tell Johnny when he refuses to eat his broccoli or other vegetables?
That the President doesn't know what's good for him?' "

I thought this would be a one-day wonder, but it took on a life
of its own. It was that rare yarn from which everyone benefits: The
media had an interesting story, and the President and the White
House saw it as a clever way to humanize George Bush. Fitzwater,
who found the whole issue amusing, decided to fuel it and see how
far it could go. At least, he told aides, it would show that the President had a sense of humor.

At a press conference that week, Bush was asked the inevitable
broccoli question and he was ready. "I do not like broccoli," the
President declared boldly. "I haven't liked it since I was a little kid
and my mother made me eat it. And I'm President of the United
States and I'm not going to eat any more broccoli!"

However, there were repercussions. Fitzwater learned from the
news wires that broccoli growers in California were sending a truck
stuffed with the vegetable to the White House in an effort to get the
President to change his mind. It had become a matter of manhood.
Bush would not back off, but he sent Barbara out to the lawn of the
White House to receive the delivery and dispatch it to a local home-
less shelter. Mrs. Bush looked hapless standing before the crush of
reporters and cameras and holding a broccoli bouquet. Smiling
wanly, she said that the President could do what he wanted, but it
was still a good idea for America's kids to eat their broccoli.

Hundreds of stories were done nationwide on the President's
stand against broccoli, and it became a standing joke on late-night
talk shows. Bush and broccoli had become part of the national culture. At one point a poll reported that nine out of ten Americans
knew that President Bush hated the vegetable. It was one of the few
issues on which he had taken a firm stand.

GIVEN THE PRESIDENT'S interests, foreign affairs became the focal
point of covering the Bush White House, and the high point jour-
nalistically was when Iraq invaded Kuwait and threatened the stability of the oil-rich Middle East. Bush made a principled stand

against the aggression. During this period the White House media operation worked with maximum efficiency and, unlike Bush's lackluster domestic-policy operation, enhanced the President's reputation.

For his part, Bush had a number of reasons for wanting to go to war with Iraq, and they were made clear over the autumn and early winter of 1990 in a series of interviews, leaks, and briefings. The President believed that Iraqi leader Saddam Hussein was an evil man bent on conquering his neighbors and that a vital American interest was at stake in the form of the region's oil supply. He felt that the United States needed to demonstrate resolve to maintain international credibility as the only remaining superpower. In addition, Bush relished the prospect of vanquishing the ghosts of Vietnam by showing that America could wage a limited war and win.

The Persian Gulf crisis also sent the President through a personal crucible that made for a dramatic story in its own right. Bush friends told me at the time that he needed to feel confident that he was sending American troops into a war they could enthusiastically embrace. This was why his trip to the Gulf, over Thanksgiving during the American troop buildup in the region, was so important. Knowing that he probably would have to order the young men he was meeting into combat, the President seemed emotional as he toured U.S. troop positions, especially one outpost in a forward area of Saudi Arabia near Iraqi-occupied Kuwait. Clad in a khaki shirt and slacks, Bush climbed into a military helicopter to make the trip to the outpost.

I was among a dozen pool reporters and photographers who followed him in a light, speedy Blackhawk helicopter. For about forty-five minutes we flew over a forbidding desert marked only by camel tracks and an occasional shrub. As we sped along above the sand, we noticed in the distance one American base after another, military islands of about one thousand soldiers apiece dotting the vista. These forward bases looked exposed and dangerous, easy targets for Iraqi missiles or aircraft. (As it turned out, the Iraqi air arsenal was incapacitated in the first days of the war, and none of these bases was hit.)

When Bush arrived for Thanksgiving dinner (he would have three such dinners that day, each with a different unit), he seemed flustered and tentative. The former World War II combat aviator stood in a chow line, watched as his plate was heaped with turkey and mashed potatoes, then asked for some coffee. When a young soldier gave him a soft drink by mistake, the President thanked him and moved on. Another enlisted man in desert fatigues thanked him profusely for the visit and Bush choked up, his eyes filling with tears. "Ninety percent of life," he muttered, "is showing up."

Friends of the President told me later that the Thanksgiving trip was crucial in moving Bush toward war. He came away convinced that American troops were eager to do their job and would perform brilliantly. In a year-end interview, I asked him how he thought the war would go if it came to that. He replied, "In, out, do it, do it right, get gone." Which is exactly what happened when the fighting began in January 1991.

THE RUN-UP TO the war showed some of the media's worst tendencies. On one side were those journalists unable or unwilling to recognize that America could fight any war morally and effectively. On the other were the journalists who had signed up for George Bush's crusade and checked their skepticism at the door. There was virtually no middle ground.

Leading the effort to stir up war fever were the television networks. Their behavior during the Gulf crisis and the subsequent conflict demonstrates that there are cases, however rare, where journalists' cynicism can be suspended and where a President can effectively marshal the media and public opinion to support his policies.

CBS anchor Dan Rather, reporting from the Gulf in September 1990, four months before the fighting would begin, went out of his way to show that he was backing the U.S. military. No peacenik here. "Some believe . . . that they may be preparing for one of the greatest battles of all time," Rather said in apparent endorsement. On ABC's *This Week with David Brinkley,* Sam Donaldson referred admiringly to General Norman Schwarzkopf, commander of the Allied forces: "Now we have a real general. Stormin' Norman is a general like we haven't seen since George C. Scott in *Patton.* . . . He arrived and said we will kick butt . . . I'm sick of those generals with their Ph.D.'s from Berkeley." (Sam seemed to have overlooked the fact that George C. Scott's Patton was a movie character, not a real-life general.)

"The gung-ho postures and one-dimensional rah-rah coverage were not happenstance," wrote media critics David Zurawik and Christina Stoehr. "The networks were reading the polls that showed widespread initial support for the military action. The networks had also started receiving record ratings for their coverage of it from Day One. Some broadcasters, though, left themselves open to charges of exploiting the situation with the manner and extent of their pursuit of the story."

At the other extreme were those journalists for whom the memories of Vietnam refused to die. Their generation, which came of age during the 1960s, was now the dominant force in American journalism. Many stories were done in the months prior to the actual fighting that made dire predictions about imminent military disaster or speculated on massive U.S. casualties in any invasion of Iraq. One number bandied about was that fifty thousand Americans might die. "It was extraordinary," says ABC White House correspondent Brit Hume. "But there was a certain premium on gloom-and-doom scenarios, and there was a certain sense that anything the United States undertook in the use of its military was likely to become a fiasco." Many in the press corps simply could not be persuaded that the American military had greatly improved since Vietnam, that its leadership was effective and honest, and that the rank-and-file troops were highly motivated and eager to prove themselves in battle.

After the U.S. bombing started, this ugly strain in the press increased. It was accurately described by Henry Allen of *The Washington Post*, who said that in the 1970s, "Big-time media were getting résumés from people who had grown up in the class segregation of upscale suburbs, day-school products who had never been in places where you don't let your mouth write checks that your butt can't cash, had never even been yelled at with the professional finesse of a drill sergeant, a construction boss or a shop teacher. The most important experience in their life had been college. During the summers, they had internships, not jobs. . . . After the draft ended, virtually none of them even knew anyone who had been in the military, much less served themselves. They were part of what sociologists called the new class, the governing class, the professional class. They were a long way from most Americans."

The military's briefings during the Persian Gulf War, however, made skeptical journalists look stupid, insensitive, and condescending, for their questions ranged from the bizarre to the ridiculous. Reporters asked how U.S. communications in the war zone could be "superb," as the military claimed, when a Marine reconnaissance team had been trapped near Khafji. They wondered if the Air Force was being unfair by bombing buildings in Baghdad that did not have twenty-four-hour surveillance to make sure civilians were not inside and if Americans were being immoral because their bombing could create a large oil spill. Journalist Bill Monroe remarked: "Consider the assumptions behind these questions: Communications can't be superb if they aren't perfect. Presumed command centers should never be bombed unless spies are reporting hourly on whether civilians have entered. General Schwarzkopf should have given the Environmental Protection Agency a veto over the liberation of Kuwait."

Once the fighting got under way, the Bush administration's orchestration of public perceptions was nothing short of brilliant and media skepticism was mostly washed away in a torrent of national jingoism. Few in the media wanted to seem unpatriotic—public support for the war was by then overwhelming—so the military commanders were portrayed as altruistic and superhuman. The troops on the ground were always brave and true. Saddam Hussein was evil incarnate, and George Bush was a combination of Franklin Roosevelt, Winston Churchill, and Dwight Eisenhower.

One of Bush's cleverest moves was to demonize Saddam Hussein. He and his advisers realized during the run-up to the fighting that the American public was becoming jittery over the coming war, so they personalized the gathering conflict as a crusade against a Hitler-like dictator who was trying to conquer his neighbors and blackmail the United States and other free nations because he would then control the flow of Middle Eastern oil.

In the war zone, the Pentagon imposed strict rules of coverage that most of the media were all too willing to accept. Reporters could not travel around the theater of operations freely, as they had in Vietnam. They needed military escorts and in most cases had to travel in small, well-supervised packs. News reports were to be submitted to military censors.

Back home, the networks, local stations, and many newspapers jumped into the jingoistic derby. "The media loved the story lines (especially the ones about their own dread magnificence)," wrote Lewis H. Lapham in *Harper's Magazine*, "and by Christmas every network and every magazine of respectable size had designed for itself some kind of red, white and blue emblem proclaiming its ceaseless vigilance and its readiness for war. When the steel rain at last began to fall during the second week of January, most of the national voices raised in opposition to the war had been, as the Pentagon spokesmen liked to say, 'attrited.' Through the five weeks of the aerial bombardment and the four days of the ground assault the version of the public discourse presented in the media turned increasingly callow. *Time* and *Newsweek* published posters of the weapons deployed in the Persian Gulf, and the newspapers gave over the majority of their editorial-page space to columnists gloating about the joy of kicking ass and kicking butt."

The Gulf crisis and the subsequent military triumph for the United States and its allies propelled George Bush off the charts in popularity for a few months. At one point, 80 percent of Americans said they approved of the job he was doing as President. But he never seriously considered using this popularity to push for a domestic program, which was a fatal error.

PERHAPS THE MOST important interview I had during the Bush years was a three-hour session with White House national security adviser Brent Scowcroft at the start of the Gulf crisis. Scowcroft had accompanied the President to Kennebunkport in August 1990, and a group of us in the press corps asked him to dinner in a private room at an elegant inn near the center of town. The group consisted of the White House correspondents for the most influential print publications: the *Los Angeles Times*, *Newsweek*, *The New York Times*, *Time*, *The Wall Street Journal*, *The Washington Post*, and *U.S. News & World Report*.

The first half-hour consisted of small talk. Scowcroft discussed his jogging routine, playing golf with the President in the rain, and how much he liked Kennebunkport. But as he speared his food, the retired general turned to policy. He gave a compelling account of Bush's thinking on the Gulf crisis and what it meant for America, and mentioned that he had been waiting to catch the President when he was not preoccupied with the day-to-day details of managing the crisis in order to discuss its long-term implications.

That day at dawn, the President had called Scowcroft at his hotel and asked if he wanted to go trolling for bluefish.

Scowcroft seized the moment, and for much of the day, as the two men fished lazily in Cape Maine, they talked in detail about a "new world order" that the Iraq crisis could create. With personal diplomacy cultivated through years of experience and friendship with many world leaders, Bush might construct a coalition that would outlast the immediate conflict and serve as a permanent structure for discouraging the "thugs of the world." With the Cold War over and the Russians seeking Western aid, Moscow was being extraordinarily cooperative with the President in confronting Saddam Hussein, even though Iraq had long been a Soviet-client state. Bush and Scowcroft believed that multilateralism, with the United States aggressively taking the lead and firmly in charge, could be the way of the future in resolving global disputes.

The national security adviser went on to describe Bush's style of personal diplomacy and how he made spur-of-the-moment phone calls to other leaders, without the extensive briefings and preparations that his predecessors, especially Ronald Reagan, had found necessary. Generally, Bush would make the calls from the small study off the Oval Office, swiveling back and forth in a big armchair as Scowcroft listened in on an extension and took notes. The national security adviser gave us chapter and verse, offering anecdotes and lengthy descriptions of the administration's geopolitical philosophy for many areas of the world.

After Scowcroft's *tour d'horizon*, several of us huddled in the parking lot reviewing our scribbled notes. We couldn't believe our good fortune. All seven publications plumbed that interview for weeks afterward. One of my stories in *U.S. News,* on September 10, 1990, entitled "The President Thinks Time Is on His Side," read:

"George Bush yelped when son Jeb accidentally embedded a fishhook in the President's right earlobe while casting off the coast of Kennebunkport last week. A White House doctor quickly removed the barb and advised an immediate tetanus shot. But the President soldiered on, trolling for another hour in his speedboat before agreeing to medical treatment. He was rewarded with three bluefish.

"Bush's friends and advisers see a lesson in that story. Anyone who thinks that he lacks the perseverance for a prolonged struggle in the Persian Gulf, they say, does not know George Bush. In fact, his decision to try diplomacy and economic sanctions, rather than a quick military strike, to force Saddam Hussein out of Kuwait reflects a familiar pattern in Bush's life. He is a man of disciplined persistence rather than bold strokes, stubborn to a fault."

The story went on to say how Bush was heartened by public support for his careful approach and saw signs that a new post-Vietnam "maturity" was emerging in America, a growing recognition that the United States must take risks to stop aggression. The piece continued: "During another trolling expedition, this one with National Security Adviser Brent Scowcroft, he ruminated about a 'new world order' that might emerge from the crisis. In it, the U.S. would forge new alliances with Arab states and work with other 'civilized nations' to contain the world's brigands through the United Nations. Bush concluded that an immediate attack on Iraq would dash that dream. By the end of the morning, he also had landed three 14-pound bluefish. Perseverance paid off, at least in the Gulf of Maine."

FOR THE PRESS corps, the highlight of the four Bush years was foreign travel. We visited exotic places all over the world on nineteen separate trips to such sites as Beijing, Buenos Aires, Cairo, Canberra, Caracas, Cartagena, Barranquilla, Berlin, Istanbul, London, Moscow, Paris, Rio de Janeiro, Riyadh, Santiago, Seoul, Singapore, Sydney, and Tokyo. While the travel was not as leisurely as it had been under Reagan, we saw some fascinating places and, especially at superpower summits and in our Thanksgiving visit to the Persian Gulf, felt fortunate in being witnesses to history.

We journalists shared the administration's initial skepticism about whether Mikhail Gorbachev was a serious reformer and whether Communism was indeed unraveling. Gradually, we all came to recognize that the Soviet Union was truly breaking up. There were plenty of extraordinary and historic events, such as the destruction of the Berlin Wall and the signing of various arms-control agreements that made the world safer. But the small moments somehow seemed more memorable. One came during Bush's storm-tossed summit with Gorbachev in Malta in December 1989. In a tense atmosphere the two superpower leaders met on Gorbachev's luxury cruise ship to discuss reductions in their nuclear and conventional arsenals. During a break in their talks, the pool of American reporters was left to idle for a couple of hours in an empty shipboard nightclub. From behind locked glass doors, we noticed Gorbachev, his hands clasped behind his back, and his foreign minister, the white-maned Eduard Shevardnadze, walking slowly toward us down a long corridor, their heads tilted toward each other and engaged in intense conversation. They were no more than ten feet away when both men looked up and were startled to see a half-dozen disheveled reporters gazing at them from behind the glass doors. There were no security officers anywhere to be seen, no aides, no apparatchiks. It was a scene that journalistic veterans of many superpower summits had never seen before: the leader of the Soviet Union and one of his key advisers caught alone in a private moment. Suddenly, Gorbachev broke into a big smile and pointed at us as if we were caged apes in a zoo. He said something to Shevardnadze, and they both laughed. At that point, we regained our composure and beckoned for them to come over and chat. The media-savvy Gorbachev shook a forefinger at us, as if to say we should know better than to suggest such a thing; then he and his adviser turned around, slowly walked back down the corridor, and disappeared.

Another moment reflecting the historic times came during a Christmas reception my wife, Barclay, and I attended at the Soviet embassy in 1989. At one point, a group of somber, hard-looking men in brown uniforms and huge round hats appeared and walked silently to the center of the room, where they stood in formation. It was the Alexandrov Red Army Chorus. They sang a few Russian folk tunes and then, to every American's surprise, these representatives of godless Communism launched into an emotional rendition of "God Bless America." The world, it seemed, had truly changed.

AS THE PRESS corps traveled, we gained many other insights into different cultures. When Bush decided at the last moment to attend the Earth Summit in 1992, the White House travel office had great difficulty finding hotel rooms for reporters in the host city of Rio de Janeiro. Few of us were surprised when journalists were split up among various hotels in the city. What did take us aback was the nature of the facilities, which were locally known as "love motels."

Mine was the Dunas, which Brazilian *Playboy* magazine had awarded five bunnies—top of the line. Couples would drive up to a check-in hut, take care of the financial arrangements (which could be billed at an hourly rate), pick up a key, and then drive directly into a series of small garages adjacent to the rooms. Once inside, the couple could emerge unobserved and walk into their love nest. My room was the "Me Tarzan, You Jane" suite, featuring a huge bedroom with a living tree growing up through a skylight. There were no closets, only hooks for one's garments. Clearly, long-term stays were uncommon. The TV showed continuous porno movies, and the bathroom featured a cavelike shower that could accommodate half a dozen people. I had the feeling that sexual acts had been performed on every surface in the room, which smelled strongly of disinfectant, so I piled my belongings in a tidy clump on a glass table to limit my contact with my surroundings.

Chick Harrity, a *U.S. News* photographer on the trip, was in a nearby love motel. If anything, his room was even more exotic. It came equipped with a "frolic pool" and a lighted, one-person disco floor so that guests could perform for each other onstage. Arriving back at the motel late one night, Harrity asked Dirck Halstead, a photographer for *Time,* to stop by for a room-service dinner. When the bellhop arrived with their meals, he looked with disdain at the two bearded, middle-aged men sitting fully clothed across the table from each other over a bottle of wine. There are cultural limits, even in love motels.

AFTER THE GULF War, the second big foreign-policy crisis of the Bush era was the Soviet coup that almost toppled Mikhail Gorbachev from power in the summer of 1991. At 11:30 P.M. on August 18, Scowcroft, clad in powder-blue pajamas, was sitting on his bed in his hotel room in Kennebunkport. Bush was vacationing at nearby Walker's Point, and the national security adviser, trying to catch a final tidbit of news before he went to sleep, sat back and flipped on Cable News Network.

But he sat bolt upright when he heard the report that Gorbachev had been removed as Soviet president. At first Scowcroft didn't think it was very important—simply a change of title or a garbled story—but two minutes later CNN reported that an emergency committee had been created to take power. This sounded ominous, reflecting private U.S. intelligence that Bush had secretly passed on to Gorbachev three months earlier that a coup was possible. (Gorbachev had replied at the time that only a paranoic madman would make such an attempt.) Scowcroft dialed the Situation Room in the White House basement for a quick intelligence assessment, but the duty officer, surrounded by computer terminals linked to the CIA, the State and Defense departments, and the best intelligence-gathering systems in the world, had no more information than Scowcroft had picked up from CNN.

Scowcroft concluded that matters were serious enough to inform the President, whom he called on a secure phone line at Walker's Point. At 11:45, he told Bush that it looked like a coup might be under way in Moscow, and Bush told him to call him back when he heard more. It was the classic Bush response—an unwillingness to act, or even consider action, until he had as many facts as possible. This caution was a leftover from his days as director of Central Intelligence in the 1970s, when he learned that the initial reports about an unfolding crisis were almost always wrong. His reaction was, in one of his favorite phrases, to "let things sort themselves out."

Bush handled the Soviet crisis deftly, organizing international support for Gorbachev and Boris Yeltsin, the advocates of reform, and speaking out against the hard-line coup leaders. In the end, the Soviet people took care of their own business, demonstrating en masse against the return of a Communist dictatorship and re-asserting control of their own government. With some intelligent leadership by Bush, things had indeed sorted themselves out.

But back at home, Bush had lost contact with his own people. Several of his friends later said that the President had ceded too much authority on domestic issues to his abrasive chief of staff, John Sununu, the conservative former governor of New Hampshire. More than one Bush aide told me of Sununu's boast at midterm in 1990: "We've accomplished all we need to accomplish on the do-mestic front. It wouldn't matter if Congress went home and didn't come back to Washington for the next two years." Such devotion to do-nothingism doomed Bush's chances for reelection.

UNDER SUNUNU'S REGIME, the White House day would officially begin at 6:55 A.M., when an informal group of insiders gathered in his suite next door to the Oval Office to receive their marching orders from the chief of staff. At 7:30 A.M., he would convene a larger senior-staff meeting in the Roosevelt Room down the hall. He would sit in front of an American flag on one side of a long, polished mahogany table, with budget director Richard Darman at the opposite side. It was show-off time. The two men, who fancied themselves the intellectual superiors of everyone else in the room, would play issue-tennis, batting topics back and forth, trading gibes and barbs, trying to impress their subordinates with their brainpower. Everyone would turn to Sununu, then Darman, as the pair volleyed ideas on the budget, the Democrats, and the media. There was no free flow of ideas, no effort to encourage diverse views. Few staffers dared to speak unless called upon. Scowcroft, disgusted with the spectacle, would not even sit at the main table, but would plant himself on a sofa off to the side to make it clear that he was not part of the proceedings and not under the thumb of either Sununu or Darman.

One morning Sununu helped himself to a platter of muffins and began talking with his mouth full. "What's in the news?" he mumbled to Fitzwater, who was generally the first to be called upon. (The Bush White House didn't want to make much news, but it did follow the media closely. Sununu would have Ed Rogers, his aide, read the major newspapers and magazines and use a yellow marker to highlight anonymous quotes from administration officials; then the two of them would try to figure out who was talking out of school, usually to no avail.)

Fitzwater said there wasn't much going on. Fred McClure, the chief congressional lobbyist for the White House and one of Bush's few black advisers, was next, and gave a summary of legislative prospects, which Darman disputed.

Suddenly Sununu noticed that Sig Rogich, the White House media coordinator, was absent. The chief of staff loved to mock Rogich, a communications consultant and advertising man from Las Vegas known for his splashy Armani jackets and Italian slacks that contrasted with the boring pinstripes of the rest of the senior staff. Exhausted after three weeks on the road to arrange a Moscow summit with Gorbachev, Rogich had indeed skipped Sununu's meeting.

The chief of staff was not pleased. "Today is save-your-job day," he announced. "Let's take attendance." After a dramatic pause, he asked, "Where is Sig?"

Bruce Zanca, Rogich's deputy, who was attending in his place, became flustered and blurted out jokingly, "He worked the night shift. He'll be here in a minute."

Sununu replied, "Let the record show that Zanca tried to save his boss's job."

"A feeble attempt," Darman added.

It was this kind of arrogance and condescension that created so much bitterness and anger toward Sununu both inside and outside the White House. For most of his three years as chief of staff, he made many enemies, who were waiting for revenge; their opportunity came during the spring of 1991.

I had begun to notice that Sununu was absent from the White House a considerable amount of time, which was unusual for a chief of staff, and I resolved to find out why. I asked around, and was told that Sununu was frequently on personal business, on vacation, or out raising money for Republican candidates. One senior official who had tangled with the chief of staff suggested that I check out his mode of travel; it could be that Sununu was using government planes for nonofficial purposes, which would violate federal rules and was certainly questionable on ethical grounds.

I began asking questions. It turned out that Sununu was indeed misusing government jets and limousines for personal and political travel, including visits to ski areas, his Boston dentist, his former constituents in New Hampshire (just in case, his critics said, he wanted to run for the Senate from his home state in the future).

In the course of my reporting, I began hearing from sources that *The Washington Post* was also making inquiries about Sununu's travel, and I had a strong feeling that the story had not only become competitive but that the *Post* was planning to run its piece the following weekend. I decided to rush my story into print, so I recruited Steve Hedges, an investigative reporter at the magazine, to help out, especially to help chase down leads I was picking up about Sununu's destinations. Under the Freedom of Information Act, we also asked the Pentagon to give us the records covering Sununu's use of military aircraft.

Late on Friday afternoon, April 19, as *U.S. News*'s deadline approached, our Pentagon correspondent, Bruce Auster, called with word that the Pentagon had given him a copy of the travel records. Hedges and I pored over the sheets, which listed a remarkable number of dates and places, and aircraft that the chief of staff had used since he arrived at the White House. One trip was to Vail, the posh Colorado ski resort. There were some abbreviations for airports, however, that we couldn't figure out. As I walked back to my office, I noticed a staffer from the *U.S. News* travel office standing at a copying machine. "Just the man I wanted to see," I said. I showed him the Pentagon breakdown, and he quickly identified the abbreviations for every airport. I checked with Sununu's office, and one of his aides said he would have no comment. Another source in the White House told me that Sununu wanted to learn exactly what I knew, and would take his chances without trying to shape the story by presenting his own defense. On Friday night, the promotion staff at *U.S. News* issued a press release on what quickly became known as the Air Sununu story, enabling us to beat the *Post* by a full day. (The newspaper ran its piece that Sunday.)

This was the beginning of the end for John Sununu. The furor became a symbol for the chief of staff's arrogance and self-importance. Throughout the rest of that summer and early fall, the news media, fed by Sununu's many enemies, produced a stream of stories on the chief of staff's unbridled ego and misuse of the perquisites of office. It turned out, for example, that he had taken a government limousine to a stamp auction in New York. When he defended himself by saying he couldn't travel commercially because he needed to be in constant voice communication with the White House through secure phone lines, he seemed to be saying he was too important to work under the rules that governed everyone else.

It got worse. The President's approval ratings began to slip as the economy stagnated. Sununu persuaded Bush to publicly urge banks to lower the interest rate on credit cards, and the Senate passed legislation designed to force such a rate reduction, but as a result the stock market plummeted 120 points and the whole episode turned into a political disaster. Sununu deeply offended Bush loyalists by telling a television show that the President had "ad-libbed" his remarks on credit cards, blaming his boss for the debacle.

The day before Thanksgiving 1991, the President asked his eldest son, George W. Bush, who was an informal adviser to the White House and later was elected governor of Texas, to canvass prominent Republicans and find out how many of them thought Sununu should go. The younger Bush, known as Junior within the official family, found virtually unanimous agreement that Sununu had alienated too many people and outlived his usefulness. This was what he told his father, and at the President's request, he also told Sununu what other Republicans were saying. But Sununu would not go gracefully; that weekend, he tried to orchestrate support for himself among congressional Republicans and others, but found it impossible to create a groundswell.

On Monday, Bush loyalists leaked a story to the media that the President's son was urging his father to oust the chief of staff. This wasn't true, but Junior, seeing an opportunity to force Sununu out, which he thought was best for his father, refused to deny the story in public. It was clear then that Junior had joined the chief of staff's adversaries and wanted him to go. That day Sununu told the President he was resigning, and Bush declined to ask him to stay.

Like Donald Regan before him, John Sununu had allowed power and privilege to go to his head, and he never built up relationships with people around Washington—certainly not with the news media, which he utterly disdained. I had seen this contempt at first hand when I interviewed him on the administration's agenda and legislative strategy months earlier. I kept asking about Bush's deficit-reduction plans, and the chief of staff kept ducking my questions. Finally he stood up, looked at me, and said, "I don't know if you've wasted your time, but I know I've wasted mine," then walked out the door.

But such scorn was mild compared with his outburst against Ann Devroy of *The Washington Post*. Just before a ceremony in the Rose Garden at which Bush signed a new civil-rights bill, Sununu shouted at Devroy, "You're a liar! Your stories are all lies! Everything you write is a lie!"

ONE OF BUSH'S defining moments in domestic affairs was the Los Angeles riot of 1992. The unrest was precipitated by what many Americans considered a gross miscarriage of justice, the acquittal of several white police officers for the brutal beating of black motorist Rodney King. The cops said King had resisted arrest, but a videotape of the incident showed that the police kicked and beat King while he was lying helpless on the ground.

The President had neglected the problems of the cities for three years. He displayed little interest in his own administration's modest proposals for enterprise zones—essentially, tax breaks for the inner cities—promoted by Housing and Urban Affairs secretary Jack Kemp. He had virtually no contact with blacks, no idea of the discrimination they faced, and no sense of the feeling of hopelessness among those on the lowest rungs of society.

As the rioting began, Bush handled the crisis management smoothly, but he rejected the larger, more dramatic option of calling on the nation to end racial injustice. His aides gave him two drafts of a prime-time television speech he was scheduled to deliver on May 1. One was an uplifting text written by speechwriter Tony

Snow, which emphasized the need for racial harmony. The second text, written by White House communications director David Demarest and speechwriter Dan McGroarty, called for law and order. Bush chose the second, calculating that it would appeal to white middle-class voters troubled by crime. Press secretary Fitzwater went further and blamed the riot on the Democratic social-welfare programs of the 1960s and 1970s, inflaming Bush's liberal critics.

Then the President decided that the administration's tone was too harsh, so he sounded a conciliatory note by promising to work with Congress to pass his modest proposals to aid urban areas. He also visited poor communities in Washington, Philadelphia, Baltimore, and other cities. But there was little follow-up, and again he looked like a vacillator who hadn't a clue about the country's domestic problems.

Even more damaging, the President seemed hopelessly out of touch about the recession that was causing deep pain and anxiety in the American middle class. Through it all, he continued to believe the bad advice he was getting from chief economic adviser Michael Boskin and budget director Darman, who insisted that the downturn would be mild and short-lived. When Bush opposed extending unemployment benefits to millions of jobless Americans, he seemed particularly callous.

Suddenly, everything seemed to be going wrong. Not only was the recession cutting deep into the middle class, but the President was being portrayed in the press as too removed from everyday America. His suspicions about the media's bias against him finally bubbled to the surface. Sometimes they bordered on the irrational, and increasingly they focused on the invasion of his privacy. One worry was that the press and his political opponents would rebroadcast embarrassing footage of his collapse from stomach flu in Tokyo in early 1992, when he threw up in Prime Minister Kiichi Miyazawa's lap. Though it got plenty of airtime when it happened, the footage was never used in the campaign of 1992.

Like every President, Bush bridled at the thought of revealing every detail of his physical problems. He told friends he didn't mind informing the country about serious ailments, but not what he considered trivial ones. He objected strenuously when aides urged him to disclose that he suffered from persistent hemorrhoids. But despite what he saw as a loss of dignity, he eventually authorized the disclosure because he feared that failure to reveal the problem might lead to the leak of an incorrect diagnosis and cause the media to speculate that he had something far worse, like colon cancer.

As the 1992 campaign year began, Bush told his friends and advisers privately that the mainstream media were responsible for much of his trouble, because they made him seem so isolated. One incident particularly galled him. He was inspecting a new type of high-technology scanner for supermarket checkout counters and expressed wonder at how the device could read not only preprinted labels containing prices—common at many grocery stores—but could also read labels that had been shredded. A newspaper reporter at the scene referred briefly to the incident in his pool report to the rest of the press corps, and *The New York Times* used it as an example of how far Bush was removed from American life. The incident became a prime example of reporters' stereotyping of George Bush's isolation: He didn't even know what a standard checkout scanner was!

There were a few journalists Bush liked personally, such as easygoing John Mashek of *The Boston Globe,* who had gotten to know Bush over the years in his past job as chief political writer for *U.S. News.* But the President had an abiding dislike for David Hoffman of *The Washington Post,* partly because of Hoffman's attempts to implicate him in the Iran-contra arms-for-hostages scandal. Privately, Bush referred to Hoffman as "that little shit."

More broadly, the President complained in private that the press didn't give him credit for his accomplishments—the same complaint that Bill Clinton would make four years later. He had tried to develop personal relationships with reporters, he told friends, but they still attacked him in their stories. Angrily, he told aides that he couldn't understand why the "talking heads" on the Sunday public-affairs TV programs were unrelentingly critical of him. (He was particularly furious with David Gergen, the former adviser to three Republican Presidents, for failing to defend him on the *MacNeil/ Lehrer NewsHour* on public television.) Bush said that the White House press corps wanted a younger, more with-it, more liberal President to fawn over and that no one cared about foreign affairs anymore now that he and Reagan had vanquished the Soviet threat and made the United States the lone superpower.

On most of those points, Bush was correct, but in public he managed to hide his animosity toward journalists until the very end of his administration. He had mastered the Republican art of hating the press privately.

Dan Quayle

One of the worst examples of media excess was the political evisceration of Dan Quayle.

Quayle's defining moment came at the very start of his career as a national political figure; unfortunately, the debut was a disaster from which he never recovered. When the young Republican senator from Indiana was selected by George Bush to be his running mate at the 1988 Republican convention in New Orleans, it set off a reaction among the media that was almost unrivaled in the annals of the press. A Bush-Quayle campaign official called it "the most blatant example of political vivisection that I've ever seen on any individual at any time; it really surpassed a feeding frenzy and became almost a religious experience for many reporters." He wasn't far wrong.

On the sweltering afternoon of August 16, 1988, George Bush made the announcement to the news-starved press corps. As Quayle tells it, he got the word from Bush confidant James Baker only a few hours before he was to be introduced at an outdoor rally in Spanish Plaza as the number-two man on the Republican ticket. Baker had made no arrangements for Quayle to reach the rally, and the young senator and his wife had to push their way through a restive crowd at the last minute to reach the speakers' platform. When the President announced his name, Quayle bounded onstage like an overeager puppy, excitedly punched Bush's arm, and shouted, "Let's go get 'em."

As Quayle recalled in his memoirs, "Looking back, I realize that the speech was too hot. I was talking like a junior senator in campaign overdrive. I was picked, in part, for my youth, but this was a little too youthful—not Vice-Presidential nor, given the nature of that office, potentially Presidential. . . . I was energized and proud, and I was wearing my emotions on my shirtsleeves. . . . But that's not how most of the media played it. I was a stranger to most Americans, and that night the commentary they heard included the memorable line (historians should note it as the first Quayle joke) that up there on the platform in Spanish Plaza I looked like the guy on the game show who'd just won the Oldsmobile."

Bush's campaign team was caught completely off guard. David Beckwith, then a *Time* magazine reporter who was covering Bush (and who later became Quayle's press secretary when he was Vice-President), says, "Let's be completely honest about this: The largest share of the blame for that debacle goes to George Bush in the way he chose to introduce Quayle and keep his identity a secret. . . . The fact is that neither Quayle nor the press corps nor the Bush staff was prepared for Quayle's introduction." Beckwith says Bush simply wanted to generate a news story for journalists to write about. Well, he got a whopper.

At one point, Beckwith, attempting to get information on Quayle for a *Time* story, went to Bush's press office in desperation. They were swamped. He told press officer Alixe Glen that he had in his briefcase a newspaper column by a Quayle friend, Ken Adelman, that made a good case for the young Indiana senator. "They photocopied a thousand copies of it, and that's all they had to hand out," Beckwith recalls.

Lacking another storyline, the media immediately turned to the obvious stereotype promoted by Quayle critics: that he was a vapid rich kid, a bumbler who didn't have an idea in his head and who had achieved his success because of dumb luck and family connections. Some of Bush's advisers, including campaign chairman

Baker, fed the stereotype by failing to vigorously defend Quayle in private interviews with reporters; he and other advisers had doubts about Quayle, too. "That gave everybody the go-ahead to trash the guy," Beckwith says, "and the story just became that he was a screw-up. Once the herd gets rolling in that direction, there's almost nothing that can be done to turn it around. The best you can do is get out of the way and wait for them to exhaust themselves, maybe picking off a dogie here and there. But you're not going to do any real good until things calm down and they're ready to go in a different direction, which occasionally they are."

Not for Dan Quayle. His image would stay with him for the next four years—and quite likely will bedevil him for the rest of his political career if he chooses to run for office again.

COVERING A NATIONAL convention is one of the most difficult and competitive assignments in journalism. The reporters who attend these events are the best in the business, and no one wants to be scooped on a story. Everyone is scratching and clawing to deliver the least tidbit of news in a hothouse atmosphere. This dynamic, it turned out, was the worst possible climate for the introduction of Dan Quayle on the national stage, because the only thing of importance going on at the convention was the choice of the Vice-President.

Like most reporters at the convention, I was shocked to see Quayle's performance in Spanish Plaza. He seemed barely in control of himself, an unguided missile ready to explode. As I and most of the other reporters began to collar delegates, make phone calls, and research his record to find out what Quayle was all about, an easy storyline emerged. Fair or not, the initial impressions of a man not ready for prime time seemed to emanate from a broader picture of an heir to a family fortune who never had to work hard in his life. (Quayle and his supporters would bitterly complain that he was hardly a multimillionaire, as some journalists suggested. He estimated his net worth in 1988 as $854,000, far less than that of the Democratic vice-presidential candidate that year, Senator Lloyd Bentsen of Texas.)

Meanwhile, Bush's senior strategists badly mishandled the

evolving situation. None of them realized the extent to which the storyline on Quayle was gelling into a caricature of a political lightweight. Pollster Robert Teeter, campaign manager Lee Atwater, and, belatedly, campaign chairman Baker tried to present a more positive picture of Quayle as someone who had been a good campaigner, who had beaten the odds to win tough races in Indiana, and who had a decent record in the Senate. In retrospect, they could have aggressively promoted their own version of Quayle's life by portraying his background as perfectly acceptable for a vice-presidential nominee who would grow in office under the tutelage of George Bush. But they dispensed little detailed information about him, only a generalized defense. None of them realized how much trouble the young senator was in.

Most damaging were the questions that reporters were raising about whether Quayle had used special influence to land a position in the Indiana National Guard during the Vietnam War, thereby escaping service in Southeast Asia. No one could ever prove that he used unfair connections, but absent any sustained effort by the Bush inner circle to provide a compelling alternative persona for Quayle, and fearing that they would get scooped by rivals in caricaturing him, reporters decided collectively that Quayle should not be given the benefit of the doubt. The press overemphasized his lackluster academic record in college, as opposed to his moderately successful record in the Senate. Another cheap shot was speculation about marital infidelities that apparently never existed.

One of the low points for journalism came on Friday, August 19, 1988, after Quayle left the convention for his hometown, Huntington, Indiana. Thousands of supporters were gathered near the courthouse steps in Huntington. As we left the press bus and made our way to the rally, we were booed. After the speeches, Quayle walked over to us on the edge of the crowd and began answering questions. Suddenly, we realized that the press conference was being broadcast over loudspeakers to the throng, which pushed up to the reporters surrounding Quayle. Our questions to the candidate were hostile, often angry. Ellen Hume, then of *The Wall Street Journal,* asked with considerable outrage in her voice how Quayle felt when "people were dying in Vietnam while you were writing press releases" for his National Guard unit. The crowd became angry, at one point chanting, "Boring . . . boring . . . boring." Quayle didn't make any real news at the event—he gave the same answers he had given for the previous three days—but something important had changed in the relationship between the press and the politicians. The public was not on our side.

I have always suspected that someone in the Bush-Quayle campaign staged the "Battle of Huntington" to embarrass us—holding the press conference amid the crowd, and allowing it to be broadcast over loudspeakers to stir up Quayle partisans. The result made him seem like a gladiator in the arena, badly outnumbered by the vicious lions of the media, and showcasing our rude and hectoring demeanor. It was a trap, and we fell for it.

Certainly the press was justified in scrutinizing Quayle's background. Fueling our interest was the fact that he was not the most qualified candidate that Bush could have chosen for his ticket. Just as important, we sensed divisions in the President's camp about Quayle's nomination. But there was a go-for-the-jugular quality to the press coverage that went beyond fair scrutiny. It was provoked by Quayle's vulnerability and the misplaced desire of the campaign press corps, dominated at the time by liberal baby boomers, to revisit the Vietnam-centered divisions of their youth and to hammer a man they suspected was a hypocrite. It was also provoked by a competition-induced compulsion to break the big story that would take Quayle out of the race.

This didn't happen, but the GOP vice-presidential nominee was badly battered. His worst moment came in his October 6 debate in Omaha, Nebraska, with Texas senator Lloyd Bentsen, the Democratic vice-presidential nominee. After Quayle tried to compare his length of service in Congress with John F. Kennedy's before he won the presidency, the avuncular Bentsen stunned him with the line, "You're no Jack Kennedy." Quayle managed to mumble that Bentsen's remark was uncalled for, but he was caught off guard and stood, grim-faced and confused, before the cameras as the Democratic partisans in the crowd cheered. The common media description was of a deer caught in headlights, one more vivid image of Dan Quayle as a nincompoop.

In the end, Americans, as always, cast their votes that fall for the top of the ticket, Bush or Democrat Michael Dukakis, rather than the candidates in the second slots, but for Dan Quayle the negative coverage was just beginning.

AFTER THE BUSH-QUAYLE ticket won the election, the new Vice-President never got a honeymoon from the media. The subtext was already embedded in mainstream journalism: Dan Quayle was a figure of ridicule. Reporters thought it was fun and easy to focus on his gaffes and missteps while playing down his positive contributions to the administration. Michael Lewis of *The New Republic,* for example, was still picking Quayle apart four years later, in 1992. In "The Boy in the Bubble," Lewis described Quayle standing at the door of his plane pointing to a nonexistent fan in the distance in order to get some favorable TV footage. "This is meant to convey the idea of a dynamic young leader bonding with a prized supporter," Lewis wrote. "And it does, unless you see him do it five times in two days, often as not to the backside of a member of the Secret Service." Virtually all national candidates pose for such photos. The broader problem was that almost all of Quayle's coverage was of this dismissive, smart-alecky, nasty variety—far more one-sidedly negative than anything Bill Clinton has endured since.

Yet Quayle was neither an ignoramus nor an incompetent. I got to know him quite well during his vice-presidency. In person, he was competent, articulate on the issues he knew well—such as tort reform and deregulation (he was chairman of the Bush administration's Council on Competitiveness, which was in charge of recommending ways to reduce federal regulations)—and unfailingly amiable despite the battering he endured. He also assembled a highly talented group of advisers, led by his savvy chief of staff, William Kristol, and including his press secretary, David Beckwith. While the Vice President was not given many important responsibilities within the administration—few holders of the office ever are—he did offer some valuable if often unheeded political advice, such as when he warned Bush against breaking his no-new-taxes pledge in the budget agreement of 1990. The Vice-President vigorously opposed raising taxes, arguing that it would turn conservatives against the President and irrevocably damage his credibility with mainstream voters. Quayle was right. He also was an early champion of term limits for members of Congress, having made his first speech in the House of Representatives on the subject in 1977. He spoke publicly on the issue again in 1990 and 1992, but was widely ignored by the press. Eventually the issue caught on around the country in the 1994 midterm elections.

Over time, Quayle, Kristol, and Beckwith were among the few members of the administration who understood how isolated George Bush was becoming from voters during the recession of the early 1990s, and they saw how difficult his reelection race would be. They thought the President should go on the offensive and attack the Democrats and Bill Clinton for being too liberal, just as Bush had done in his 1988 campaign against Dukakis. Yet no one in the President's high command was willing to listen. Senior advisers in the White House and Bush himself simply could not imagine the American people voting him out of office for someone as personally flawed as Clinton.

Quayle's biggest problems were not his positions on political strategy or substantive issues, but his failure to communicate effectively on television and his penchant for making silly mistakes on camera just when he was starting to get some favorable press treatment. My theory is that Dan Quayle has a "garble chromosome" in his makeup. The man who in small groups seemed in command appeared to fall apart, freeze, or bumble on television. While Ronald Reagan was magnified by the tube, Quayle always seemed smaller than life. He appeared to be callow, much younger than he was in person, with every stumble suggesting ignorance or panic.

BECKWITH, QUAYLE'S PRESS secretary, had the worst job in Washington. At first he thought Quayle was redeemable in the media's eyes, and he developed three options for a media strategy early in his boss's vice-presidency:

1. Go underground completely and remain out of the media's sight. No interviews; no speeches in public. The goal was to allow the media herd to exhaust itself and forget the nincompoop image. Then the Vice-President would be reintroduced after two years. However, Quayle was too proud to adopt this strategy; hiding out, he said, would be capitulation to his tormentors.

2. Take a big gamble and put the Vice-President in high-visibility situations where he could prove he was not a clown. His problem, some advisers theorized, was based on only a few issues and gaffes, and he should roll the dice and try to shatter his negative image. One idea was to appear on late-night television shows and trade quips with, say, Johnny Carson or David Letterman, who were making fun of him. This strategy was rejected because it was too risky. The Vice-President was not adept at repartée and couldn't be relied upon to acquit himself well in off-the-cuff confrontations.

3. Proceed as if Quayle didn't have a problem. Let Washington reporters get to know him and the quality of his work. He would go about his business quietly, grow "an inch a day," and over the expected eight-year Bush-Quayle administration, he would stand tall.

In the end, the Vice-President adopted the third strategy, but it was doomed to fail. Not only did he have only four years instead of eight in which to redeem himself, but the media would not cooperate in reassessing him. Beckwith recalls, "Because some members of the press had so much invested in Quayle's being as bad as they had written—either because they were ideologically determined to make a conservative look bad, or because they had predicted in print, or psychically had committed to making him look like a bozo—they were unwilling to let him up off the mat."

For the next four years, Quayle's accomplishments were overlooked and every gaffe was pounced on with a vengeance. Beckwith would call reporters and editors to complain about cheap shots, and was ignored. He tried to plant stories about the Vice-President's political acumen—such as his support for congressional term limits, and his consistent call inside the Bush administration for holding the line on taxes—but few news organizations took him seriously.

Quayle would do his job quietly and effectively, then would commit a gaffe that contributed to his reputation. In April 1989, only three months after being sworn in as Vice-President, he arrived at the Pago Pago airport in American Samoa for a refueling stop en route to other destinations in Asia. Noticing many enthusiastic children in the crowd, he said that they looked like "happy campers." American reporters on the trip wrote dispatches portraying his off-the-cuff remark as an insult to the people of Samoa.

Picking up on the stories, Eni F. H. Faleomavaega, American Samoa's nonvoting delegate to the U.S. House of Representatives, wrote Quayle to complain that "some individuals have even drawn the conclusion that you were implying that people of Samoa are simple, illiterate natives happily camped out in the jungle." These remarks, however unfair, were widely quoted. It was another case of media overkill, but it gave the late-night talk shows plenty of fodder.

On a trip to Chile, Quayle picked up an anatomically correct doll in front of reporters, gleefully examined it, and purchased it as a souvenir, which made him look like a horny adolescent on holiday. He also mangled the phrasing of the United Negro College Fund slogan "A mind is a terrible thing to waste." Quayle's version: "What a waste it is to lose one's mind, or not to have a mind is being very wasteful. How true that is!" Just when he seemed to be on an even keel, he would sabotage his progress with a silly mistake.

When the Vice-President traveled in the United States, he usually received favorable local news coverage, because he was accessible, friendly, and informed about local issues. Initially, he was optimistic that this localized and low-key strategy would work in changing his image; after all, it was what he had done as a member of the House and as a senator from Indiana, and his constituents liked him. But eventually Beckwith and Quayle's other advisers realized that such positive local coverage would never correct the negative image in the national media. Not even a largely favorable series of articles about Quayle by *Washington Post* superstars David Broder and Bob Woodward in January 1992 could turn the tide. The pieces were largely ignored in the press.

Kristol, Quayle's chief of staff, says, "The media sees itself as a debunker of all established institutions and all powerful figures." In response, a politician has three choices: try to discredit the media, win them over, or redefine the perceptions by which the politician is being judged. In 1990, the Vice-President and his advisers decided to take the latter course by redefining Quayle's agenda and perceptions of him so that the press was no longer dwelling on the question of his gaffes and intelligence and was focusing instead on his ideological positions. "Better to be attacked as a right-wing fiend," Kristol recalled later, "than as a fool."

So Quayle took on three inflammatory issues: legal reform, in which he argued that America was overly litigious and that fat-cat lawyers were unfairly benefiting from the system; cutting down on federal regulations that he said crippled business interests, a familiar Republican theme over the years; and family values. The goal, Kristol recalled later, was to provoke "presidential-level events and fights" to show that Quayle was not an empty suit but a tough ideological partisan. What happened was that the Vice-President did come across as a right-wing fiend but never lost his image as a fool, so he was in twice as much trouble.

The defining issue was Quayle's critique of a popular television series, *Murphy Brown*. On May 19, 1992, three weeks after the rioting in Los Angeles that followed the Rodney King verdict, he gave a speech in San Francisco about how a "poverty of values" was the real cause of the bedlam in Los Angeles and how everyday violence and drug-dealing made it all the more difficult for single mothers to raise children in the ghetto. But the single sentence that would ignite what Quayle later called "the real ideological firestorm of my Vice Presidency" came later in his speech. Quayle said, "It doesn't help matters when prime time TV has Murphy Brown—a character who supposedly epitomizes today's intelligent, highly paid, professional woman—mocking the importance of fathers by bearing a child alone and calling it just another 'lifestyle choice.' "

Negative reaction to the speech was swift. By 10 P.M., when Quayle arrived in Los Angeles for his last events of the day, a horde of reporters was waiting. They wanted more details about his displeasure with *Murphy Brown*. Quayle had never seen the show in question (he had read news reports about it), so he avoided talking about the program in specific terms. But he tried to make the broader point that Hollywood did not reflect America's traditional morality in the values it glorified in movies and on TV.

The White House, especially new chief of staff Sam Skinner, was nervous about the negative media reaction to Quayle's speech, especially from the networks. George Bush agreed, telling aides he didn't want to be part of any effort to take on a popular television character. But Quayle didn't back down. He continued to take on Hollywood, arguing that the entertainment industry was promoting immorality and violence, which provoked a healthy national debate about the moral values conveyed by the mass media that has persisted. But the Vice-President was not properly credited for starting the debate. The media image was of a man blundering into a culture war he wasn't ready for and mistaking a fictional character for a real person. Neither interpretation was true.

On June 15, not quite a month after the *Murphy Brown* speech, came the most damaging gaffe of all. Quayle was supervising a spelling bee at a junior high school in Trenton, New Jersey, when twelve-year-old William Figueroa went to the chalkboard to spell out the word *potato*. Quayle had been given a cue card by school officials on which the word was spelled incorrectly as *potatoe*. The Vice-President double-checked his cue card and then urged young William to add an *e* to his correct spelling, which the boy did with obvious reluctance.

So was born the potato incident. Beckwith and Kristol were in a holding room outside the event, having paid only scant attention to the spelling bee, and as a result they were unaware of any problem. But the second question to Quayle at a news conference immediately after the spelling bee was, "How do you spell *tomato*?" Quayle laughed and went on to another question. But Beckwith was puzzled. He hung around after the news conference and asked a reporter, "What's this business about *tomato*? I've never heard anything about that." The reporter looked up and said, "You will."

Beckwith told a military aide to get out of a waiting limousine and got in beside Kristol. By now it was clear that the media had noticed that the Vice-President had misspelled *potato*. The two aides tried to convince each other that it wasn't a big deal. Maybe it had happened too late in the evening (about 5 P.M.) to be a big story on the nightly network news; maybe, they told each other, they would get lucky.

The next day CNN began running a video clip of the incident. "I counted eighteen times they ran it between the time I got to work and the time I left," Beckwith recalled. "It just kept running over and over. They made it into a big deal. I was in the position of trying to put a finger in the dike. We tried to think of some humorous thing about spelling to make fun of it." Beckwith thought he could say it was an Old English version of the word. The trouble was, he had used that theory to explain why Marilyn Quayle, the Vice-President's wife, had misspelled "beacon" on the family Christmas card.

The potato incident was the perfect stereotype of Dan Quayle as a fool, precisely the image he had been trying to shake off for so long. This gaffe was an error of the most basic and embarrassing sort, and it was on videotape, played endlessly on all the networks. Once again it made him the butt of jokes in offices, around dinner tables and cocktail parties everywhere, and an easy target on late-night talk shows. NBC's Jay Leno, for example, said, "Maybe the Vice-President should stop watching *Murphy Brown* and start watching *Sesame Street.*"

Again Dan Quayle was a laughingstock. All his quiet work behind the scenes, all his savvy political advice to the President, and all his successful missions abroad had been futile. "One story supporting the stereotype blows everything else out of the water," Kristol recalls. Beckwith adds: "It gave us a new appreciation of how little progress overall we'd made in two or three years, if it could all be undone by one incident like this. It goes to show that unless they are jolted out of it forcibly, the first impression that people have ends up being the one they retain."

The Vice-President went on to give a solid speech at the 1992 Republican convention in Houston that August and avoided any major mistakes for the rest of the campaign. Yet the jokes kept coming. A study by the Center for Media and Public Affairs in Washington found in August 1992 that Quayle's news coverage was three times more negative than positive, while Democratic vice-presidential nominee Al Gore's coverage was 91 percent positive.

Throughout the campaign, Quayle generally appeared in smaller television markets, as Vice-Presidents normally do, while the President took on the large ones and the truly competitive states. Quayle did as he was told, even though he realized that the Bush campaign was being too defensive and that Clinton was dominating the agenda day after day. The high point for the Vice-President came in his October 13 debate with Gore in Atlanta. He followed advice from Baker and Teeter and focused not on ways to make himself look good in contrast to Gore but on attacking Clinton for character flaws such as flip-flopping on issues and having "trouble telling the truth."

From time to time, Quayle supporters and family members would urge him to take a bold gamble to resurrect his image. After Clinton appeared on MTV, the music-video channel, Quayle's children advised him to do the same. He took what they said seriously and raised the idea with his advisers.

"What's your favorite kind of music?" asked an aide, posing as a skeptical MTV interviewer.

"Rock 'n' roll," Quayle replied.

"Oh yeah? What's your favorite group?" the aide asked.

"Rolling Stones?"

"Okay. What's your favorite Rolling Stones song?"

Silence. At that moment, the idea of appearing on MTV died.

In fact, nothing worked, either for Quayle or for the Republican ticket. During the two years following the election, Quayle wrote a book defending his record in public life and continued to appear before conservative audiences. He was trying to cement his base in the Republican party's right wing as he prepared to run for President in 1996. But in early 1995, he announced that he would not run after all. He admitted he was having health problems, but said they weren't the reason; rather, he wanted to spend more time with his family and to spare them the ordeal of another ferocious round of media-bashing. His decision was wise; in the end, Dan Quayle realized he could not escape from his own stereotype.

8

The 1992 Campaign

Bob Teeter, George Bush's pollster, discerned the early tremors of an anti-government earthquake in late 1991. He told his colleagues that he had never seen the American public so alienated from Washington, not even during the Watergate scandal. His public-opinion surveys and focus groups showed that voters were particularly furious at Congress for inaction, pettiness, and isolation. "People ask, 'What are these guys doing?' " Teeter said to an associate. " 'Education needs fixing. Roads need fixing. And these pompous asses down there in Washington are talking to themselves.' "

A congressional check-writing scandal, in which many legislators were caught floating loans to themselves through their government checking accounts, intensified public revulsion against Capitol Hill. Teeter also found that the Senate hearings on Clarence Thomas, Bush's controversial Supreme Court nominee, had made matters worse; Americans felt that the Senate Judiciary Committee had sunk into a swamp of innuendo and character assassination.

All these resentments would eventually culminate in the historic midterm elections of 1994, when voters gave Republicans control of the House and Senate for the first time in a generation. But back in the fall of 1991, Teeter thought the problem was manageable, at least in terms of reelecting George Bush. A quiet, bespectacled man with a professorial air, Teeter was an optimist and could not envision the voters rejecting his old friend, who had demonstrated his competence in winning the Persian Gulf War and managing the breakup of the Soviet Union. In any case, the Michigan pollster, who had been an architect of Bush's 1988 victory, did not want to come across as prophet of gloom and doom. Bush hated this stance, and Teeter wanted to move beyond the confining role of public-opinion analyst and become the head of the campaign. In 1992, the President gave Teeter his wish. It was a mistake.

Over the years, Teeter's view of the press had hardened. Like many veterans of national politics, he had seen too many erroneous stories about strategy, process, and people—"stories about the wrong people in the wrong room at the wrong time saying the wrong things," according to one Teeter associate. He resolved to do things differently in 1992—to shut down leaks about the Bush campaign, deny reporters access to junior staffers who might talk out of school, and return to Ronald Reagan's technique of funneling all information through a handful of top people.

This strategy would prove extremely harmful to the Bush campaign, because it went too far. In addition to keeping reporters in the dark, Teeter managed to keep most of his own staff out of the loop. No one knew the overall strategy, let alone the plan for the next month or even the next week. "It's all in Teeter's head," was the constant explanation from Bush's other advisers. Whether he ever had a master plan is doubtful—he seemed to think that the election would be won or lost in the last ninety days—but certainly the campaign behaved as if no overall plan ever existed. "Teeter trusted no one," says a senior Bush adviser from 1988 who was shut out of the planning. "It was the worst, most unimaginative, most stupid campaign I ever saw."

Teeter thought Bush's biggest advantage was that the American people liked him personally. "They think he's real," Teeter told me and other reporters on various occasions. This always struck me as a flimsy basis for a campaign, yet everyone on the President's reelection staff deferred to Teeter, including the other members of his inner circle—campaign chairman Robert Mosbacher, operations manager Fred Malek, pollster Fred Steeper, and political deputy Mary Matalin.

Teeter reflected Bush's cautious incrementalism. He argued that the President need only address modestly a handful of major issues—drugs, crime, the environment, education, and the deficit—to remain popular and meet the country's limited expectations. But Americans were increasingly eager for change, and while Teeter picked up the anti-Congress resentment in his polls, he underestimated the public's growing scorn for the status quo. Even though 75 percent of the voters approved of the way Bush was doing his job in mid-1990, according to internal White House polls, only 16 percent gave him favorable ratings on improving education, only 24 percent liked his performance on the environment, and only 40 percent approved his handling of the economy. The danger signs were there, but the President's inner circle ignored them, thinking that the Democratic candidates were so weak that voters would, in the end, settle on the incumbent instead of taking a risk with a replacement.

By the last ninety days of the 1992 campaign—the period when Teeter said Bush could turn everything around—it would be too late. Bill Clinton and the Democrats, with help from the press, would label George Bush as irrelevant for his times, and it would be impossible to change this impression.

A big problem for the President was that Teeter's anti-media bias became infectious both in the White House and around 1030 15th Street, the spartan downtown Washington office building that the Bush campaign used as its headquarters. Campaign leaders were slow to return reporters' phone calls, even when they were being asked to respond to attacks by the Democrats. Often these attacks would go unanswered, because the Bush team took too long to reply; when the response came, it was too late for the news cycle.

While Clinton kept hammering at the message of a failed economy and Bush's insensitivity to America's distress, the President had no coherent message to counter this accusation. "George Bush would do six events a day and take questions at each of them," says one of his campaign advisers. "At the beginning of his Presidency, you had the image of an energetic President who was very much in charge and who would continue the conservative policies of Ronald Reagan. But he was a different personality and had a different management style than Reagan. By the end, George Bush had stopped defining himself. External events—and Bill Clinton—were defining him through the media, and he looked like he was out of sync with the country." This adviser adds, "There is a daily media machine you have to feed and react to. If you lose the agenda, someone else will take it."

But Bush disliked what he called "stagecraft." He thought governing and campaigning should be totally separate and was confident that he could switch to a "campaign mode" at the very end of the race. Then, and only then, would he allow himself to be managed by his media handlers.

A deeper problem was that on substantive issues the President was adrift. Despite the anti-Congress mood that Teeter had identified, Bush refused to go on the attack against the Democratic power brokers on Capitol Hill. A former House member, he told his aides that if he started criticizing Congress, he would hurt Republican incumbents as well as the majority of Democrats.

Teeter's theory was that the President could pull out a victory by attacking the Democratic nominee at the conclusion of the campaign, when voters were paying most attention. Early on, the Bush forces thought it would probably be New York governor Mario Cuomo, Nebraska senator Bob Kerrey, or Arkansas governor Bill Clinton and that the election would turn on whether the voters thought the Democrat was "a risk we cannot take." Hence the goal of the Republican campaign would be to save its ammunition and savage the Democrat for the last month or two, just as Bush had savaged Michael Dukakis four years earlier.

"The country got to watch George Bush every day on TV dealing with a real crisis [in the Persian Gulf]," a senior Bush adviser told me in late 1991. "There is a real record. There are no doubts about his handling of the job. The uniqueness of the President's job is foreign policy, and people will not take the risk and bring somebody out of the bushes."

There were big flaws in this strategy, of course. With the Communist empire in ruins and no immediate threat of nuclear war, Americans felt the need to turn inward and no longer cared much about international issues. Further, the President no longer had a first-class attack politician at his side, certainly no one comparable to Lee Atwater, who had died in 1991. Hard-nosed media expert Roger Ailes could have played such a role, but he had opted out of the '92 cycle to pursue private interests, and Bush and his advisers never seriously tried to bring him back. They thought Ailes would be too controversial and would divert attention from their planned attacks on the Democratic nominee.

Most important, George Bush himself had become the issue, as incumbent Presidents usually are, and as Clinton would become the issue four years later. As the recession deepened, Bush blithely proclaimed that times would get better as he played golf and sped around Cape Maine on his cigarette boat. Last, neither Bush nor his inner circle realized how deeply he had hurt his credibility when he broke his no-new-taxes pledge in a budget deal with Congress in June 1990. It was the one promise that everyone had remembered from his 1988 campaign. When he repudiated it on the advice of White House chief of staff John Sununu and budget director Richard Darman, he no longer seemed to stand for anything. He had lost his best "wedge" issue against the Democrats—holding the line on taxes. Republican conservatives were furious, and many of them would demonstrate their anger by supporting GOP challenger Patrick Buchanan in the 1992 primaries.

AS I BEGAN reporting the outlines of the '92 campaign from Bush's standpoint, I realized how little the President and his team had thought about what he would do in a second term. Teeter and Bush batted around the idea of spending $5 billion in each of the most distressed cities as an experiment in finding the best ways to do the most good. The idea was to look for the best anti-drug programs, the most effective programs for the homeless, and the best education programs, and then apply them nationally. Initially, the President liked the concept, but then—under the influence of budget director Darman, who tended to shoot down proposals that weren't his own—he lost interest. If he were to make such a request, he told aides, the Democratic majority in Congress would only add their pet projects to each state and district, bloating the cost. "You wind up breaking the bank," Bush said.

Throughout early 1992, I kept asking administration officials and Bush's political strategists—including Teeter, Fitzwater, political adviser Mary Matalin, and chief of staff Sam Skinner—what the President would do in a second term. The answer was always the same: We haven't thought much about that yet, but there is no reason to think a second term would be any different from the first. Of course this became Bush's fundamental problem: He was becoming a defender of the status quo.

Everything seemed to go wrong. Even Bush's malapropisms and bizarre phrasings, which at first seemed endearingly goofy, were cited by critics as evidence that he was frazzled, foolish, and fearful of electoral disaster. In January, when he was campaigning in New Hampshire, he seemed deeply shaken by the attacks of conservative commentator Patrick Buchanan, who was running against him for the GOP nomination. When a voter asked if he would support an extension of unemployment benefits, he replied, "If a frog had wings, he wouldn't hit his tail on the ground. 'If.' Too hypothetical." At another point he spoke about "Mrs. Rose Scenario," and later declared, "I'm a country music fan. I love it, always have. Doesn't fit the mold of some of the columnists, I might add . . . of what they think I ought to fit in, but I love it. . . . Nevertheless, I said to them, you know there's another one, the Nitty Ditty Nitty City—that they did. And it says if you want to see a rainbow you've got to stand a little rain. A lot of families are hurting."

YET THERE WERE several points at which I believe Bush could have salvaged the 1992 election. Some of his advisers urged him late in 1991 to unveil a new economic program consisting of more aggressive marketing of U.S. exports (a huge element of the U.S. economy), expanded unemployment benefits, job-retraining programs, and other ideas designed to alleviate the middle class's economic insecurities. Clinton would later use all these themes to good effect. Darman, however, persuaded Bush to wait until his State of the Union address in January 1992 to make the proposals, and this delay again allowed the Democrats to portray him as out of touch. "Waiting until the State of the Union was a terrible mistake," says a senior Bush strategist, because it made the plan look like an election-year gambit.

Similar delays and inaction cost Bush dearly over the spring and summer as his campaign foundered. It was clear that the high command—Teeter, Malek, and Mosbacher—was not up to the job of wrestling with Clinton and his hard-charging Democratic strategists such as James Carville, Paul Begala, Mandy Grunwald, and George Stephanopoulos. But Bush refused to shake up his team, even though he had James Baker, the secretary of state who had overseen Bush's successful 1988 operation and was one of America's best political strategists, at his disposal. Baker, however, didn't want to be considered a political handler anymore, so he resisted suggestions from Bush loyalists that he take over in early summer. The President deferred to his old friend and let him remain at the State Department until it was too late.

In the late spring of 1992, Bush called a meeting in the Roosevelt Room to discuss his reelection campaign. He had been hearing from friends around the country that he was in serious trouble, and he wanted to ask his senior political advisers what the real situation was. As the meeting opened, Fitzwater slipped a scrap of paper to George W. Bush, the President's eldest son and political troubleshooter. "What's our message?" the scribbled note asked. "What's our plan?" The younger man asked precisely these questions, but no one answered. After a few moments of silence, the President repeated the questions, and again there was no answer. Bush then declared, "I need a plan."

A few weeks later, Teeter produced an inch-thick document that he billed as the "reelection plan." It was nothing of the sort. The document turned out to be a state-by-state analysis of trends and polling data, not a prescription for the next four years, or even a statement of the campaign's overriding messages. It was a pollster's guide, not a blueprint for action. Bush let the matter slide because he thought Jim Baker would take care of everything.

WHEN BAKER AND his aides from the State Department finally arrived at the White House after the GOP convention, they found the campaign in shambles. Not only was Bush unable to show that he had a political vision, but he was unable to respond effectively to the daily attacks of Democratic nominee Clinton and independent candidate Ross Perot.

Trying to shake things up, Baker and aides Dennis Ross and Robert Zoellick began work on what they told reporters would be a "major speech" at the Detroit Economic Club in September. They tried to invent an economic vision for Bush in a matter of days and, defying the odds, the address got good reviews in the media. Bush admitted that millions of Americans were suffering economic pain, and for the first time he set forth his principles and goals for the economy. He said that the recession, then in its twenty-sixth month, had occurred because of "profound changes now at work in our economy," including layoffs in the defense industry and huge debts accumulated by companies and households during the 1980s. He wanted to "keep tax rates low and make them lower, to keep money sound, to limit government spending and regulations, and to open the way for greater competition and freer trade." He also derided "the mirage that my opponent offers of a government that accumulates capital by taxing it and borrowing it from the people, and then redistributing it according to some industrial policy."

But the President did not continue to hammer home the economic theme. "His heart just wasn't in it," said an aide after the election. "I guess that shows that he really didn't understand the middle class's economic insecurity."

Baker and his deputies also found that the campaign's television ad campaign was a mess. Months earlier, Teeter had assembled some talented advertising strategists from New York to work as a team, but their collegiality broke down and no one took charge. At one point they went to Camp David and sat Bush down to make some commercials. They asked the President to speak into the camera and sell the country on his administration. "They thought putting George Bush full-face on screen would humanize him," a White House strategist told me later, but it turned out that he didn't have much to say. "We didn't have a message or a plan or an explanation of why George Bush should be reelected, except that he was better than Bill Clinton," this strategist said. In keeping with their effort to humanize Bush, other commercials were produced of the soft and fuzzy variety, mainly biographical ads similar to the ones he had used in 1988. At a cost of $5 million, these told voters nothing new or compelling about the President.

Baker took one look at the ads, scrubbed them, and immediately sought help from Sig Rogich, the new ambassador to Iceland, former White House media coordinator, and onetime Las Vegas public-relations executive who had produced many of Bush's most effective commercials in 1988. Baker persuaded Rogich to come home and take charge of the ad effort, but by then the momentum of the campaign had moved irrevocably away from the President. "We were running the whole campaign out of our back pocket," recalls a senior administration official.

WHILE THE REPUBLICAN campaign was stumbling, Clinton's operation was gaining in competence and confidence. James Carville had taken control of much of the campaign management that fall and was keeping Bush off balance with day-by-day attacks. A wise-cracking self-styled "ragin' Cajun" from Louisiana, Carville also kept the campaign and the candidate focused most of the time on the economy. The sign he kept in the "war room" in his Little Rock headquarters—"It's the economy, stupid"—served as the Clintonites' political mantra. No matter how the Republicans tried to divert them, the Democrats focused again and again on the recession and blamed Bush, Reagan, and the GOP. "Labor has been devalued for a dozen years," Clinton said in a typical stump speech. "We have stayed too long with trickle-down economics, and we have paid a terrible price for it." In the end, most voters decided that Bush had not paid enough attention to domestic issues, especially the economy. Even if Clinton and Perot were not fully palatable as alternatives, most citizens simply didn't want George Bush to be their leader anymore.

STILL, THERE WERE many signs of trouble for Clinton that would not fully emerge until after he became President. The Democratic team was brilliant at tactical warfare—the news-cycle-to-news-cycle mastery of rapid response to any charge or criticism that surfaced. Clintonites saw the campaign as a game and treated the press as an enemy force to be manipulated and circumvented. To that end they used paid advertising and creative exploitation of "new media," such as Clinton's appearances on radio and television talk shows and MTV, to get their message across. Many of Clinton's senior advisers—including Carville, media consultant Grunwald, chief spokesman Stephanopoulos, and press secretary Dee Dee Myers—treated journalists in a dismissive or condescending way. At least reporters thought so.

I got these impressions not only from other reporters who followed Clinton, but also at the Democratic convention, which I covered for *U.S. News,* and in trips with Clinton during the campaign. The contempt came from the top. Bill and Hillary Clinton were furious at the way the press had treated him on the character issue, especially during the New Hampshire primary and the subsequent Democratic primaries in the winter of 1992.

Many members of the White House press corps, however, were laboring under the illusion that the media would be given a clean slate if Clinton became President-elect. These journalists were exhilarated by the prospect of getting to know a young, vigorous leader who promised to do dramatic things in Washington. But such a friendly relationship was never in the cards. "That was an unrealistic expectation, considering that the first thing you told the world about him was that he was a philandering, draft-dodging pot-smoker," recalls Myers. But she failed to make the crucial distinction between the political reporters, some of whose members *had* portrayed Clinton in this way, and the White House press corps, which by and large did not cover him during the primary campaign. Myers now admits the difference, but adds, "You have to understand how that set Clinton and Mrs. Clinton up to view the press generally."

Clinton's media problem was unmistakable when I made visits to his transition offices in Little Rock after the election as I prepared to begin covering his administration. I would call ahead from Washington to make an appointment with Clinton aides, and would be told by their assistants that I could come on down if I wanted—a four-hour plane trip via Atlanta or Cincinnati—and they would see if they could fit me into their schedules. It was as if I were asking for an appointment with the pope.

Inside the Clinton operation, it wasn't hard to see why the media were being given short shrift. The transition from winning candidate to Inauguration was turning into a disaster. Fearing news leaks, Bill and Hillary were keeping their decisions so close to the vest that even their senior aides didn't know what was going on. The President-elect's tendency to discuss issues to death was also hurting him. He was taking too long, aides later conceded, to select his cabinet, and was neglecting the even more basic task of choosing his White House staff. He was also procrastinating over what priorities he would set for his first one hundred days, which he claimed would rival Franklin Roosevelt's in their historic impact. He was quickly gaining the reputation that no President wants—of being incapable of making quick decisions.

Making it worse for the staff was their own uncertainty. With the exception of political consultants Carville, Begala, and Grunwald and pollster Stan Greenberg, virtually all of Clinton's campaign aides wanted jobs in government; but they were unsure of their fate during most of the transition. The result was an atmosphere of chaos and tension. "I don't know what previous transitions have been like from a Democratic administration to a Republican administration, but the pace of the transition was so demanding," Myers recalls. "It was worse than any time during the campaign. It was worse than almost any time during the administration, in my opinion, because the demands were extraordinary. There was no time to try to put together a government in sixty days in the midst of tremendous personal uncertainty. The atmosphere was poisoned."

For the press, there were periods of virtual news blackout in Little Rock. Stephanopoulos, the chief spokesman, was part of the problem, because he was unsuited for his job. For years he had worked as an aide to congressional Democrats, including House Democratic leader Richard Gephardt of Missouri, and was a gifted legislative strategist and faithful liberal, but he was not a communications specialist. Yet he was given the responsibility of briefing reporters every day in Little Rock, a function he carried with him into the White House. Soon the atmosphere at his briefings became hostile and chaotic. When frustrated reporters pressed him for information, he seemed to delight in denying their requests or dismissing their questions.

During the first months of the Clinton era, Stephanopoulos, with his boyish good looks, tousled hair, and aura of power, enjoyed a brief flurry of attention from the tabloids as the sexiest man in the President's inner circle. Gossip columnists wrote stories on his dating habits, his taste in restaurants, and other personal aspects of his life. The media and other critics around Washington saw his hand in all manner of decisions—so much so that he once told me he was amused that he had such an "Oz-like quality." But this sense of humor was generally lost on the press corps. Like many of the other Clintonites, Stephanopoulos wanted to be a policymaker; the care and feeding of the press corps was secondary.

Dee Dee Myers also was miscast as White House press secretary. A Californian who was Clinton's campaign press secretary, she had worked for a succession of losers: Walter Mondale in 1984, Michael Dukakis in 1988, and California gubernatorial candidate Dianne Feinstein in 1990. Compounding her problem, Myers, like Stephanopoulos, had no experience in the executive branch, and bore a huge grudge against the press for its focus during the primaries on Clinton's draft record and his reputation for womanizing. Reporters complained that she didn't take their questions seriously, failed to order her staff to cooperate, and was never interested in learning the way that White House reporters operate. Eventually, she might have been an excellent press secretary if she had been given more seasoning as a deputy. With her youthful appearance and flippant approach to major issues, she seemed to lack *gravitas*. She also was kept out of many important meetings, which further crippled her ability to deal with the issues of the day. Many reporters wondered why she had accepted the job in the first place, since she was denied truly senior status. When the Clinton administration formally took over, she was not even given the large office normally assigned to the President's press secretary; Stephanopoulos took this space for himself. Instead, she accepted a much smaller office two doors down, the room that a deputy press secretary had occupied in previous administrations. The first female press secretary to a President deserved better.

A few Clinton aides, especially the more mature ones who had experience in the business world, were more considerate than the younger ones. Mickey Kantor, the chief of staff during the transition, was one of them. He would reserve time for reporters, and always attempted to be cordial and helpful. He was a successful lawyer in Los Angeles and a strong manager—too strong for the younger Clintonites and Mrs. Clinton, who thought he was too dictatorial. But Kantor could be counted on to deliver on a promised interview. We would meet at a quiet coffee shop not far from the transition headquarters, and he was able to provide a sense of how Clinton was organizing his government, with an emphasis on ethnic, racial, and gender diversity. Later, Kantor became the U.S. trade representative, where his managerial skills were put to good use, and would emerge as one of the successes in the Clinton cabinet.

Despite the difficulties, I found my visits to Little Rock to be indispensable in one way: I gained an understanding of the Arkansas part of Bill and Hillary Clinton's lives. Although Little Rock is a medium-sized city, the political environment is that of a small town. All the politically active people know one another. Skip Rutherford, a local public-relations man helping out with the transition, was kind enough to show me around, and wherever he went, he was forever waving to pals and shouting hello across downtown Little Rock's streets. It was the same with other political and civic activists. In restaurants where the Arkansas political and civic elite tended to congregate, such as Doe's Eat Place, they would table-hop and I would be introduced graciously. Everyone in Little Rock seemed enormously proud of Bill and Hillary. Their friends were eager to tell positive stories about them, especially how the soon-to-be President and First Lady were preternaturally smart, savvy, and altruistic. I could see that for the Clintons, leaving Little Rock would be like leaving the womb. It seemed to me that they would find the adjustment to Washington, a harsh and unforgiving place where they could no longer dominate their political environment, very difficult indeed.

When I interviewed Bill Clinton for the first time shortly after the election with a team of *U.S. News* reporters, I got the impression that he was a bright, engaging man of great charm and enthusiasm. Clinton welcomed us warmly at the Governor's Mansion and called us by our first names as he sat in a favorite chair sipping coffee. He said he was tired—he had dark circles under his eyes that would rarely disappear thereafter—but he was eager to take Washington by storm, ready to sweep away the old methods of doing things and to throw himself into a crusade for historic change. He also displayed no awe or doubts about the office or his ability to master it.

I came away from that interview, however, with the feeling that Bill Clinton was a politician who didn't have a sense of his own limits or those of his government. He reeled off a list of policies he would reverse, legislation he would persuade Congress to pass, executive orders he would sign. It was as if he considered Washington a high school political-science laboratory where he could test his theories, and he was both the smartest kid in class and teacher's pet (which in fact he had been long ago in Hot Springs). Yet in Washington many of his rivals would be just as smart as he was, and the political culture would be much more resistant to change than he had ever dreamed.

9

Battle Stations

The relationship between the Clinton administration and the news media started with a fight. Scores of reporters returning to the White House after Clinton's swearing-in found that the Upper Press Office—a small gathering place outside the press secretary's office—had been closed to them for the first time. Helen Thomas, correspondent for United Press International and doyenne of the White House press corps, spent much of Inauguration Day in a fury, shouting at Dee Dee Myers. "This is an act of war," she fumed. Thomas and a growing number of her colleagues badgered Myers and other White House officials whenever they showed themselves. A press staff, they argued, needs to be accessible. "What have you got to hide?" Thomas demanded.

The next morning the fuss intensified. As communications director, George Stephanopoulos showed up to brief the media on camera and got a rude surprise; the administration was less than twenty-four hours old, and the press corps was already in revolt. Stephanopoulos wanted to talk about Clinton's economic plan and his timetable for filling out his cabinet and senior staff, but the reporters, fidgeting in their assigned seats in the White House briefing room, had a much more parochial issue on their minds—what they called the new "no-fly zone" in the Upper Press Office.

With considerable hyperbole, Thomas argued that not even Richard Nixon had displayed such arrogance toward the fourth estate and had such a penchant for secrecy.

"We were walled in from the moment we got there," Thomas recalls. "It was like an Edgar Allan Poe story, like the 'Cask of Amontillado.' They were putting in one brick after another, closing us in. Can you imagine . . . reporters not being able to go to the press secretary and police blocking the way? I was in shock. . . . Who were these people? Suddenly we're personae non gratae; we're going to be . . . ghettoized, so we were screaming bloody murder."

Other wire-service correspondents, including Terry Hunt of the Associated Press and Gene Gibbons of Reuters, and a vocal group of reporters for regional news bureaus, agreed. It was, they insisted, a matter of survival. What happens, they asked, if we need reaction to a local story or some international development? What if we need to confirm that an important dignitary will be in town to meet the President? We're paid to find out such facts, they said, no matter how trivial they may seem to the policy mavens at the White House, so we need immediate access to the press secretary.

The reporters had a point about survival, but they didn't realize how big a war they had on their hands. Bill and Hillary were intent on circumventing the White House press corps. Other administrations had tried it, of course, but the roots of this particular flanking strategy ran deep. The Clintons were convinced that the news media had contributed to his loss of the Arkansas governorship in 1980 by not giving him proper credit for his accomplishments—a complaint that would become common during their White House years. Journalist David Maraniss points out that in 1982 the Clintons and their inner circle in Arkansas "decided that they would never again rely on the 'free media'—newspaper, radio, and television reporters—to define Clinton and his programs. Interweaving means and ends, they would use paid media, commercials, and grass-roots mailings whenever they wanted to get their message to the public, even during a mid-term legislative session. Individual journalists might be courted, especially the peskiest ones. . . . But for the most part, the press was not part of the plan." Going around the mainstream media became their modus operandi, an essential part of a permanent campaign.

The day after his Inauguration, Clinton laid down the law at his first meeting with his senior staff: As a matter of policy, they were to make an end run around the White House press corps. They would arrange a series of town meetings around the country starring the new President and First Lady, which would be carried live on television, and they would set up frequent appearances on *Larry King Live* and other television and radio call-in shows to get the administration's message directly to the country.

It was a fundamental error. Stephanopoulos and his senior communications staff, none of whom had extensive journalistic backgrounds, were not only trying to restrict reporters' access but to isolate the media as no administration had since Richard Nixon's. Reflecting the Clintons' feelings, they could barely camouflage their disdain for mainstream journalism, and this was the way they were perceived by reporters whose questions were left unanswered, whose requests for interviews were regularly turned down, and whose phones rarely rang with callbacks from White House officials.

"When Clinton became President, there was a sense that they could just simply go over the heads of the networks and deal with the local affiliates," says NBC commentator Tim Russert, "because when they got off that campaign plane in Iowa, New Hampshire, Illinois, and other places, they would just abandon the national press and go right for the local TV, and it would get them through that hurdle. What they didn't realize is that it was a traveling circus, which went from town to town and state to state, and people were thrilled for that one-week period because the circus was in town. Now the circus has returned to home base and is there for four years, and you can't take it on the road every day or once a week to try to win that particular town. Suddenly you have to govern a whole vast country, where people get their information in a lot of different ways, and most people still get their news and information through the traditional news media."

Many Washington veterans saw the problem coming. James Lake, a Republican media consultant who had advised both Reagan and Bush, was flabbergasted when he read a story in *The Washington Post* about how Clinton aide Jeff Eller was boasting that the administration was going over the heads of the mainstream media. He pointed the story out to Michael McCurry, a new associate in Lake's public-relations firm who had worked for several Democratic presidential candidates in the past. "Well," Lake said, "you guys have done some things right and some things wrong, but this is the dumbest thing you've done so far." Every White House tries to circumvent the mainstream press corps, Lake added, "but we never bragged about it." In the end, he said, the mainstream media will always drown out the regional or alternative media.

Mistakenly, the Clintonites thought the world had changed. They adopted a theory that was summarized by *The Media Studies Journal* in its spring 1994 issue: "There's a view that holds that the 1992 presidential election marked a major, irreversible turning point for the news media, for politicians and—especially—for the American people, who have depended on the former to keep an eye on the latter, while mistrusting both. Long-heralded communications technology, this view maintains, changed all that: In 1992, the people were no longer dependent on the press to understand their leaders, and leaders would no longer have to trust the press to get their messages to the people intact. The media middleman, so this wisdom goes, has lost his monopoly franchise.

"Bill Clinton, perhaps sensing the public's malaise with the traditional media, recognizing an electorate's increasing love affair with interactive media—from video games to talk shows—and himself not entirely willing to hand over control of his message exclusively to the press, undertook many now famous end runs. TV talk shows from *Arsenio* to MTV to *Larry King Live* to *Donahue*, radio call-in programs from New York to Los Angeles, televised 'town meetings' of 'average Americans' (with the media watching on monitors outside)—all were designed to permit Clinton to take back control of his message from a press corps he didn't trust."

The Clintonites' obsession with new technology became comic—and counterproductive. The press staff urged each reporter to lease an electronic beeper so the White House could keep everyone up-to-date on the earth-shaking developments expected in their new Camelot. (In the past, a telephone recording system had worked just fine; reporters would call in and listen to a message outlining the activities of the day.) The beepers represented a valid theory, but they became a costly bother. All day the President's schedule and his staff's "media accessibilities" would change; routine briefings would be called for 1 P.M., then slip to 2, then 3:30, then 5, all dutifully transmitted by the little beepers. The constant updates drove home the point that the Clintonites were hopelessly disorganized.

The Clintonites might have enjoyed the company of individual journalists on occasion, but they reasoned, as many other White House staffs had before, that as an institution the press must be kept at arm's length. Just as troubling, Clintonites seemed to consider White House reporters as "George Bush's press corps," leftovers from the Republican years who had wanted Bush to win and couldn't forgive Clinton for beating him. This perception was totally false.

There was no strategy to deal with each segment of the media—ranging from the networks to the big daily newspapers, the newsmagazines and regional newspapers, radio reporters, print columnists, and television commentators, in addition to the "new media" such as Larry King and radio-talk-show hosts in local markets around the country.

The irony was that in January 1993 the White House press corps was eager to make a fresh start. Most journalists covering Clinton wanted to get to know this fascinating and energetic new President, along with what appeared to be a new age First Lady. Here was a President who wanted to go back to the days of activist government, and there would be news. The White House press corps was ready for a honeymoon.

The Clintons and their advisers bungled the opportunity. For all their supposed brilliance and public-relations skills, they didn't understand the rules of Journalism 101. They never realized that more than anything else, journalists want good stories, positive or negative, and that getting an exclusive is one of the best prizes in the business. The White House could easily have committed itself to feeding the beast, as the advisers to Bush and Reagan described the process of satisfying the media's appetite for news. They could have placed positive stories with reporters all around Washington, guaranteeing themselves favorable coverage and good relationships with those who benefited from the information.

Yet the Clintonites could never get over their animosity toward the press. A middle-level press staffer spoke for her colleagues when she angrily complained to reporters, "You people act as if you own this place." She had a point about our arrogance, but the White House reaction was to increase the tension level and make the relationship worse for everyone.

BECAUSE HE STAYED isolated from the mainstream media, Clinton's image problem intensified. In those early months his Arkansas reputation as "slick Willie" took a firm hold in the White House press corps. During the campaign, he had often refused to give straight answers in dealing with sensitive issues, such as allegations of marital infidelity and the military-draft question. The same pattern now reemerged on many other subjects. The new President appeared more interested in leaving himself wiggle room than in explaining himself clearly. He seemed a man without moorings, with an adolescent tendency to make excuses.

For their part, Clinton and his aides quickly had their suspicions confirmed that the press corps was more than ever obsessed with trivia and playing what the President called "gotcha" journalism, in which the main objective was to catch the White House in mistakes or inconsistencies. Indeed, one story followed another about White House ineptitude and loss of credibility, but the press didn't make them up; they were all based on administration blunders. Taken together, a portrait emerged of a presidency that was courting disaster.

Immediately after his election, Clinton began breaking some of his key campaign promises. He abandoned the middle-class tax cut he had pledged to support, although he would resurrect the idea after the Democrats suffered severe losses in the 1994 midterm elections. He reversed himself on U.S. policy toward Haiti by refusing to accept any more refugees. He decided that trade liberalization was more important than pushing for human rights in China.

Examples of White House bungling and presidential indecisiveness were legion. The most important was Clinton's withdrawal, within a few days of his Inauguration, of Zoe Baird as his nominee for attorney general after disclosures that she had hired an illegal nanny. Then he moved to name Kimba Wood attorney general, but she had a similar problem and again he backed off. Finally, he selected Florida prosecutor Janet Reno. He appointed Lani Guinier to be head of the Justice Department's civil-rights division, then retreated and withdrew her name when she was attacked for having excessively liberal views.

There was also the ongoing controversy over gays in the military. Shortly after the election, the President-elect boasted that he would overturn many years of Pentagon policy and allow homosexuals and lesbians to serve in the armed forces. The story got huge play, and his proposal stirred up a gigantic controversy, even among fellow Democrats. It seemed another case where Clinton couldn't get his priorities straight and was veering toward the left despite portraying himself as a moderate and "new kind of Democrat." When he backed off and adopted a more amorphous policy toward gays in the military, it reinforced his image as a waffler.

Then there was the ham-handed firing of the White House travel-office staff. Many reporters felt they were repeatedly misled about the reasons for the dismissals. There was also Clinton's $200 haircut on *Air Force One* at Los Angeles International Airport, which seemed to violate his self-proclaimed image as a populist.

"We got off to a rocky start," admits Dee Dee Myers, "but then the press started immediately with the 'Is Clinton's a failed presidency?' within the first couple of weeks. . . . There was [an] unbelievably harsh rush to judgment. And from then on we could do no right even when we did right. The failures took on grand symbolism and the successes were basically ignored. . . . When the economic-stimulus package failed, which was only a $16 billion package, it became a symbol for the administration's incompetence, an inability to get legislation passed through a Democratic Congress, the President's lack of a relationship with the Hill, blah, blah, blah, even though ultimately Clinton got his $1.5 trillion budget resolution passed without any Republican support. It was [as if] all these setbacks, which were part of the give-and-take of the legislative process, took on symbolic importance because the press had a storyline after the first couple of weeks, which was 'young, arrogant, incompetent.' We couldn't figure out how to get out of that box for the first two years that I was there. . . . Take age. Everybody in America thought this was a White House being run by thirty-year-olds. Well, the chief of staff was forty-seven. The budget director was fifty-five. The national security adviser was fifty-five. The deputy national security adviser was fifty. The chief domestic policy adviser was in her fifties. The National Economic Council director was fifty-five. [The media] ignored the people who were making policy."

Myers's explanation is only partly valid. The senior policymakers she mentions were indeed mature individuals, but many other policymakers in key positions were young and inexperienced in the ways of the White House—including Stephanopoulos, Myers herself, economic adviser Gene Sperling, domestic advisers Bruce Reed and Michael Waldman, communications strategists David Dreyer and Mark Gearan. Many members of the White House staff responded to the perceived misperceptions about their inexperience in precisely the wrong way—with hostility and a lack of basic manners, especially the junior staff members who had frequent contact with reporters.

A senior administration official who had regular dealings with the White House press operation was aghast. The attitude of the press-office staff, he says, was "We're the zookeepers and we're here to mind the animals and make sure that they don't bite the tourists."

Helen Thomas recalls: "The simplest thing, the time of day, would be rebuffed. They came in with an attitude, and that attitude . . . must have been inspired from the top. Mrs. Clinton had it too . . . Usually we have a honeymoon. . . . We never did with them. They came in with so much hostility. It was almost like being back in the arena in the Nixon days. . . . Why don't they feel that reporters have a legitimate role in this democracy?"

Stephanopoulos's curt assistant, Heather Beckel, would schedule interviews with reporters, only to change the appointments two or three times in the same day, disrupting the journalists' schedules with no apparent regard for deadlines. When an interview finally did occur, "Steph," as his friends on the staff called him, would sit with his feet on a table, or sometimes sprawled out on a couch in his office, and deflect one question after another. Generally he seemed preoccupied with other thoughts; then he would abruptly say, "Gotta go," and walk out of his office.

". . . It was more than the new team's inexperience that was creating massive ill will in the press corps," says political scientist Stephen Hess. "Every President seeks opportunities to go over the heads of White House reporters—televised speeches from the Oval Office and weekly radio addresses, out-of-Washington press conferences and luncheons for editors and publishers. Clinton, however, was the first President to conclude that he didn't need White House reporters, that it was not necessary to be filtered through the press corps. While all new Presidents tell reporters that they will have the most open administration in history (even though they all close up sooner or later), Clinton didn't even make this gesture. On the contrary, he told radio and television correspondents at their annual dinner in March 1993, 'You know why I can stiff you on press conferences? Because Larry King liberated me by giving me to the American people directly.' "

"The message here may be very simple," says Frank Mankiewicz, a Washington public-relations executive and former press secretary to Senator Robert F. Kennedy. "You can get elected from outside the media mainstream, and the 1992 election may even have set a permanent precedent, but it is just as difficult to govern without the Establishment Media as it has ever been. The Clinton administration must either wait for a generation of media Bigfeet to pass from the scene, move the Capitol to Tulsa, or figure out some way to involve the media outlaws early on in government, as well as in politics."

In retrospect, Stephanopoulos has a different and far simpler explanation for the early missteps: "So much of our problem was a late start; [we were] overtired; too much was going on, and then certainly it got out of control with gays in the military and [the controversies over] the attorney general, which clouded everything." He admitted that he was vastly overtaxed, because essentially he had two full-time jobs, senior policy adviser to the President and principal link to the news media, and couldn't do both. As a result, he neglected the media relationship, something he now regrets. But he was not persuaded that the coverage would have been much different even if the White House had run more smoothly; the press, he said, was just looking to find fault.

THE WHITE HOUSE caused many problems for Clinton by running what the President called "a permanent campaign." This meant oversimplifying issues, emphasizing public relations, and attacking adversaries, all with the goal of generating voter support and re-electing Clinton. Every issue, it seemed, was to be treated as a political battle. The new President had promised the country the most productive first one hundred days since the New Deal, and to accomplish this he needed to work with the Democratic majorities in Congress. Hence, Clinton really should not have been looking for enemies to fight but for allies to work with. Yet the White House set up a series of "war rooms" in an attempt to replicate the creative turn-on-a-dime atmosphere that had developed in Little Rock during the campaign.

When I visited the budget war room—the most famous and important of them all—in the spring of 1993 in the Old Executive Office Building, it was clear that the Clintonites had at least succeeded in re-creating the Little Rock atmosphere of chaos and combativeness. A press escort brought me to the site for an interview with Roger Altman, a poker-faced millionaire Wall Street investor who had joined the Treasury Department. Altman was running the budget war room to win passage—narrowly but successfully, it turned out—of the Clinton economic plan. Self-important young aides bustled everywhere, shouting messages to one another as they cupped their hands over telephone receivers. Blaring television sets tuned to live coverage of congressional proceedings on C-SPAN intensified the din. Computer keyboards rattled. Half-eaten slices of pizza and soft-drink cans were strewn about.

Suddenly I noticed Altman, in shirtsleeves, across a desktop with a telephone at his ear. I waited until he looked up, then hurriedly introduced myself. "I'm busy here," he announced. Someone shouted, "He's on the phone"—a reference, it appeared, to a senator—and Altman lowered his voice so that I couldn't hear his conversation. I waited. Realizing that I might never get this close to Altman again, I told him I really needed to talk to him. He gave me a cursory five-minute interview, then declared that he had to go. I was ushered out, wondering why the White House had bothered to bring me there in the first place. The chat had provided no useful information, which was standard for most White House interviews in those days.

ON THE EVENING of July 20, 1993, Clinton was doing a live interview with Larry King when White House chief of staff Mack McLarty whispered into his ear during a commercial break. They had an "important appointment," McLarty said somberly, and the President left immediately.

A few moments later, in private, McLarty broke the bad news: the body of deputy White House legal counsel Vincent Foster had been found in Fort Marcy Park just outside the capital. He had been shot in the head, and it was an apparent suicide.

The next morning at 11:30, the President told the White House staff, "No one can ever know why this happened." He was deeply shaken. Foster had been an old friend from Hope, Arkansas, and he always seemed to be a rock of stability and good sense. But to the media, what followed seemed less a case of grieving friends being thrown off stride by the tragic death of a beloved colleague than a bungled investigation and possibly a cover-up.

There were many questions. Foster had handled legal matters for the Clintons both before and during his White House service. Was he hiding some sinister developments in the Whitewater affair, a failed Arkansas land deal that the Clintons had been involved in years before? Had he found something embarrassing or criminal in the Clintons' financial affairs, which he was in the process of reviewing? Why were files relevant to Foster's death kept from government investigators? It turned out that Foster had been involved in the controversial firing of the White House travel office staff. Was he worried about some facts that had not yet come to light? Editorials in *The Wall Street Journal* had lambasted him for being at the center of a conspiracy of Clinton advisers who were alumni of the Rose law firm in Little Rock. Was his death related to those charges? Foster had told friends that the White House press corps was more interested in savaging people, including himself, to create a sensational story than in covering the administration fairly. Was he driven to kill himself by the media?

Sensing that the White House was hiding something, the press corps jumped into the story with a vengeance. Adding to the impression of a cover-up was the fact that no one sealed off Foster's office until 10:15 A.M. the day after his death. Yet White House staffers had rummaged around his office the night before—to look for a suicide note, they said. Some of Foster's files were sent to the Clintons' private lawyer and not to investigators. On July 26, six days after Foster's death, an undated, unsigned note torn into twenty-seven pieces, with one section missing, was found in the bottom of Foster's briefcase. It was apparently a suicide note outlining things that were troubling the deputy counsel, including his "mistakes from ignorance, inexperience and overwork" and his feeling that "the WSJ [*Wall Street Journal*] editors lie without consequence." Foster wrote, "I was not meant for the job or the spotlight of public life in Washington. Here ruining people is considered sport." Yet the note was held by White House staffers for thirty hours before it was turned over to the Park police, and wasn't made public until August 10, more than two weeks later.

In the end, the handling of the Vince Foster case was a blemish on both the White House and the press. The Clintonites made a series of blunders because of their inexperience and grief. While journalists were correct to be suspicious, they went overboard, suggesting without much evidence that a big scandal was brewing. The effect was a worsening of relations between the White House and the press.

AND OF COURSE there was Whitewater. The basic facts were simple: In 1978, Bill and Hillary Clinton had invested in a resort in northern Arkansas being planned by Whitewater Development Corporation, and the resort had never been built. From there, the story became more and more tangled, and few journalists, let alone voters, could figure out exactly what the point of it all was. Much media analysis painted Whitewater as a scandal that showed the conflicts of interest and incestuous relationships among rich and powerful people in Arkansas. There were allegations that the Clintons had taken improper tax deductions, that Whitewater documents were missing, that Mrs. Clinton had been hired by Madison Guaranty, a small savings and loan owned by James McDougal, a partner with the Clintons in the Whitewater deal, to help prevent a state agency from closing it down after it was found to be insolvent. Later there were questions about whether Madison Guaranty funds had been used to pay off a Clinton campaign debt from his 1984 gubernatorial race. The press also raised questions about whether there had been improper contacts between officials in the White House, including legal counsel Bernard Nussbaum, and those in the Treasury Department, including deputy Treasury secretary Roger Altman, about the government investigation into Whitewater and related matters.

Many media organizations, including *The Washington Post, The New York Times,* and *U.S. News & World Report,* assigned reporters to investigate Whitewater. The stories poured forth, often without context and without apparent significance. Not wanting to miss the next "Watergate," the media never gave the Clintons the benefit of the doubt, and there were plenty of errors. There was the *Time* cover story suggesting that Stephanopoulos had tried to obstruct justice by demanding that former Republican prosecutor Jay Stephens be removed from the Whitewater investigation being conducted by the Resolution Trust Corporation. It turned out that *Time*'s charges were overwrought and unfair, and to make matters worse, the magazine used on its cover a misleading four-month-old photo as if it were contemporaneous with the Stephanopoulos-Stephens story.

Newsweek also took severe criticism for reporting that Hillary Rodham Clinton didn't use any of her own money in making a controversial commodities investment in 1978 that earned her $100,000. It turned out that *Newsweek,* caught up in the feeding frenzy over Whitewater, got it wrong; Mrs. Clinton had invested $1,000 in the transaction.

Yet the overall impression given to the public was that something rotten and of great consequence had happened and that the Clintons and their cronies were trying to hide it. In the end, the Clintons decided that they had to ask for a special counsel to investigate Whitewater; otherwise, they told friends, the press would never let up and the administration would be so distracted that it couldn't govern effectively.

As of late 1995, the outcome of that investigation still remains to be seen, but for many months in 1993 and 1994, Whitewater infected everything. One key Clinton adviser called it a "Chinese water drop." When McLarty stepped into the briefing room one day at the end of 1993, he intended to announce the appointments of Pat Griffin as the new chief congressional lobbyist for the White House and Harold Ickes to be the new deputy chief of staff, with responsibility for health-care reform, but most of the questions were about Whitewater. When the President was presiding over an East Room ceremony to publicize his program to retrain American workers for jobs of the future, CBS's Rita Braver spotted McLarty and shouted, "Are you gonna resign?" The chief of staff was shaken. After all, he was one of the senior White House aides who had not been subpoenaed to appear before a congressional committee investigating Whitewater, yet he was being dragged into the swamp. Later he told a friend that he finally understood what character assassination was all about.

When Clinton visited Prague in January 1994, he got more publicly frustrated by the Whitewater coverage than ever before. ABC's Ted Koppel was on the trip, and the other networks were complaining that he was being given unfair access. Consequently, the White House gave each of the other networks the chance to ask a couple of questions during brief presidential interviews. Rita Braver asked about a tripartite agreement just signed among the United States, Russia, and Ukraine. Then she asked about Clinton's summit with Russian president Boris Yeltsin, and finally she posed a general question about Whitewater, which Clinton answered. Then came Jim Miklaszewski of NBC, and all of his questions were about Whitewater. Clinton blew his stack and walked off the set. In private, he lambasted Dee Dee Myers with the worst tongue-lashing she ever endured from the President.

"Here we are halfway around the world," Clinton screamed at his press secretary. "I don't know why we talk to reporters if they're not interested in what we're doing. Why do they bother to come? Why don't they just stay home if this is all they care about?"

ANOTHER FLASHPOINT WAS a new round of accusations about Clinton's sex life. For years there had been rumors about Clinton and adultery, but except for Gennifer Flowers's claims during the campaign about a longtime affair with Clinton while he was governor, there were no names attached to the accusations. But in December 1993, *The American Spectator,* a conservative magazine, published an article by David Brock that quoted four Arkansas state troopers—two of them on the record—about the President's sexual past. The men claimed that throughout his governorship and his presidential transition, Clinton had used them to procure women for him, play lookout while he was having sex, and keep his liaisons secret from his wife. The article also suggested that Clinton had offered one of the troopers a job if he refused to cooperate with reporters who wanted information about his indiscretions. Since, at the very least, there was a legitimate question of whether Clinton had abused his office by misusing the troopers at his command, the mainstream media covered the story in considerable detail. CNN interviewed two of the troopers, and the White House was thrown into a frenzy. Finally, the White House issued a denial through adviser Bruce Lindsey, an old friend from Arkansas now working in the West Wing: "The allegations are ridiculous . . . and there is nothing here that would dignify a further response," he said.

But it turned out that Clinton *had* talked to at least one of the troopers to persuade him, without success, not to go public with his stories. To many reporters, this seemed out of bounds and reckless, and showed how deep the presidency had sunk: The chief executive was now making phone calls to shut down stories about his alleged sexual dalliances. The *Los Angeles Times* published its own version of the troopers' allegations a few days later, and the press gave the story widespread coverage. Here were real people, not anonymous sources, making serious accusations that were both salacious and substantive in terms of possible abuse of power. Adding fuel to the story were the White House's halfhearted denials. Several officials told me that no one except Bill Clinton knew the full truth, so no one could make a categorical denial. It was widely acknowledged by Clinton friends and associates that he had strayed from his marriage vows, although in his famous interview with Hillary on *60 Minutes* in February 1992, he had suggested that the indiscretions were in the past.

"Troopergate" eventually faded as a story, only to be resurrected the following May, when an Arkansas woman named Paula Jones filed suit to charge Clinton with sexual harassment. She claimed that the then-governor had asked her to perform oral sex in a Little Rock hotel room in May 1991. A federal judge in Little Rock ruled that Clinton was immune from a trial while he remained in office but the judge allowed Jones's lawyers to continue gathering evidence. Subsequent legal maneuvers promised to delay a final resolution for years, but the case once again embroiled Bill Clinton in a tawdry mess. He was increasingly the target of ridicule for his overindulgences, sexual, culinary, and political, and the overall impression left with voters was of a glib and reckless teenager with little self-control and an excuse for everything.

The night before Jones filed her suit, White House communications director Mark Gearan was in his office watching the network news, as were virtually all other members of the senior staff. A young aide flipped on all three of Gearan's television sets and raised the volume as one network after the other aired its Paula Jones piece in anticipation of the filing of her lawsuit the next day. Gearan shook his head sadly. Every network was giving the story a big ride. Andrea Mitchell, NBC's veteran White House correspondent, blended together a number of developments from the day, including congressional passage of a ban on some types of assault weapons, the ineffectiveness of the administration's Haiti policy, and the sexual-harassment suit. Gearan was annoyed because he felt that NBC's approach put Paula Jones's allegations on the same plane of credibility as other more important issues. Still, he didn't call the network to complain because he knew it wouldn't do any good.

The next day, the press corps eagerly awaited the arrival of Jones's lawyers in Little Rock to file suit, the last day possible under their interpretation of the statute of limitations in Arkansas. At one point the mellifluous voice of Mutual Radio correspondent

Peter Maer rose above the din in the White House press room: "She's filed." With their customary irreverence, reporters latched on to the juiciest part of the lawsuit, Jones's claim that she could identify "distinguishing" characteristics on President Clinton's genitalia, observed when he supposedly exposed himself to her in the hotel room. Members of the press corps compiled a humorous list of hypothetical identifying features on the presidential groin, including a Wal-Mart logo, the words *It Whistles Dixie,* a Razorback snout in honor of the mascot of the University of Arkansas, a "Home of the Whopper" tattoo, a Confederate flag, a "Bubba" tattoo, a happy face, a Big Boy bib, and Astroturf.

THE CREDIBILITY OF the White House sank to a new low in the press, and Clintonites responded by shutting down virtually all information about the Clintons' personal lives and lifestyle. The rift with the media became so wide that the shell-shocked White House was more reluctant than ever to cooperate on even the most benign story ideas.

It was a familiar pattern. In the early spring of 1993, I began collecting information about a theme that seemed to be both positive and interesting: Bill and Hillary Clinton as working parents. I wanted to examine how the President and the First Lady coped with the problems faced by millions of other baby boomers, balancing work with their commitment to each other, to their daughter, Chelsea, and to their self-fulfillment as individuals. I believed the story would have resonance and would allow the Clintons to describe their personal and professional lives so that Americans could connect with them.

But, as always, anything smacking of the personal was a hard sell at the Clinton White House. It took weeks of diligent reporting to get enough insight and a sufficient number of anecdotes to form a story. Time and again, friends of the couple told me that Bill and Hillary were so suspicious of the media that they probably wouldn't cooperate. Given their experience with the press during the campaign, their doubts were certainly understandable, but in this case their suspicions were unfounded. I was, after all, pursuing an essentially positive story.

I learned something else. Arkansas friends of Bill Clinton, such as Carolyn Staley, David Leopoulos, and the Rev. Rex Horne, the President's longtime pastor at Immanuel Baptist Church in Little Rock, tried to be helpful, but it gradually became clear that Bill Clinton had walled off large chunks of his life from even his best pals. Staley, a close friend from their days as teenagers in Hot Springs, said she never knew of any womanizing by Bill. He never mentioned anything of the sort and never hinted about the troubles in his marriage, which he later admitted on national television during the campaign.

Eventually, the Clintons agreed to sit down for an interview about my story on achieving balance in their lives. When the day came, I showed up at the White House with my *U.S. News* colleague at the time, Matt Cooper. Like so many aspects of the White House operation, little had been planned in advance. Press secretary Myers and other press staffers first took us to the Diplomatic Room in the residential quarters of the East Wing, then deemed it too dull and formal a setting, so while we waited for the Clintons to arrive, they ushered us into a garden patio. As we sat waiting on wrought-iron furniture, a strong wind chilled us to the bone and everyone began shivering. Suddenly, the President emerged from the East Wing carrying a steaming cup of coffee, with the First Lady a few paces behind. He announced that it was too cold, so following his lead, we all pulled our chairs across the Rose Garden lawn into the sun.

The interview went well. It was clear that the Clintons could be warm and ingratiating, and their personal story had relevance for millions of Americans, especially young and middle-aged professional people. I used the occasion to probe into the sensitive area that most Americans and White House reporters were interested in: the relationship between Bill and Hillary, and the family environment they were creating for their daughter.

The Clintons talked about how Chelsea always came first and how they intended to give her as normal a life as possible in the White House. The President said he planned to continue getting home each night in time for a family supper at about 7 P.M., which was something he did manage to do on most evenings. This was vital emotionally to all of them. "You know," Mrs. Clinton told me, "we've worked really hard to establish some time in the evening so that when we have dinner together, it's a real family time and not something that is structured. We also try to spend time afterward just talking, finding out what's going on . . . helping with homework and just really being with each other." The President gave Chelsea the run of the White House, and she took advantage of it. Sometimes she did her homework in the private study off the Oval Office from which George Bush had run the Persian Gulf War, while her dad sat at the big desk that John F. Kennedy had used and which his son had hidden under.

Earlier, the Clintons' aides and friends had confirmed rumors that Bill and Hillary did argue frequently and explosively—they had for years—although they denied a rumor that she had once hurled a lamp or a vase at the President in their residence. Intimates said that such temper flare-ups quickly faded. "Do they argue?" said a friend. "Sure they do. It's over who will supervise Chelsea's friends when they come over or how to stop phony Secret Service leaks about what's going on between them or about the way the White House is being run. It gets intense. They are both intellectually competitive people."

Friends also told me that it appeared that whatever serious trouble the Clintons may have endured in their relationship had been resolved long ago. Rather than futilely quiz them on such painful subjects—and risk the almost-certain cutoff of the interview and irreparable damage to my relationship with them—I stayed on the theme of how they kept balance in their lives. "That quest for balance is more difficult than ever for Bill and Hillary Rodham Clinton," I wrote in U.S. News. "Despite the advantages of the White House, with its large household staff and perquisites, they still face many of the same problems that other working couples experience in juggling jobs, friends, and family. But the new problems and tensions of the White House have highlighted some of their differences as professional managers, as political operatives, and as parents. Like other working couples, they battle with outside interferences to set priorities, they worry about getting time for private satisfactions, and their marriage is very much a work in progress. They are constantly forced to make compromises that sometimes leave them with doubts. 'We're still trying to get it right,' the President told U.S.

News. 'All I can say is that we have really struggled with it, and we've worked at it for 20 years.' "

ANOTHER REVEALING INCIDENT occurred after the July 1993 suicide of Vincent Foster. Reuters correspondent Larry McQuillan was covering the Clintons when they attended Foster's funeral in Arkansas, and the President was in obvious emotional pain. He stopped his motorcade at a watermelon stand that he had patronized since he was a boy and walked up to the media pool. He rambled on aimlessly, telling reporters how to grow prize-winning watermelons, relating how a farmer needed just the right amount of water and how the whole process took a lot of savvy. "At that point," McQuillan recalls, "he just wanted to talk to people. There was a rush of olden memories." The President went on to reminisce about a cow-chip-throwing contest that he had won long ago in Hope, Arkansas, his hometown. The local folks, Clinton said, kidded him that his victory was unfair; as a politician, he was a professional in tossing cow manure. "I had never seen the man open up like that," McQuillan says. "It told me there was a human person there—more than I had been exposed to."

The problem was that such humanizing glimpses into the Clintons' lives were all too rare. "Bill and Hillary Clinton are the most guarded presidential couple I've ever seen," says McQuillan, who has covered the presidency since Gerald Ford's administration. "You rarely get the sense you are seeing the real person. . . . Everything they do seems calculated. . . . There's a sense they're performing when reporters are around."

The Clintons were becoming caricatures, ridiculed by conservative talk-radio hosts and late-night television stars such as David Letterman and Jay Leno. The press was setting a negative news agenda for both the "old media" and the "new media" that the White House was so eager to cultivate. "No amount of contact with regional papers, radio talk shows, or alternative media will define you as much as the press corps that sees you every day," says Susan Page of *USA Today*. Bill Plante of CBS News adds: "It's not very easy to go over the heads of the press and Congress directly to the public unless you have a commanding presence, and one of the things that this President lacks, in my view, is a presidential presence. That hobbles him in dealing with the American public, and going through the new media or the old media isn't going to change it."

AS THE RELATIONSHIP between the press corps and the White House deteriorated markedly in the spring of 1993, White House chief of staff Mack McLarty realized that something drastic had to be done. He had known Bill Clinton since they were playmates in kindergarten and grew up together in Hope, but they were not intimate friends, as was commonly supposed in Washington. In fact, throughout much of the 1980s the two men had seen each other only three or four times a year. Since McLarty did not play a major part in his old chum's presidential campaign, he was floored when Clinton offered him the job of White House chief of staff. He told the President-elect that he knew little about Washington and would prefer to serve as a senior counselor in the White House, but Clinton insisted. For chief of staff, he wanted someone who was loyal, had business and management experience (McLarty was head of Arkla, a natural-gas company based in Little Rock), and was a stable family man. Mack qualified on all counts, and he couldn't say no.

McLarty realized immediately that he had big problems. He knew it was natural for a President-elect to bring some of his top campaign people into the new administration, but his common sense told him that Bill and Hillary were going too far. They were rewarding their political advisers without adequate consideration of whether they were qualified to govern the country. He also realized that he had none of his own longtime friends and confidants on staff, but once again he deferred to his old kindergarten pal.

The new chief of staff was troubled by the new administration's hostility to the mainstream media. He would not dream of acting in an arrogant or dismissive way, but he saw evidence of such behavior all around him. Early on, he told the President-elect that the new administration needed to "interface with the national press" by holding frequent news conferences and giving regular interviews, and Clinton agreed, but Hillary was an insurmountable obstacle. According to several Clinton strategists, her advice was to "roll over them." This is what was passing for a media strategy.

Actually, the administration's record during that first year was messy but modestly successful. Clinton won congressional approval for several of his priorities, including a budget plan that cut the growth of the deficit, a bill guaranteeing workers unpaid family leave to take care of their children during emergencies, and a national-service program that authorized government financial aid for education in exchange for a period of community service. Just as important, even though Clinton exhibited a troubling tendency to ignore foreign policy, U.S. relations with Russia, which everyone around the President considered the most important single foreign-policy issue, were going well. Even though Russia retained nuclear weapons, the tensions of the superpower relationship had dissipated.

But the President was not getting credit for much. Instead, the press corps was focusing on his many missteps, gaffes, and policy reversals. McLarty told friends that the drumbeat of negative publicity was hurting Clinton badly and that something needed to be done.

In May of 1993, with Clinton's approval, McLarty decided that Stephanopoulos had to be moved out of media relations and into a more private policymaking role. To shore up the communications team and to bring in a mature Washington insider, he began negotiations with David Gergen, best known as a political commentator for public television and editor-at-large of *U.S. News & World Report*, to be a senior counselor in the White House. Gergen had long admired Clinton, and often praised the former Arkansas governor in his columns and TV analyses.

After a few weeks of contacts, Gergen was poised to take the job, but he wanted to be sure he would have full access to the President whenever he wished and would not be solely a "spin doctor" shaping public-relations strategy; he wanted to be a full-time policymaker. In the end, word leaked that Gergen was talking to the White House, and of course we at *U.S. News* knew what was going on, but the final deal awaited a face-to-face meeting between him and the Clintons. Since both Gergen and the President were notorious procrastinators, no one at the magazine was surprised when, as our deadline approached on Friday night, May 28, the key tête-à-tête had still not taken place. Gergen let us know that he was scheduled to meet with the First Lady and the President no later than 9:30 P.M. Since we expected the meeting would take about half an hour, we thought we could get a story into the magazine in time. Merrill McLoughlin and Michael Ruby, the co-editors of *U.S. News,* decided to postpone our press deadline, a story was prepared, and we waited for final confirmation.

At about 9:30, Gergen let us know that the meeting was delayed. The co-editors decided to hold the magazine until no later than 1 A.M. Back at the White House, Gergen did not meet with Hillary Clinton in the residence of the East Wing until 10 P.M. and did not start his meeting with the President, who had been in Philadelphia, until 11 P.M. Gergen finally called Ruby at about 2 A.M. with word that the deal was done and that the President would announce his appointment later that morning, but there was nothing we could do; the magazine had closed without the story.

BILL CLINTON WAS not getting universally unfavorable press coverage during his first year. Once in a while, when he showed signs of living up to the expectations he had created during the campaign, he earned positive coverage. One such occasion was his speech in Memphis on November 13, 1993, to a convention of African-American church leaders. Speaking from the pulpit where Martin Luther King, Jr., had preached on the night before he was assassinated, Clinton gave an inspirational, emotional sermon urging Americans to build a new sense of community in national life. He said that the memory of Dr. King was being dishonored by all the hatred, violence, and immorality in the land, much of it involving children. He was clearly at home with black preachers; they punctuated his speech with applause, choruses of "Amen" and shouts of "That's right," and cheered when he finished.

I was fortunate to have scheduled an interview with Clinton that day on his views about religion and spiritual life. In fact I had slipped out of the speech just after it ended to position myself, as directed by White House aides, at the door of his limousine. When Clinton came out and saw me climb into the backseat, I heard him say, "Isn't anyone riding with me and Ken Walsh?" Clearly, he didn't want to be alone during an interview with a reporter. Jeff Eller, the only aide in the vicinity, hopped into the car as an official witness.

Clinton reached down to the floor, picked up a white pitcher filled with coffee, poured himself a cup, and settled into his seat. For the next twenty-five minutes, as we sped to his next stop, he regaled me with his thoughts about his own spiritual quest, his lifelong dealings with the black church and its importance in the African-American community, the breakdown of the family in America, and his weekly phone calls to the Rev. Rex Horne, his minister in Little Rock, for spiritual guidance. When we arrived at the next engagement, he was so wound up that he wouldn't get out of the car, even after a Secret Service agent opened the door for him. The interview ran ten minutes overtime, and I could see why Clinton was late so frequently. He just couldn't pull himself away from an interesting discussion.

In this case, of course, this tendency worked to my advantage, and I got some wonderful insights into the man. In my story for *U.S. News*, I wrote: "Clinton admits he is still 'working through' where his spiritual journey will take him and the country. But he has begun a series of prayer breakfasts with small groups of religious leaders to discuss moral and social issues; last week's session focused on helping victims of AIDS. His advisers are arranging for various theologians, historians and university presidents to hold similar conversations with the President on other topics over the next few months. His fascination extends to recent books, like Yale Law Prof. Stephen Carter's *The Culture of Disbelief* and George Washington University Prof. Amitai Etzioni's *The Spirit of Community,* which talk about the need for spirituality in modern life.

"It is increasingly evident in his own. The night before the historic signing of the recent Mideast peace accord on the White House lawn, Clinton stayed up until 3 A.M. reading the Book of Joshua and rewriting his speech to make it more inspirational. He told aides he was fascinated that one sliver of land had produced so many great religions and said that he hoped some day to understand why."

The President also showed glimpses of the altruism that had

lured so many voters to him in the first place. On his first trip to Moscow in 1994, when he sat next to Boris Yeltsin at dinner, the Russian leader lowered his baritone voice to a confidential whisper. How, Yeltsin asked, do you govern a democratic country? Clinton was nonplussed and later said to a friend, "How do you answer a question like that?" But after a moment's silence he counseled Yeltsin to stay close to his people and to get out of Moscow regularly to avoid becoming too insular. Of course, this was the visionless philosophy that Clinton was using to govern the United States, but it wasn't working here, and it wouldn't work in Russia.

DAVID GERGEN HAD high hopes of solving the White House's public-relations problems. He made clear to friends that his main interest in returning to government was to strengthen the institution of the presidency rather than to assist Clinton as an individual, and he tried to use the same methods he had learned while advising Richard Nixon, Gerald Ford, and, especially, Ronald Reagan. This meant feeding the beast, maintaining a constant flow of positive news, providing selected reporters with tidbits of exclusive information, and creating media events to gain positive attention, rather than leaving journalists to their own devices. Gergen's philosophy was that reporters with no news to cover and time on their hands will almost always find something negative to write about, and he was right.

Gergen immediately restored reporters' access to the Upper Press Office as a symbol of the White House's new openness. He persuaded Bill and Hillary to host what would become a highly successful barbecue on the South Lawn for the members of the press corps and their families, and he arranged for the First Couple to host small dinner parties and luncheons with such satraps of the media establishment as R. W. Apple, Washington bureau chief of *The New York Times;* David Broder, political columnist of *The Washington Post;* Jack Nelson, then Washington bureau chief of the *Los Angeles Times;* and network anchormen Tom Brokaw of NBC, Peter Jennings of ABC, Dan Rather of CBS, and Bernard Shaw of Cable News Network. Reporters' phone calls were returned more quickly, and there were more one-on-one interviews with key sources, even though White House officials still divulged little about what was going on.

Gergen defined success mostly in terms of the television coverage the White House was receiving on the nightly news. On the bitterly cold evening of December 16, 1993, he sat in his overheated office wearing a crumpled white shirt, with his tie tugged three inches below his neck, and interrupted an interview to flip on the network news at 6:30 P.M. This had been part of his daily routine for years, even when he was in print journalism. He sat transfixed as ABC News correspondent Brit Hume announced that President Clinton had chosen a new defense secretary, former CIA insider Bobby Inman, to replace outgoing Les Aspin. Gergen had been worried about media reaction to the choice, but as it turned out, he had little initial cause for concern. When the ABC correspondent pronounced the selection a good one, Gergen broke into a big smile, nodded his head, and silently pumped his fist in celebration.

Within a few weeks, however, Inman would self-destruct, coming up with a bizarre and unfounded conspiracy theory about how the press was out to get him, and withdrawing his name from nomination. But most White House staffers lived moment to moment, news cycle to news cycle, and on that particular night in December, the Inman announcement seemed a winner.

GERGEN'S PREOCCUPATION WITH television was shared throughout official Washington. For many years, White House aides had defined success in terms of media coverage of the President, and of course television had become the dominant image-maker. When the network coverage was good, everyone at the White House was happy; when the coverage was bad, the White House thought it had failed on that particular day. In effect, television had become a major force—sometimes *the* major force—in shaping policy.

Fueled by Gergen's fascination with television, innumerable White House staff meetings, including many involving the President, were dominated by discussions of how to manipulate the media, get positive attention, and avoid damaging stories. "Much of the time," a key Clinton aide told me, "that's all we do."

This trend became particularly troubling in foreign-affairs matters. Perhaps the best example was the way in which television coverage of suffering and death in Bosnia pushed the President into a series of hasty, ill-considered actions. In the early spring of 1994, those televised images prompted Clinton, through the United Nations, to bomb Serb positions around the besieged Bosnian Muslim enclave of Goradze. However, the attack turned out to be an ill-planned, weak effort that destroyed only a few trucks and a tent, so the President backed off and reverted to military inaction while making hollow threats. A clear pattern emerged: Pushed by gut-wrenching television coverage, the President would lurch toward action to change the perception that he was incapable of moving aggressively, only to back off when the coverage began to focus on the possibility that he was moving the country toward a debilitating Vietnam-like war. The result was a cycle of indecision that undermined his administration's credibility during Clinton's first two years.

By late 1995, Clinton had adopted a more steadfast approach. A sustained bombing campaign by the United States and its allies led to a U.S.-brokered peace agreement in Bosnia, enforced by an international military contingent that included thousands of U.S. ground troops. Clinton, for once, disregarded negative media coverage and took what he called a "risk for peace."

Another example of the media's impact on foreign policy was Somalia. George Bush had responded to television pictures of mass starvation in this African nation in 1992 by organizing a humanitarian relief effort anchored by U.S. troops, and Clinton signed on to the plan when he took over. But that was soon to change. The President was on a political trip to California in the fall of 1993 when he flipped on the television in his hotel room, and what he saw turned his stomach: A dead American serviceman was being dragged through the streets of Mogadishu, and a beaten and bruised U.S. helicopter pilot was being interrogated by the local thugs who had captured him. It was all on videotape, being shown on CNN. Immediately, Clinton called his national security advisers in Washington and demanded that they get their act together. "Goddamnit," he said. "When I come back, I want options on the table. I want some new ideas."

Over the next two days, the televised pictures caused widespread public and congressional revulsion. No one, it seemed, wanted continued U.S. involvement in Somalia. Clinton responded by saying he would send another 1,700 troops to Somalia to deter hostile forces over the short term but also announced that he would pull out all except a few hundred U.S. personnel within six months. Once again television had forced a President's hand on foreign policy.

BUT NOT EVEN David Gergen's substantial skill in media management and knowledge of Washington could turn Clinton's image around. The President seemed powerless to improve his popularity, and his image remained that of an indecisive accommodator. Then, during the course of 1994, Gergen's influence faded dramatically. For one thing, many longtime Clinton loyalists did not trust him. Here was a Republican in their inner councils, a man who had helped Nixon and Reagan, two demons of the Democratic pantheon. "I didn't fight the Republicans for a decade to take orders in the White House from David Gergen," said David Dreyer, a former congressional aide from the Democratic party's liberal wing.

In addition, Gergen's reputation as a first-class leaker during the Reagan years hurt him badly, even if the charge was unfair. "He was fatally marked as a spin doctor, even though he was much more substantive than that," says a senior White House official who worked with Gergen. "Inside, he was perceived as a leaky faucet, someone not to be trusted." However, there was never any evidence that Gergen had leaked information designed to make either of the Clintons look bad.

Another factor in Gergen's demise were the generational and cultural gaps between him and the younger White House staff members who surrounded him. Gergen preferred a hierarchical management system—generally, Republicans do when running the White House, while the Democrats are more free-form and undisciplined. He said publicly that the young White House staffers were admirably energetic but inexperienced, a plain fact, and this angered them.

Most important, Gergen ran afoul of Hillary. The Sunday before the President was to deliver his State of the Union address in January 1994, senior policymakers gathered in Clinton's residence over coffee and soft drinks to work on his speech for the last time. The question was whether the President should promise to veto any health-care bill that did not provide universal coverage for all Americans. Blinking hard, Gergen spoke up: Wouldn't such a promise box the President in, remove his options in bargaining with Congress, and make it tougher to negotiate a deal with moderates who might object to the cost of such a pledge? There was a dead silence in the room. Then Hillary, an outspoken advocate of universal coverage, took aim. Universal coverage, she said, is nonnegotiable; it *will* be in any new health-care system, and the President will say so. Gergen had been slapped down, and no one defended him.

This was a turning point. Gergen had run afoul of the First Lady, and she was angry about it. From that moment on, White House aides said, Gergen was excluded from key deliberations on health care, economic policy, and other important issues. Finally, in June 1994, the hammer fell; Gergen agreed to be removed as White House counselor and reassigned by the President to the State Department, where he was given the title of senior adviser. The transfer, administration officials said, was really a way to ease him out of the White House while avoiding the media frenzy that an outright resignation would have created. At the end of 1994, David Gergen left the government, considerably disenchanted. He would return to *U.S. News* as editor-at-large in mid-1995.

AS HIS PRESS relations worsened in April 1994, Clinton did some soul-searching with Paul Begala, one of his political advisers from the campaign. Despite his frequent Washington-bashing rhetoric, Begala was then a capital insider who retained strong links to many reporters. He knew that though he couldn't affect their coverage, at least he could get some feedback on what they were thinking and planning.

Why, Clinton asked him, do they give me such a rough time? He pointed out that some of his other advisers were convinced that the media were only interested in rumors and lies. Surely, he said, journalists can't be that jaded and corrupt. Begala said that he wanted to be an optimist, but he wasn't sure it was realistic. Today's press culture frowns on reporters who do positive stories about the presidency, he said, so the premium is on finding a negative slant on the news.

Actually the problem went much deeper. Over the years, the press regulars had become cynical about any President and any politician, not merely Bill Clinton. From Vietnam to Watergate to Iran-contra, the government had told too many lies to warrant trust. At least, this was how many journalists felt. Reporters, especially the White House press corps, had become an engine of anti-incumbency.

10

Hillary

It was Hillary Rodham Clinton who was most pained about the sad state of her husband's administration. The lack of privacy was the worst part. Just before she moved into the White House, when the new First Couple was still riding high, she told friends that she would insist on a "zone of privacy" that would protect her and her family from what she considered excessive media scrutiny. She felt that her personal life, her family finances, and particularly the activities of the Clintons' teenage daughter, Chelsea, were off limits to the press.

In the end, the mainstream media would tacitly agree to only one of the Clintons' informal rules: Chelsea was left alone, but everything else was fair game. Even more than her husband, Mrs. Clinton was having a difficult time forgiving the press its trespasses.

Mrs. Clinton—professional lawyer, unabashed advocate of feminism, children, and health-care reform, and senior policy adviser to the President—started out as a unique First Lady. Like all pioneers in American life, she had to test the boundaries of public acceptance of her new role. Meanwhile, the press struggled to find a fair way to cover her. There was considerable failure on both sides.

From the start, Mrs. Clinton wanted to break the shackles that had constrained previous First Ladies. Her goal was to become a highly visible policymaker, not simply a helpmate to the President and a White House hostess. To that end, shortly after the 1992 election, Clinton named his spouse his personal minister in charge of health-care reform, a task that affected potentially one seventh of the American economy.

Mrs. Clinton never reconciled herself to the media scrutiny that her job inevitably entailed. As a result, she made only sporadic efforts to let Americans see her real personality and, more important, to explain her views to the country—something that every powerful policymaker owes the voters.

The First Lady had developed a bitter and angry view of the media during the 1992 campaign. She was furious at the coverage of her husband's alleged past sexual escapades, and she felt the media had humiliated her by forcing her to publicly address the adultery issue or else see her husband lose the nomination. "Whatever has gone on in their marriage," says a family friend, "Hillary doesn't think it's anybody's business but theirs."

Administration officials have said privately that much of the hostility toward the media came from Hillary, not Bill. In the first few months of the administration, Mrs. Clinton considered a plan to move the press out of the West Wing, the central staff area of the White House, into the Old Executive Office Building next door, and White House planners went so far as to scout out the OEOB for new media quarters. The Secret Service even began studying ways in which the reporters could gain access to the building without slipping into officials' offices unannounced. In the end, Mrs. Clinton abandoned the idea, largely because it would have caused another furor in the press corps, something the White House didn't need.

Journalist Bob Woodward says that Mrs. Clinton was not only upset at media criticism directed at her personally, but about coverage of her efforts to reform the health-care system. According to Woodward, "The coverage often lacked seriousness, she felt, with stories appearing in the lifestyle sections of the newspapers, which traditionally covered First Ladies, rather than on the front pages as a critical question of national policy. She had learned to detest the media during the campaign, and knew all too well that journalists were drawn to stories about controversy or failure. It spooked her at times. To ward off potentially negative stories, she decided that the meetings with 500 experts who were going to advise in the drafting of the legislation would be conducted in private. She also refused initially to release the experts' names. The cloak of secrecy prompted much criticism and even a lawsuit, bringing health care out of the lifestyle sections onto the front pages. Hillary was upset that the dispute took so much time and attention from the designing of the policy."

In turn, the press corps became deeply suspicious of Mrs. Clinton—perhaps more so than any First Lady in history. "Hillary Clinton is the first First Lady to have a legitimate policy role in the administration," said Ann Compton of ABC News in February 1994, "and she is the first one I have covered out of five who has totally ignored and avoided the White House press corps. I've never traveled on her plane. I've never interviewed her. I've never even so much as said, 'Good morning,' or asked her a policy question in over a year now." Also in February 1994, Deborah Mathis, a White House reporter for Gannett News Service who had covered the Clintons in Arkansas, said, "I don't see Clinton as soured on the press; in fact, I think he still enjoys talking to [them]. But Hillary clearly despises the press—she always has. . . . For him to be too kind to the press is something of a betrayal of Hillary, so he has backed off some because of the pressure he's getting from her to look at the press as an enemy. If he had his druthers, we'd see more of him. He'd pick up the phone and call more reporters. . . . He's that kind of operator. But he's also surrounded by—aside from Hillary—a group of people who have [the] first line of contact with the press and who don't like us."

Mathis went on: "There's a certain mystique surrounding Hillary Clinton that is not accidental, a glamour that comes with being mysterious. And what better situation than to be the premier woman of the land and have people wonder what you're really about? I think the idea of a hybrid of an Eleanor Roosevelt and a Jacqueline Kennedy has passed through Hillary Clinton's mind more than once. Not that she's all a concoction, but I think that she fancies herself as being a kind of a blend of those two First Ladies. And she's pulling it off pretty well. I also think she does not trust the press because she believes that we deal superficially. She's of the school that believes almost everything is deeper than it appears, and she doesn't trust us either to understand or be interested in those depths."

A year later, in January 1995, Mrs. Clinton gave credence to this theory when she told *The Washington Post*, "I don't think you can ever know anybody else. And I certainly don't think you can know anybody else through the crude instruments available to us of exposing bits and pieces of somebody's life. . . . I think that does a disservice both to the person, but more broadly to the common human enterprise of each of us trying as best we can to come to grips with life's challenges. So I find it very difficult to understand the dissection of bits and pieces of people, the categorizations of 'Aha! Now I know!'—filling in some fact that, unrelated to any other context of some person's life, is expected to be revealing. I just don't understand that."

Hillary continually complained to friends that she never expected the level of scrutiny that she was receiving as First Lady; it was so unfair. "No one can ever prepare you for this job," she told several friends on several different occasions. She took the scrutiny personally, as if she were the only public figure to be criticized, ridiculed and, in her mind, misinterpreted.

The media were intensely interested in Hillary for a good reason: The public was fascinated by her. She was news—a strong, articulate personality with an agenda of her own and, at least at the beginning, no qualms about promoting it. Younger professional women considered her a role model, and the Clintons fed the idea that she would be a full partner in governing.

During the campaign, the Clintons enjoyed it when supporters introduced them with the phrase "Buy one, get one free." For a few months they encouraged the idea that they would have a full-fledged presidential partnership, with the First Lady serving as a member of Clinton's policy-making inner circle, but when polls showed that conservative voters were worried that her role would be too central, the campaign hierarchy stopped encouraging the "co-presidency" idea.

Yet no matter how much she downplayed her role, there remained an intense public interest in Hillary Clinton that was shared by the press. Every tidbit about her was voraciously consumed, ranging from her constantly changing hairstyles to rumors that she had furious arguments with her husband in their East Wing residence. This fascination stemmed in part from all the talk of philandering that had surfaced during the campaign and Hillary's decision to "stand by her man." Reporters, and much of America, wondered what kind of marriage they really had. What kind of deal did she extract from her husband before she saved his campaign by defending him from the adultery charges? These questions and many more may have been unfair, but they became the stuff of conversation at dinner tables, taverns, cocktail parties, and newsrooms across the country. Mrs. Clinton's "roll-over-them" approach did nothing to help the administration, because it made her seem even more aloof and brittle.

For her part, Hillary felt a rapid erosion of the zone of privacy she had always been able to maintain in Little Rock. Accompanied by a handful of Secret Service agents, she would take Chelsea for a two-mile walk to the National Zoo, wearing sunglasses and a scarf to avoid recognition, only to find a story about the jaunt in *The Washington Post*'s style section the next morning. "Someone would always call the *Post* and tip them off," says an associate, and it drove her crazy.

As her father neared death in a Little Rock hospital in April 1993, Hillary spent two weeks at his bedside. "That was a benchmark," says a friend. "She was very close to her father, and she couldn't believe how intrusive the media were. There was a stakeout at the hospital. She would ask, 'Why is this happening?' " Reporters from tabloid newspapers would nose around asking staffers, friends, and hospital workers how she was dealing with the experience. When the President went to Little Rock for the funeral, the situation became worse, because virtually every major news organization accompanied him. Mrs. Clinton's grief over her father's death was tinged with bitterness at the media, especially the tabloids, which, she felt, knew no bounds and would not allow her to suffer in private.

Hillary's feeling about the press affected her policy role. When she and Ira Magaziner, her staff aide in charge of health-care reform, began hammering out their complex and far-reaching proposal to overhaul the nation's medical system, they did so in near-total secrecy. When health-care professionals, other interested parties, and the press corps complained about the secrecy, they were told there was no legal requirement for such meetings to be open because Mrs. Clinton was not a government employee. Technically this stance may have been valid, since she was drawing no income, but it denied that the public, through the media, was entitled to know how this historically significant package of reforms was being formulated. In the end, the secrecy surrounding Mrs. Clinton's health-care task force had serious political repercussions. Potential allies, such as Republican moderates in Congress, were excluded and alienated, and the public got the impression that Mrs. Clinton was concocting some huge Rube Goldberg project that could not be explained or justified—an impression that led to its eventual demise in Congress.

"Mrs. Clinton really came in hostile to the press, cutting us out," says UPI's Helen Thomas. "To her own detriment, she blocked any coverage of the health-care plan, [failing to] open that window for public debate and dialogue. They would have gotten the feedback to find out where the danger spots were, where the opposition was . . . this is what democracy is all about, win, lose, or draw. But she definitely was avoiding the Washington press corps. We [asked] Lisa Caputo [Mrs. Clinton's press secretary] . . . 'Why can't we have more Washington press conferences with Mrs. Clinton?' Caputo, who was leaving the room, shot back, 'She does hold them. Why don't you go out of town when she holds them?' So I called up Gergen and said, 'Look, my office spends thousands of dollars to make sure that we cover the President properly . . . and for her to say that we have to go out of town if we want to cover Mrs. Clinton at a news conference is beyond the pale." But such protests had little effect.

As support for her health-care ideas faded among voters and on Capitol Hill, Mrs. Clinton became even more resentful. Clearly, she was not accustomed to failure, and she saw the press as the reason for her setbacks. By March 1994, she was upset that the media had "trivialized" the Clinton presidency. Beset by criticism of her handling of the family finances in the Whitewater affair and by reports that she had made $100,000 on a $1,000 investment in the commodities market in the 1970s after getting special advice from a family friend with business before the state of Arkansas, she stopped reading the newspapers. This was her habit during times of particular stress.

In April 1994, amid a media feeding frenzy over the commodities issue, Mrs. Clinton attended the fifty-fifth birthday party of her friend Michael Berman, a Washington consultant. She tried to relax by dancing the boogaloo to sixties music with old pals, but she was clearly troubled. She sounded off angrily about how much the administration was being damaged by the press, and argued naïvely that journalists should simply focus on the administration's public-policy agenda, not the First Family's personal lives, finances, or the mistakes of their staffs. Of course this attitude only got her into more trouble. Since she considered most press inquiries to be illegitimate intrusions, it caused reporters to think she had something to hide.

THROUGH THE FIRST two years of the Clinton presidency, Hillary and her staff seemed to have little idea of the animosity they had engendered from the press. When White House reporters complained that they were being shut out, her staff replied that Mrs. Clinton was entitled to handle the press any way she wanted to. Besides, they said, she had permitted various interviews with medical and economics reporters in 1993 and 1994 on health care, and made a habit of doing interviews while she was on the road with local newspapers, television, and radio stations. Of course this only incensed the White House press corps, as Helen Thomas predicted; now they were being told that even though she was an important policymaker, the First Lady would give the media virtually no access in Washington. Lisa Caputo told me in May 1995 that Mrs. Clinton had held more than fifty "press availabilities" and had done more than four hundred interviews in nearly two and a half years as First Lady, but the overwhelming majority of them were on the road with local media.

Hillary and her staff eventually set down a rule: She would give interviews to the national media in Washington only when news organizations came up with themes she wanted to talk about, such as her spiritual life or her opposition to House Speaker Newt Gingrich's proposal to open more orphanages. Rarely would she submit to questions of a general nature, and this became a big problem, because she cut herself off from any sustained contact with the journalists who were covering the White House. Her aides said she was too busy, and in any case didn't want to talk about herself.

Mrs. Clinton's staff became heavy-handed. At one point in 1993, I began negotiating with Caputo for a general-interest interview for *U.S. News*. Apparently under instructions from the First Lady or her chief of staff, Margaret Williams, Caputo pressed me to tell her what topics I wanted to ask about. I said I was sure I'd want Mrs. Clinton to discuss children's issues and education, which was where her press secretary was steering me, but I couldn't rule out asking about the news of the week or such other topics as the Whitewater affair. After much negotiating on the telephone, Caputo said we couldn't have our interview unless we agreed to limit it to children's issues and education—and further, we had to agree *not* to use her photograph on the cover of the magazine. Clearly, the First Lady did not want to contribute to the common impression that she was co-President. But the restrictions were too much. The co-editors of *U.S. News*, Merrill McLoughlin and Mike Ruby, rightly refused to accept the deal, and we didn't get our interview.

CERTAINLY THERE WAS a salacious side to the press corps' interest in Hillary, but her keeping a distance from White House reporters did nothing to lessen America's curiosity about the Clintons' private lives. My view has always been that if journalists ask about matters the First Couple considers private, they can always refuse to answer. As a matter of public-relations strategy, they can take the initiative and make news of a positive sort, such as announcing a new policy development, or do something innocuous like mentioning the books they are reading. But Mrs. Clinton and her aides refused to feed the beast. Lisa Caputo did come up with recommendations for media interviews, but they were almost always dropped from the schedule because there wasn't enough time.

While Barbara Bush and Nancy Reagan had behind-the-scenes roles in their husbands' administrations, they were not members of the inner circle of policymakers. Yet each had met with key journalists on at least some occasions, and their staffs were helpful and accessible. During my time covering the Reagan and Bush administrations, I chatted over lunch regularly with Elaine Crispen, Mrs. Reagan's press secretary, and later with Anna Perez, Mrs. Bush's press secretary, and I sometimes felt they learned as much from me as I did from them, at least about press perceptions of the President and the First Lady or their staffs. This is part of a healthy symbiotic relationship, but the Clintons never seemed to figure it out. In mid-1995, Caputo began to make time for such informal interviews, but the relationship was never as easygoing and productive as it had been with Crispen and Perez. Lisa always seemed to be under too many restrictions from her boss on what she could say.

The strange part of all this was that when Mrs. Clinton did meet with reporters, she almost always did herself a world of good. In April 1994, she held a press conference to discuss her controversial commodities trading practices from years past. The media had been keeping the issue on the front burner, and finally the First Lady decided to hold a let-it-all-hang-out press conference to clear the air. She did brilliantly from a public-relations standpoint, answering some questions with candor but deftly sidestepping others, and her performance drained much of the power from the story, because she was no longer stonewalling. Nevertheless, thereafter she returned to her policy of keeping her distance from the White House press corps.

A revealing insight came during the Clintons' trip to the Philippines and Indonesia in November 1994. The Democrats had just lost the House and Senate—their biggest losses in a generation— and polls suggested that President Clinton's unpopularity was a big factor. Just as important, Mrs. Clinton's health-care-reform plan had been a drag on the party, because voters considered it a big-government intrusion on the medical system. Thus, in a way the election was also a repudiation of Mrs. Clinton as a policymaker.

As the President and the First Lady left for Asia on the Friday after the election, they were still in a state of shock; indeed, the entire White House staff was stunned by the magnitude of the loss. Naturally, Mrs. Clinton was sought out by reporters, who wanted her assessment of the election results and to ask her what she would do next. Somehow her press secretary got the impression that the First Lady wanted to discuss the meaning of the election, and she hastily arranged for a small pool of reporters, representing the larger press corps, to interview her after a tour of a Buddhist temple near the city of Yogyakarta in Indonesia. Caputo even encouraged the journalists to ask the First Lady specifically about what the voters seemed to be saying.

But the press secretary had misread the situation. Hillary bridled at the queries, and the interview was a near-disaster. Asked if it would be more difficult for her to take a policymaking role with the Republicans in charge, she seemed nettled. "Who knows?" she replied huffily. "I have no idea. That's why I don't know how to have these conversations. I don't mean to be difficult. I don't know how to have them. It depends upon what they do." Her suspicious and defensive attitude only reinforced the impression that the last thing she ever wanted to do was to talk to reporters.

Like her husband, Mrs. Clinton began to take solace in the lives of her predecessors. While the President read about the tribulations of Thomas Jefferson, Abraham Lincoln, Franklin Roosevelt, and Harry Truman, his wife read more and more about Eleanor Roosevelt. She was deeply impressed with Doris Kearns Goodwin's *No Ordinary Time,* a book that describes how Mrs. Roosevelt, like Hillary, was the target of widespread criticism and considerable abuse for delving deeply into public policy. Mrs. Roosevelt reinvented her role, giving up the civil-defense job in her husband's administration that was causing controversy, and subsequently devoted herself to informal goals such as promoting rights for immigrants, minorities, and women. She maintained her role as an advocate for liberal causes long after Franklin Roosevelt's death, and wrote a newspaper column for many years. (Hillary would emulate Mrs. Roosevelt by starting her own column in July 1995.)

Yet Mrs. Clinton had too much pride in her own abilities and considered herself too much a feminist icon to back off completely from making policy. From November 1994, when the Democrats suffered their catastrophic losses, to January 1995, the Clintons talked regularly about the role she would play in the next two years, and finally they came up with a new public-relations plan. After analyzing opinion polls and discussing the matter with key advisers and friends, they settled on a revised political formula that would govern Mrs. Clinton's activities as First Lady: She would be an adviser but not a manager. She would advocate whatever policies she chose, both publicly and privately, but she would not be in charge of anything.

This, the Clintons concluded, was the key distinction. "People want her to be an advocate for causes she believes in," said a senior administration official, "but not operationally in control. . . . People feel it's okay having her as a staffer, but having her run a piece of the action is something the American people find hard to understand."

In the final weeks of 1994, Hillary began acting on this formula. After keeping a low public profile for months, she allowed aides to tell reporters that she would be focusing on small- and medium-scale projects in the following two years, such as encouraging women to have mammograms for early detection of breast cancer, promoting improved educational opportunities for women and young people, and helping veterans of the Persian Gulf War who were suffering from an unusual malady called Gulf War Syndrome. All of these projects were quite traditional in nature and might have been taken on by Barbara Bush or Nancy Reagan, but Mrs. Clinton also resumed attending senior-staff meetings at the White House, including strategy sessions on health care. Her participation concerned some of President Clinton's other advisers, who worried that she would persuade him to push for another massive overhaul of the medical system at some later date. Those advisers questioned whether Mrs. Clinton, who was generally less eager than her husband to compromise, really understood how much her health-care-reform plan had hurt Democratic candidates in 1994. Other White House officials said that she did comprehend the problem. "She gets it," said a senior administration official in late November. "She's the first to recognize that the big government issue on health care blew us out of the water." Yet the skeptics said Mrs. Clinton didn't believe that her original plan represented too much government; she would concede only that her opponents had successfully portrayed it in that way.

As 1995 began, Mrs. Clinton reasserted her influence beyond health care. She began participating in senior-staff discussions at the

White House on welfare reform and personnel appointments, in which she remained a strong advocate for gender and racial diversity. She also drew up plans to be an active fund-raiser for the Democratic party in 1995 and 1996, especially among feminist and liberal audiences, and began conferring with her husband's aides about who would run his reelection campaign.

Hillary favored a series of "nonhierarchical teams" to take charge of polling, media strategy, and other areas, rather than relying on Bill Clinton's key advisers from 1992. She was said to be unhappy with White House pollster Stan Greenberg and political strategists Mandy Grunwald and Paul Begala because they had helped persuade the President to make the midterm elections a referendum on his administration and harshly attack Republicans as Reagan clones. This strategy had proved disastrous. Voters, White House polls suggested, saw the gambit as a return to the divisive political battles of the 1980s rather than as an attempt to find workable solutions for the future.

In the winter of 1994–95, Mrs. Clinton also deeply involved herself in shaping the administration's 1996 budget. At a key meeting between the President and his senior staff in December 1994, White House budget director Alice Rivlin argued that the administration should propose another big deficit-reduction plan. White House chief of staff Leon Panetta, Rivlin's predecessor as budget director, agreed. They said the administration just might be able to work with the Republicans on Capitol Hill to position the government on a glide path to a balanced budget within a decade.

Agreeing with economics adviser Laura D'Andrea Tyson, Mrs. Clinton would have none of this. According to a participant at the meeting, she argued that it was not "politically smart" to take another big chunk out of the deficit, because too many popular programs would have to be cut. Voters didn't care about the deficit, Mrs. Clinton and Tyson said; they wanted a tax cut, and the administration should provide it. One by one, senior policymakers chimed in to support the First Lady, including George Stephanopoulos and economics adviser Gene Sperling. The President quickly sided with his wife, and there was no further debate.

The administration's budget proposal was bitterly disappointing to those who wanted the President to take the lead in reducing red

ink, including many moderate Democrats. Clinton's budget projected annual deficits of nearly $200 billion for at least five more
years. Partly at Mrs. Clinton's urging, her husband had decided to
take the low-risk course and pass the buck to the Republicans instead of moving aggressively toward a balanced budget. The President would reverse himself a few months later, first by proposing
a ten-year balanced budget, and then accepting a seven-year bal-
anced-budget timetable pushed by the GOP. But the incident
showed that Mrs. Clinton's liberal instincts remained strong, and
proved that she could still exert a powerful influence on her husband.

IN FEBRUARY 1995, Hillary began to go public with her new, soft-
ened I-am-not-a-manager image. It was a repetition of her
makeover during the 1992 campaign, when she soft-pedaled her
policy-making side after being derided by opponents as a liberal har-
ridan. Mrs. Clinton again decided she should humanize herself, and
we in the media were only too happy to oblige.

A similar strategy had worked before. Pilloried for her expensive
tastes in the White House, Nancy Reagan had made a surprise appearance at a Gridiron Dinner, an annual show presented by newspaper reporters in the capital, and won over many journalists with a
self-deprecating performance of "Second-Hand Rose." Hillary decided against a high-risk theatrical event but was willing to do a burst
of media encounters. In mid-February, she even led reporters on a
tour of the newly redecorated Blue Room in the residential quarters,
just as Nancy Reagan or Barbara Bush might have done.

One of Hillary's efforts to reach out was a strange, rambling interview she gave to *Washington Post* food critic Phyllis Richman in
February, which the newspaper described with the headline "Chewing the Fat with Mrs. Clinton." Richman wrote: "Mrs. Clinton is full
of surprises this day. At a time when there is much hand-wringing
among Democrats about her image, her role and her effect on her
husband's political fortunes, she is fearlessly willing to follow the advice: When the going gets tough, the tough go to lunch. At this particular one, she is either totally at ease or doing an amazing job
playing the part of Harriet Nelson." Mrs. Clinton went on to joke

and laugh with her staff at the table, talk about her daughter Chelsea's cute new sweater, her love for Tabasco sauce, and how her husband was not really a junk-food addict but ate "a really good diet" and loved bananas. If this lighthearted, traditional side of Hillary was there all along, and not concocted for the moment, why did she hide these facets of her personality for so long?

After my unhappy experiences in trying to arrange an interview with Mrs. Clinton for the better part of two years, early in 1995 I decided to travel with her to see if being on the road would improve my luck. A trip to Mrs. Clinton's hometown of Park Ridge, Illinois, seemed to be a good possibility. On Tuesday, February 14, I flew to Chicago, and I met Mrs. Clinton at her alma mater, Maine East High School, the next morning. White House staffers positioned me and the other national reporter covering the trip, Julia Malone of Cox Newspapers, with local reporters and photographers behind a rope in a long corridor of the school. Mrs. Clinton said hello to us and headed into a classroom, where she met privately with a few students. Then she toured a computer lab where freshmen were learning about ancient Greece, visited a group of student leaders across the hall, and fielded general questions from the young people. Finally, she addressed a Maine East assembly to enthusiastic cheers, telling the students and faculty of her admiration for how ethnically and racially diverse the school had become since her day, when it was nearly all-white.

Thereafter, Mrs. Clinton spent two hours at a local health clinic urging elderly women to have mammograms for early detection of breast cancer, then proceeded to a restaurant owned by a former high school classmate for a reunion of a hundred old school chums. She seemed to have a wonderful time, laughing easily and bursting into raucous cheers when the bananas flambé arrived.

One thing that struck me on this trip was that while Hillary certainly mingled easily with people, there was a uniformity to her audiences and staff. I wondered how in touch she could be when she was surrounded so often by professional women such as herself and talked mostly to idolizing groups of working women, liberals, social activists, feminists, and earnest achievers. Where were the working-class folks? Where were the homemakers? The conservatives? Other First Ladies rarely talked with critical audiences, but other First

Ladies were not policymakers like Mrs. Clinton. What she saw and heard helped to shape decisions at the highest level, and I wondered whether she was getting a genuine cross section of views.

Just before Mrs. Clinton left the health clinic, a staff member rushed out to the van where Julia Malone and I were waiting and asked Julia to step inside; Mrs. Clinton was now ready to do the interview Julia had requested. I sat in the van and stewed, fretting that I wouldn't get my chance.

When Julia returned, she seemed reticent about discussing the interview with Hillary's staff members present in the van. Later she told me Mrs. Clinton had turned spiky when asked about her role in the administration, and specifically on what influence she'd had in crafting the President's State of the Union address a month earlier. Hillary went on to lash out against the media, arguing that reporters often disseminated lies about her. It was questions about process like the ones Malone was asking that angered her, she said. Thereafter she became uncooperative, and Julia had a hard time extracting a straight answer on a variety of other questions.

It is common for one reporter to warn another about such problems with an interviewee, and I took what Julia said seriously. After Hillary's lunch with former high school pals, I was escorted to a cluttered basement office in the restaurant, where I was told I would talk to her in a few minutes. I resolved to tread carefully, at least at the start of the interview.

I started out with softball questions, then moved on to the tougher ones. *U.S. News* was preparing a cover story that week on fatherhood, so I asked Mrs. Clinton to describe the most important things that fathers could do for their children.

Ignoring the jangling phones and the uncomfortable chairs in the small office, the First Lady was eloquent in her response. "Sometimes it's difficult for fathers to put aside their own aspirations about their own lives and what they expect from their children," she told me. "But a father who's able to put his child first and help that child develop whatever skills he has is giving a great gift. . . ."

I recalled that Mrs. Clinton had spoken with reverence about her own father's role in her life, and she smiled. "Oh, my father did that for me. And I was thinking today that he said something several times when I was very young that made . . . a huge impression on me. He would tell me that he would always love me no matter what I did, but that didn't mean he would always like or approve of what I did, but he would always love me as a person. And I can remember as a young girl I would say, 'Well, does that mean if I murdered somebody, you would still love me?' And he would say, 'Yes, I would love you and I would support you, but I wouldn't like what you had done.' And there's something about that absolute, solid security of knowing that you're loved, especially as you get to be a teenager and you don't agree . . . that is . . . an anchor that every child needs."

When she delved into other subjects, especially her relationship with her husband, Hillary seemed far less genuine. I asked how she could best help the administration—a variant on the familiar question she always received from reporters on what role she would play for the next two years. What she said surprised me because it was so traditional; in fact, it could have been uttered by every other First Lady in American history. "My first responsibility, I think, is to do whatever my husband would want me to do that he thinks would be helpful to him," she said. "So that's what goes to the top of my list, whatever it is. I mean, it may be something of great moment, but more likely it's just to kick back, have a conversation or even play a game of cards and just listen to him ruminate. . . . I mean, whatever it takes to kind of be there for him . . . is the most important thing I have to do, because I don't believe anyone who has not been in this position can appreciate the extraordinary burdens that come with it. And it would be very difficult to try to handle that alone and not have a sounding board, not have somebody there you can talk to."

Given her longtime commitment to governmental policy-making and her interest in serving as a pathbreaking role model for feminists, what Hillary said struck me as contrived. It seemed only the latest reinvention of Hillary Clinton, designed to make her more appealing to tradition-minded voters.

The First Lady added to this softer image in mid-March 1995 by appearing in a video produced for the Gridiron Dinner. She played the female version of the title character of *Forrest Gump*, the movie that was a box-office smash that year, and she performed well, complete with a goofy Southern accent and simplistic aphorisms worthy of the simpleton played by Tom Hanks in the film. "My mama always told me the White House is like a box of chocolates," she drawled, referring to the movie's most famous line. "It's pretty on the outside, but inside there's a lot of nuts." Her parody was a hit among the Gridiron Club members.

In late March and early April, Mrs. Clinton embarked on a twelve-day, 20,000-mile goodwill mission to Bangladesh, India, Nepal, Pakistan, and Sri Lanka. Again it was the kinder, gentler Hillary who took this trip. She made a serious effort to mingle with the reporters traveling with her, and she shied away from such contentious issues as nuclear proliferation and human-rights abuses and called for improved education and health care for women and girls. Accompanied by fifteen-year-old Chelsea, she cuddled babies, tended the sick, watched local entertainers perform, and wore the traditional *shalwar kameez* tunic and pantaloons of Pakistani women and other native garb. She was, in effect, playing the traditional role of First Lady, showing empathy and concern, but not delving publicly into the toughest policy issues.

In late summer, she scored another PR coup by addressing an international women's conference in Beijing. She avoided taking any extreme positions, was well received by the delegates, and got positive coverage at home.

Still, Hillary's distrust of the news media lingered, especially the attempt to stereotype her. "There's a constant attempt to label her and define her and put her in a box," says a friend, "to say she's this and that, when she's so many things. She's not a First Lady to whom you can affix a label. She's not just one thing. She's a mother, the hostess of the White House, the point person on health-care policy, a political adviser, interior decorator, children's advocate, family advocate. She's all of these things."

In January 1996, as Mrs. Clinton was about to begin a publicity tour for a book she had written on child rearing, the Republicans and the media resurrected still another image of Hillary: the conniver. The news peg was a series of newly discovered billing records from Mrs. Clinton's days at the Rose Law Firm in Arkansas. The records revealed bills to Madison Guaranty, a financially troubled savings and loan at the center of the Whitewater affair, for a larger amout of legal work than she had earlier claimed. This raised a new question about how deeply she was involved in Whitewater. Senator Alfonse D'Amato, a New York Republican and chairman of the Senate Whitewater committee, said the belated release of the documents, which his panel had been demanding for many weeks, was part of a White House pattern of "conduct that borders on contempt, obstruction, and making false statements."

"On January 26, Mrs. Clinton testified under subpoena before a Washington grand jury investigating Whitewater. The proceedings were, of course, secret, but the fact that she was the first presidential spouse to appear before a grand jury added to the sense that she was under an ethical cloud. By this time, 51 percent of the electorate had an unfavorable opinion of Mrs. Clinton, the lowest popularity rating of any First Lady in the history of polling.

The media and the Republicans also focused attention on a recently unearthed White House draft memo, written by former presidential aide David Watkins, suggesting that Mrs. Clinton was a central player in White House Travel Office staff firings in 1993—something that both Mrs. Clinton and White House officials steadfastly denied.

The root of the problem was clearly Mrs.Clinton's penchant for secrecy. Every time she found herself mired in controversy, she would attempt to stonewall her critics and the press. This was the worst possible strategy for someone who claimed she had done nothing wrong, and it stemmed in part from her failure to come to terms with the scrutiny that public life entailed. "She gives off a sense of arrogance," GOP pollster Frank Luntz told me during the furor. "It's an attitude of, 'How dare you question me?' And no one likes that."

To me Hillary seemed an increasingly poignant figure, a talented, aggressive, and well-intentioned woman limited in what she could do and say by her husband's desire to be reelected, as well as by her own sense of limits on what the country would accept from a First Lady in the 1990s.

As her friends have often said, Mrs. Clinton has been an immensely successful professional woman in her own right, able to excel as a lawyer and politician far beyond Arkansas. But her husband's career preempted the full blossoming of her ambition. For all her importance as a feminist role model, she was being forced into a more traditional subserviency to her husband, and her friends said she was not happy about it.

AS I WAS leaving the White House one day in late 1994, I suddenly saw the First Lady six feet in front of me, all alone, with no aides, Secret Service agents, or hangers-on. She was walking briskly, staring straight ahead and lost in thought, carrying a sheaf of papers across her chest. Later I found out that she had abruptly dashed out of a 1 P.M. meeting that had run overtime and exited the building through the West Lobby, where dignitaries come and go, rather than using a more private route. She walked past a few TV technicians, unaccustomed to seeing any First Lady alone, passed the media briefing-room doors, and proceeded about ten yards to an entrance to the residential quarters of the East Wing. About fifteen seconds later, a Secret Service agent came running after her, talking into his sleeve microphone, nervously looking for the First Lady, who had eluded him.

It turned out that Mrs. Clinton often gave her protectors the slip while she was on the White House grounds. She would leave meetings at unexpected times, use the stairs when her handlers were waiting at the elevators, or take a different exit from the one her security guards anticipated. Nearly always, she gained a few seconds alone—that was all. "She considers the White House her home," says a friend. "She doesn't want to always be surrounded. She wants a normal life."

But of course that was the one thing she could never have, and at that moment Hillary seemed to me a sad and solitary figure.

11

A Failed Charm Offensive

By the late summer of 1994, with his popularity among the voters declining and his legislative agenda in deep trouble, Clinton and his aides decided to try another round of media schmoozing. For their part, most of the White House press regulars were hoping for signs of rapprochement. The atmosphere had become too hostile, they felt, and the aloofness and antagonism of the Clintonites were keeping them from properly explaining the administration to the country.

Some reporters saw darker impulses at work: an attempt to fuzz over nearly two years of distortion and dissembling with a phony charm offensive. On August 21, White House correspondent Ruth Marcus of *The Washington Post* wrote: "In Washington, White House special counsel Lloyd N. Cutler likes to say, trust is the coin of the realm. By that measure, the Clinton White House is flat broke when it comes to its dealings with the reporters who cover it. To borrow a phrase from the law of libel, the Clinton White House often seems to be following a pattern of knowing or reckless disregard for the truth. Apparently putting its short-term political interests ahead of accuracy, it regularly fails to provide trustworthy information—whether out of inability, unwillingness or both."

Marcus went on to cite several examples of the problem. Among them were conflicting explanations for the firing of the White House travel office staff in 1993; conflicting explanations of how Hillary Clinton came to make $100,000 from her $1,000 investment in commodities; whether the President voluntarily turned over Whitewater papers to the Justice Department or whether he did so under an imminent subpoena; and conflicting explanations of the disposition of Whitewater papers removed from deputy counsel Vince Foster's office after his suicide in 1993.

"Nineteen months of repeated falsehoods and half-truths have corroded the relationship between this White House and the reporters who cover it," Marcus concluded. "The corrosion breeds cynicism among reporters, which in turn contributes to a siege mentality inside the White House. To judge from the public opinion polls, that is hurting the administration at least as much as it is annoying the White House press corps."

In response, White House chief of staff Panetta wrote a letter to the *Post* defending the administration's honor. He said that both the White House and the press corps had been guilty of making errors, but he added: "What Ms. Marcus fails to appreciate is that we all—White House and press alike—operate under fierce time pressures, and factual mistakes sometimes occur precisely because the White House is trying to respond to the pressure of a press corps scrambling to get out the news. This is not to excuse mistakes when they occur, but it is to say that mistakes made in a good-faith effort to be responsive are a far cry from deliberate dissembling."

But we in the press corps weren't satisfied with Panetta's explanation. The White House had been too slippery, dismissive, and condescending for too long.

We wanted immediate improvements in the whole operation. As president of the White House Correspondents' Association, I sent a series of memos late that summer to Clinton and his key aides, including Panetta, outlining a series of recommendations approved by the W.H.C.A. governing board aimed at correcting the situation. My view, which was shared by most of the press corps, was that we had developed few real relationships with senior or middle-level White House staff members. We didn't know whom to trust, and they didn't know us as individuals. I quoted the 1988 report of the Harvard Commission on the Presidential News Conference that "all parties would benefit from restoring the habit of frequent, routine and undramatic news conferences, and from introducing a variety of alternative formats that are likely to stimulate better communication between the President and the public." Among my suggestions were regular "conversational" interviews with the President by small groups of journalists, and more frequent press conferences and interviews with senior staff members and other administration policymakers.

Within a week, I got a call from the soft-spoken White House communications director, Mark Gearan. "Can you come over," he asked, "for an off-the-record chat with the President tomorrow?"

The following evening at six, I showed up at the White House briefing room, joined there by *Washington Post* White House correspondent Ann Devroy and television commentator Mort Kondracke. Ten minutes later, we were ushered into the Oval Office, where the President stood up, came around his big mahogany desk, and shook hands with us all. Gearan, Stephanopoulos, and Myers stood quietly at the far end of the room.

I can't disclose a large amount of what we discussed—we agreed that most of it would remain off the record—but I can say that on that hot, muggy night, Bill Clinton was a troubled man. Over cookies, soft drinks, and hot tea on the patio behind the Oval Office, the President complained, sometimes angrily, that he was getting no credit for his accomplishments, such as cutting the deficit and passing a bill guaranteeing family leave for middle-class couples, and was being unfairly criticized by the press. His treatment was far worse, he argued, than what his immediate predecessors had suffered. He said he felt "disabled" as President and was frustrated because he didn't know what to do about it. It was a revealing insight into a man under fire who felt helpless to change his fate. In a spate of press conferences and other interviews during the next two weeks, Clinton made this point again, if less vividly.

The strategy was clear: Clinton's complaints about unfair coverage of his presidency and a barrage of similar grumbles from his staff and supporters were designed to shame journalists into giving him a more favorable assessment. To some extent it worked; stories appeared in newspapers, magazines, and on television and radio questioning whether the media had treated Clinton too roughly. Hence the press began portraying a newly reflective, sympathetic Bill Clinton. I reported in *U.S. News* that Clinton had finally recognized the depth of his problems and was searching for new answers. Ann Devroy of the *Post* took much the same approach.

A number of news organizations, including *U.S. News* and *The Washington Post,* referred to a media critique called *Out of Order,* by political scientist Thomas Patterson, who argued that the press has been increasingly unfair to Presidents for many years and has been particularly savage toward Clinton. His views were supported by the continuing studies of the Washington-based Center for Media and Public Affairs, a nonpartisan think tank. The Center found that for the first seventeen months of the Clinton administration, about 62 percent of the evaluations of the President on televised nightly newscasts were negative.

Yet as the 1994 midterm campaign reached its crescendo in October and early November, Bill Clinton was much more focused on tactics than on themes. This was a key error, because he had established no overall rationale for his administration. He was immersed in the presidential cocoon, feeling that the cheers and applause he was hearing at carefully orchestrated rallies across the country reflected America's mood. He became so absorbed in the esoterica of the campaign that he never saw the tide running against him. He enjoyed analyzing political commercials on television, and aides arranged for the Democratic Congressional Campaign Committee and the party's Senatorial Campaign Committee to send him videocassettes of commercials by both parties' candidates around the country. Clinton watched these tapes in his residence at the White House or in the small study off the Oval Office. Often he critiqued the videos and offered observations to his aides about what he liked and what he thought candidates were doing wrong, especially when they responded weakly to attacks.

For his own part, on the advice of his pollster, Stan Greenberg, and other strategists, the President was nationalizing the election. In speeches around the country and in Washington, he warned that the Republicans were trying to return to Reaganomics and were attempting to take over Congress with campaigns of divisiveness and fear. He was trying to rerun the campaigns of the 1980s, which the Democrats had already lost many times.

A week before the election, Clinton sat down with his aides and chortled over Republican television ads that "morphed" the image of local Democratic candidates into his own image, trying to connect the locals with the unpopular President. "They just can't help themselves," the President said. "The Republicans are so eager to run against me that they've got it all wrong. I'm not what this election is all about. They're overplaying their hand." As it turned out, he was only fooling himself.

WHILE THE PRESIDENT was trying to score points with his charm offensive, most of the White House staff was still locked in a harsh campaign mode. For many Clintonites, the '92 campaign had been the most important experience of their lives, and through it they had developed their contempt for the mainstream media. "In the campaign, you use anyone who has a single brain cell as long as they're willing to work," a Clinton adviser told me in late 1994. "For a lot of these kids, no one had paid much attention to them before. When they got to the White House, they thought it would be the same. But in the White House, competence is much more important. It took us a long time to figure that out."

Yet the emotional high of the campaign would not be forgotten. The veterans of '92 constantly returned to that experience to explain Clinton or give anecdotes to flesh out his character and beliefs. The problem was that he was now President, and the voters wanted to know what he was doing as the leader of the country, not as the man who had campaigned in the New Hampshire primary.

Moreover, governing the country was only a secondary experience to the young Clintonites, and it showed. Running the White House, they learned, is hard, tedious, and grueling work, and now the hated press corps seemed to have the upper hand.

Some officials in the White House knew enough to build relationships with individual journalists and to treat them with respect. Mack McLarty, Clinton's first White House chief of staff, had been in that category. He would see regulars in the press corps, often at lunch, every few weeks to discuss how the administration was doing. Unlike many of his colleagues, he was always factual, never mean-spirited, and never indulged in backbiting. Often he seemed to learn more from reporters about trends and media perceptions of the White House than we learned from him. While McLarty's careful attention to journalists didn't protect him from criticism—he was often singed for allowing too much chaos at the White House—in the end reporters realized that much of the problem was caused by Clinton's lack of discipline, not by McLarty's failure to manage properly.

McLarty also was on the right side of many issues, although his retiring nature and sense of loyalty kept him from making public his behind-the-scenes role. After the successful congressional vote on Clinton's budget plan with only Democratic support in 1993, he confided to a friend, "This is the last partisan thing we should do. This is it. We've got to go to the center and put a moderate coalition together."

But Hillary Clinton and the White House's liberal faction, including health-care strategist Ira Magaziner and George Stephanopoulos, persuaded the President to overrule McLarty later in 1993. They pushed Clinton into proposing a dramatic package of health-care reforms, easily caricatured as a big-government takeover of the medical system, and the President made these reforms his top priority. Since neither Mrs. Clinton nor other members of the liberal wing in the White House wanted to work closely with moderate Republicans on the issue, another partisan battle ensued.

In the end, McLarty was correct. Clinton's health-care plan, attacked in a multimillion-dollar ad campaign by its opponents, became so out of favor that it was a big factor in the President's high disapproval ratings. The unpopular plan also helped bring about the Republican takeover of the House and Senate in November 1994.

McLarty might have held on to his chief of staff job longer had he leaked more information to reporters about his role as the leading centrist at the President's side because he would have appeared more indispensable to his boss. But he refused to "beat his chest," said his Arkansas confidant Skip Rutherford, and it violated his concept of loyalty to talk about internal administration debates.

Yet when McLarty was switched from chief of staff to senior counselor to the President, the media treated him with kid gloves. He had developed such respect among Washington journalists that no one wanted to jump on him when he was down, which had happened to Donald Regan, Reagan's chief of staff, and John Sununu, Bush's chief of staff, when they lost their jobs. McLarty had built up an immune system in Washington that protected him from being savaged.

His successor, former budget director Panetta, didn't start out well. He told reporters that he would usher in a new era, one in which he as chief of staff would have full authority to manage the Clinton White House, discipline the staff, and control the flow of people and information to the President. He also served notice that he would be tough-minded in reorganizing the staff and that some people would be demoted, fired, or given different jobs. Since Panetta had a solid reputation as a truth-teller from his days as chairman of the House Budget Committee and as Clinton's budget director, reporters tended to believe him. But then the President pulled the rug out from under him, fueling more media cynicism.

White House officials leaked the news that he was about to demote press secretary Dee Dee Myers to traveling press secretary— meaning that she would become the press person accompanying the President on the road. Panetta planned to give the White House press secretary's job to State Department spokesman Mike McCurry, a respected veteran of Washington's media wars. The night before the announcement was to be made, Myers slipped into the Oval Office and told Clinton she would quit if Panetta demoted her. Not wanting to offend a loyal aide and worried that an angry Myers departure would make him look insensitive to women, Clinton relented. Myers also told the President that in all likelihood she would leave the government at the end of 1994.

This decision undercut the new chief of staff in the first test of his authority. For his part, Panetta felt compelled to dissemble the next day by saying he had never wanted to demote Myers, even though McCurry's résumé had landed on Myers's desk by mistake the day before as Panetta was preparing to make the announcement.

As the fall campaign began, the White House charm offensive had sputtered and failed. It was left to the voters to send the ultimate message to Bill Clinton about how he was doing.

12

Midterm: Disaster

The midterm elections in 1994 were the biggest disaster of the Clinton presidency up to that point. Not only did the Republicans take control of the entire Congress for the first time in a generation, but the President was widely blamed for the debacle, and with good reason.

Public-opinion surveys showed that he was extremely unpopular. A *U.S. News* poll found that 20 percent of the electorate hated him and another 25 percent "somewhat" disliked him—a 45 percent negative base. I had done extensive mood-of-the-voters interviews that fall, and my findings underlined what the polls were showing. Many Americans thought Clinton was incompetent, a phony, a liberal, a liar, and not fit to be President.

Yet during that crucial autumn of 1994, as the midterm campaigns raged across the country, the White House basically shared the President's delusions about what was happening. "We started believing our own spin," says a senior Clinton adviser ruefully. One misperception was that it was Congress that was dragging the President's popularity down, not Clinton who was hurting Democratic congressional candidates. Actually, both were in deep trouble. The

Clintonites also continued to believe that the President's character was not an issue, and that a last-minute emphasis on policy matters—especially a batch of "reform" proposals on welfare, campaign finance, lobbying, the budget, and congressional procedures—would turn everything around for the Democrats.

On Election Day, Panetta brought Clinton the bad news at about 3 P.M. Stan Greenberg's exit polls showed that a number of Democratic senators were going down to defeat, including both Democratic senatorial candidates in Tennessee, incumbent Jim Sasser, and then-Representative Jim Cooper, who was running for Vice-President Al Gore's seat. Clinton seemed shell-shocked.

Yet on election night, the worst traits of the White House's spin patrol were on display. At about 11 P.M., when the dimensions of the Democrats' losses were clear to anyone with an exit poll—and the White House had plenty of them—George Stephanopoulos appeared on CNN to say that the Democrats were "having a pretty good night so far." As Mickey Kaus said in *The New Republic* of November 28: "The point isn't simply that this was a typical, ludicrous Stephanopoulos lie. The point is that anyone who had taken note of the trend toward cynicism in American politics would know that such lies don't work anymore—especially lies delivered in the flat, robotic intonation that has become Stephanopoulos's trademark."

The next day Clinton told reporters that he would accept whatever responsibility he deserved for the losses. But he suggested that the result was not a repudiation of him but only a *cri de coeur* from voters to induce changes in Washington faster than he had managed so far—in other words, a continuation of the theme of change that had propelled him into the White House two years earlier. In interviews with me and other reporters that week, White House aides and the President's friends tried to reinforce the argument that Clinton really wasn't the main target of the voters. Several friends said that in the end he could not bear the thought that the citizens of the country, whom he so desperately wanted to love him, had actually repudiated him.

The White House was in disarray for weeks. By the end of November, over breakfast at a Washington hotel, a senior Clinton adviser slumped back in his chair in dejection. "This place just doesn't get any better," he told me as he sipped his orange juice. "Things are really fucked up. At this point I don't think things will *ever* get any better." For the next hour and a half he complained bitterly that no one at the White House seemed to realize how important it was to establish clear themes for this presidency. Certainly Clinton, wounded and angry, seemed strangely out of touch with the reality of his dangerous political predicament. "He's numb," the aide said. "He's not the person he was. I'm sure the old Bill Clinton must still be in there somewhere, but he shows very little ability to talk about what and who he is. And that's what he really needs to do right now. When I look back on the last two years, I see one missed opportunity after another. We don't have the luxury of missing any more opportunities."

This adviser said that Clinton needed to get away from the White House and do some serious thinking about what he wanted to accomplish in his next two years. "He doesn't have any time to think anymore," the aide told me, "and he doesn't function well when he can't spend some time thinking."

Of course this is a peril of the modern presidency: It absorbs time like a sponge if the President doesn't discipline himself. However, Clinton had never demonstrated the ability to do this. He was all over the lot, trying to do everything, exhausting himself in the process, and he had no sense of pace.

Increasingly, the President's more savvy advisers, especially those outside the White House bubble—people like Al From, head of the centrist Democratic Leadership Council and a sometime Clinton adviser, and Democratic governors like Roy Romer of Colorado, who had survived the 1994 GOP landslide by running a centrist campaign—thought Clinton was at a critical crossroads. He had three to six months to show that he was a moderate, that he would no longer push big-government programs like Hillary Clinton's original health-care-reform plan, and that he would work with Republicans. This, they thought, would be his last chance.

For his part, the President was increasingly upset with his staff. This was hardly new, but his dissatisfaction seemed especially severe in the weeks after the Democratic debacle. He would attend meetings with his senior advisers and come away with the idea that however brilliant and altruistic they were, his aides were basically a group of highly educated, well-off elitists who had never lived from paycheck to paycheck. "I'm the only one around here who understands the working stiff," Clinton told a senior policymaker during a late-night phone call in late November. This aide, a millionaire businessman, agreed. "None of us really understands what it's like trying to make ends meet on $15,000 a year," he said. He added that the Democrats had lost working-class males by a two-to-one margin in the election. "I just don't know how you can make up that deficit with other constituencies," he pointed out.

In private discussions with aides, Clinton returned repeatedly to the idea that the press was far too negative toward him and his administration. I never get credit for anything, he complained, but when I screw up, they're all over me. Journalists don't trust anyone with power, he said, and it makes governing almost impossible.

One of the few bright spots was Panetta, the new chief of staff. Finally, he was taking charge. "For the first time since we got here," a senior White House aide told me, "we have a center of the universe. Everything goes through Leon." He had imposed discipline on the operation, kept aides from "dropping in" on the Oval Office and wasting Clinton's time, and cut meetings short; most important, he had begun to insist that the White House demonstrate its commitment to staying in the political center.

In a late November 1994 interview, Panetta told me: "There is one overarching theme that is absolutely essential: President Clinton is committed to the average citizens of this country. He wants to improve their lives." He added that he wanted the President to focus on a few issues—welfare reform, a scaled-down health-care proposal, continued deficit reduction, and perhaps a few other initiatives—and not waste his time tilting at too many windmills. He added that one of his top priorities in managing the White House was to bring more discipline to the staff. "People have to be able to respond to directions," he said. "They have to know their responsibilities and the lines of authority, so that when issues come up, it's not just hit and miss. . . . It's very basic. . . . You tell people to do a job and they do it. You don't have to tell them twice."

Shortly after taking over, and after being overruled on Dee Dee

Myers's immediate demotion, Panetta had reassigned communications director Mark Gearan to take charge of strategic planning so Gearan could focus on long-range strategy, something the White House lacked. Panetta was also counting on his two new deputies, Harold Ickes and Erskine Bowles, to control the staff even further.

The son of Italian immigrants and a former midlevel official in Richard Nixon's administration, Leon Panetta served for sixteen years as a Democratic congressman from California, rising to the chairmanship of the House Budget Committee, and his knowledge of Capitol Hill was encyclopedic. When he moved from Congress to the White House as Clinton's budget director in January 1993, he was widely considered an excellent choice. Now, as chief of staff, he seemed to be on the right track. He adopted a more hierarchical system of management than the one used by his predecessor, Mack McLarty, and insisted that he be included in virtually all meetings, even the national-security sessions that McLarty had sometimes not attended. Panetta wanted to be "the primary conduit to the President," though it was unclear whether Clinton, who liked to be his own chief of staff, would allow him that much control.

Panetta was obviously in sync with the President in one important respect. Both were political veterans who had suffered the ups and downs of elective office. The two men were also increasingly troubled by what they saw as a mean-spirited atmosphere taking root in the capital. "I have never seen [such] depths of personal attack," Panetta told me in late November 1994. "They really do undermine people's trust in the process, and they undermine the ability of elective leadership to do its job. People deep down need to understand that elected leaders are trying to do the best they can. We've reached the point where attacks on the President or Congress are harmful to our democracy. . . . People in office have to . . . work to solve problems and not demagogue issues. People on talk shows and reporters need to be conscientious about what's good for the country as well as bad. We need a better balanced picture of reality, not just the negative. We do pay a price for this talk-show kind of emphasis that's always negative."

Earlier that week, Senator Jesse Helms of North Carolina, the incoming chairman of the Senate Foreign Relations Committee, had provided a perfect example of the slash-and-burn politics that Panetta was talking about. First Helms questioned Clinton's fitness to be commander in chief because he had avoided military service during the Vietnam War and had tried to allow gays to serve legally in the armed forces. A few days later, he said that Clinton was so unpopular that he would need a "bodyguard" if he visited military bases in North Carolina. The President had been annoyed by Helms's first remark, but he was insulted by the second and wanted to go to North Carolina immediately. Panetta calmed him down, and they agreed that the wiser course was for the chief of staff to condemn the conservative senator's rhetoric as "dangerous and irresponsible." The next day, Helms admitted that his remarks were a mistake; still, the incident only reinforced for Panetta how little respect the President commanded.

Just as important, the White House was filled with trepidation about what the new congressional majority of Republicans would mean for the economy. Robert Rubin, then a senior economics adviser to Clinton and soon to become secretary of the Treasury, was working fourteen-hour days trying to develop budget and economics options for the President. Rubin, aides said, was deeply worried that the congressional Republicans would make irresponsible tax cuts and impose what he considered a phony tabulation system for projecting deficits, with the feared result that the red ink would get worse.

In their soul-searching, some Clintonites began to look back with grudging admiration at Ronald Reagan—for his approach to leadership, and especially his belief in the symbolic importance of the presidency, his management style, and his skills at manipulating public opinion.

"What was it Ronald Reagan had?" a senior White House official asked me with considerable frustration. "He managed to really connect with people. How did he do it?" The official was baffled and galled. Reagan was not nearly as smart as Clinton, he said, or as engaged or hard-working, yet he managed to get credit for his successes and to avoid blame for many of his failures, thus earning himself the nickname of the Teflon President. Could his staff have been *that* good? Could it have been pure luck?

Good staff work and luck are always important, but what Reagan had that Clinton lacked was vision. He set forth three directions for the country, three governing themes, and he kept to them constantly. He could compromise, but the country knew that for all his faults, Ronald Reagan was committed to less government, lower taxes, and standing up to the Communists. It was a clear, compelling message, and if voters disagreed with him on some specific policies, such as his opposition to abortion or his endorsement of U.S. aid for the contra rebels in Nicaragua, they appreciated and agreed with his three governing principles.

Some of the Clintonites—McLarty, Begala, and Panetta among them—saw other advantages to Reagan's leadership style. Though he was too disengaged from events and decisions around him, Reagan did know how to delegate responsibility. He had assembled an experienced and talented White House staff, which included key aides James Baker and Michael Deaver, and had given them plenty of authority. Clinton's original White House staff lacked executive branch experience, his advisers now admitted, and Clinton tried to do too much himself. Gradually, he began to allow his chief of staff to run more of the operation. It remained to be seen whether this pattern would continue.

A former Hollywood actor and television performer, Reagan believed that a celebrity needed to create a special aura to keep fans interested, and he knew by instinct that a President could easily wear out his welcome with Americans by being too visible. The "Great Communicator" carefully rationed his appearances and always tried to convey optimism and dignity. Reagan, aides to Clinton admitted, was never photographed in skimpy running shorts; nor did he ever tell an audience what kind of underpants he wore. Clinton had done both. "There's more appreciation for the way Reagan conducted himself as President," a senior Clinton adviser said. "There was more mystery around him."

Yet in the fall of 1994 Bill Clinton was still breaking all the Reagan rules. More important, he seemed too personally flawed to serve as the moral exemplar that Americans wanted in their President. There seemed to be no end of questions about his personal life and about his ability to stay the course when under attack, and he was becoming an object of national ridicule that seemed embedded in popular culture. Late-night television talk-show hosts

David Letterman, Jay Leno, and Conan O'Brien vied with one another to see who could make the most cutting jokes at his expense. On December 13, 1994, Leno said on NBC's *Tonight Show,* "Reportedly President Clinton spent today drawing up the big speech scheduled for Thursday night where he's gonna promise a middle-class tax cut. Now, why is he writing a new speech? Why doesn't he just reread the one he kept making during the campaign?"

That same night Letterman said on CBS's *The Late Show:* "The White House is now saying that when President Clinton agreed to send twenty-five thousand troops into Bosnia. . . . he was not flip-flopping on his policy regarding Bosnia. . . . It was only an expansion of his policy. . . . Yeah, I guess in the same way that Paula Jones or Gennifer Flowers are just an expansion of his marriage."

Clinton friends and advisers were troubled that the country didn't see the good side of the President or the First Lady. "The Clintons have never understood the power of biography and personal life as a selling point for a presidential candidate or a President," a senior White House official said. "He believes that what you should talk about are the issues. That's what's important—the real issues that affect people's lives. In the campaign he felt that if he opened discussion of his background and his life, it would open up areas he didn't want people to know about. So he . . . said we've had problems in our marriage, and now let's go on to the EITC [earned income tax credit]."

In fact, the narrative of Bill Clinton's life had ended when he took office. Wittingly or not, he sent the message that his life as President was off limits to the public, when in fact the country was hungering for details about him. In my mind—and, I suspect, in the view of most journalists—the country was entitled to those details. When citizens become President and First Lady, they become public property.

"In the campaign, he was the man from Hope, and the country had high expectations for him," says a senior White House official. "Look at what people know about him as President—the haircut, Paula Jones, Whitewater. They have no insight into the Clintons as a family unit, no sense of the love in that family, no sense of his broader joys and appreciations small and large, like watching football games with his daughter, or how learned he is."

Sadly, all this remained in the "zone of privacy"—the phrase that the Clintons now used to describe the areas of their lives that they wouldn't let anyone see or understand. Certainly, a President and First Lady are entitled to some privacy, but this First Couple overdid it, and as a result they were easily caricatured. No one knew what to believe about them.

IN THE WEEKS following the November 1994 elections, as the Republicans prepared to take over, the soul-searching by the President and his advisers led to some important changes at the White House. In fact, it turned out to be one of the pivotal periods of the Clinton presidency. One of the Clintonites' conclusions was that the heat would be off the White House for the foreseeable future. The media and the country, they correctly thought, would focus on the new GOP majority in Congress. "The Republican party is now fully responsible for the most unpopular human institution in the United States," White House political consultant Begala told me, referring to Congress. "May it do for them what it did for us. Congress is now the Republican party and the Republican party is Congress." Senior administration officials also concluded that at some point in 1995 the President would have to endorse a middle-class tax cut or else the Republicans would have this powerful issue all to themselves, even though such a cut could well balloon the deficit. Within weeks of the 1994 elections, Clinton endorsed the tax cut.

The Clintonites decided to gamble that the Republicans would be their own worst enemy. White House strategists predicted that the new GOP majorities in the House and Senate would promote extreme positions on social and economic issues, such as trying to severely limit abortion, rescind the 1994 ban on assault weapons that the Democrat-controlled Congress had approved, and slash aid to the poor and the elderly. "On all those issues," a Clinton adviser told me in November, "the Republicans are on the wrong side of the middle class." Begala added, "The Republican party exists to serve power and privilege and serve the economic elite."

A large part of the White House's soul-searching focused on

how to deal with the press. Some Clinton advisers suggested another end run, the same concept that had failed so miserably in 1993. But this time there was a new wrinkle: The Democratic party would raise huge amounts of money to finance advertising campaigns on behalf of presidential initiatives. Clinton had used this approach when he was governor of Arkansas, and it had worked. However, the problem was not only that such a strategy could further contaminate relations with the press, but that no one could raise the kind of money that would be required. Opponents of the health-care-reform bill had spent $300 million to defeat the measure, Clintonites estimated, and it would take far more than that to sell welfare reform or other administration projects, so the strategy was abandoned for the time being.

White House advisers developed two theories to explain why Clinton was having so much trouble with his public perception. First, voters had no qualms about throwing out their elected leaders every few years. With the Communist menace gone, stability was no longer as important, and elected officials could be dumped with impunity, including a President.

The second theory focused on what Begala called "the explosion of bad information about government—all the criticism, the proliferation of journalism, the explosion of analysis over straight news . . . News is more analytical than twenty years ago, and the analysis is far more negative." Yet, he added, "I don't believe the press has an anti-Clinton bias."

Actually, as will be shown later in this book, the changes in the news establishment are far more profound. Washington editors and reporters are barraged with news all day long from CNN and the wire services, and with countless instant-analysis television and radio talk shows. Too often Washington journalists, assuming that the public already knows the basics, feel they have to give their readers, listeners, and viewers something to distinguish themselves from the competition. The current trend is for journalists to take the easy way out—instead of doing a better job of reporting, they add attitude, edge, criticism, and a harsh voice to their coverage. One senior Democratic strategist said, "If you're trying to move up the career ladder, it pays to have an edge and to analyze. Making ridiculous prognostications is more likely to get you on the front page or on television talk shows," which in turn increases your lecture fees and distracts you from real reporting.

Begala's theory was that there is an ever-increasing number of media outlets. In Reagan's day the White House didn't have to deal with this proliferation, and consequently it was easier to control the administration's message through the TV networks, which dominated news dissemination. But by the time Clinton was elected, the broadcast networks' market share was down and journalists were much more cynical about manipulation, so they were far more difficult to control.

In the 1992 campaign, some Clintonites understood all this. James Carville had a favorite saying: "Feed the beast or the beast will eat you. . . . Give him a cheeseburger or he'll eat your leg." So, said a Clinton aide, "we cooked up a lot of cheeseburgers."

By late 1994, a growing number of Clinton strategists realized that they needed to return to these first principles.

THE TRADITIONAL HOLIDAY festivities for the press corps reflected the somber mood at the White House. On the night of December 13 two press parties were held, one starting at five-thirty and the other at eight. To their credit, the Clintons went ahead with these events, and they even managed to stand in a receiving line shaking hands with some two hundred of their antagonists for an hour at each event.

Many of the reporters felt a strain in the atmosphere, and the Clintons were subdued. Virtually no senior White House staffers deigned to show up, even though in the past the attendance of such officials had been customary. Even press secretary Myers passed up the parties, which many reporters considered a snub.

What the Clintonites did not understand was that the holiday parties are most valued by the families of the press corps, not the reporters themselves. It remains a thrill for spouses and kids to visit the gloriously decorated East Room, to sample the White House buffet, and to greet the President and First Lady. My wife, Barclay, and I were part of the second shift, and at precisely 10 P.M., the military ushers firmly announced that the residence was closed and abruptly began herding everyone out. It seemed an ungracious way to end the evening; in the past, the journalists had been allowed to linger at their leisure, since the President and First Lady could easily escape by retiring to their private quarters on the second floor.

MUCH STILL NEEDED to be changed in the relationship between the White House and the media. The press corps still felt that the Clintonites had a deep contempt for the journalistic profession. "Their lack of understanding of the way we work is profound," said Terry Hunt, chief White House correspondent for the Associated Press, in December 1994. Some of the problems were basic, he felt. White House planners didn't seem to realize that if they scheduled a presidential speech to the nation at 9 P.M., as they had that month when Clinton released his post-election plan for new tax cuts and spending reductions, about 20 percent of the morning newspapers on the East Coast would miss the story. Nine P.M. was simply beyond their first-edition deadlines. Time and again Hunt and other White House correspondents suggested that the White House issue an advance text and embargo it for release until after the President had delivered his remarks. In that way morning papers could have stories on the speech, based on a text prepared ahead of time. But the President either procrastinated too long in preparing his remarks, making an advance text impossible, or the White House staff lacked the savvy and interest to meet press deadlines. Even two years into the Clinton administration there was no one on the press staff who had substantial daily journalism experience. And still there was trouble at the top. Senior administration officials and close friends of the Clintons told me that the President and the First Lady were as angry at the media as ever. They blamed the press for helping to create an anti-Clinton climate that enabled the Republicans to make their historic gains. The First Family was "pretty well convinced that the cynicism will dominate the relationship between the press and the presidency while they're here," a senior White House adviser said, "and they don't think there's any way to get at that because it's just fundamentally the nature of the relationship. . . . It makes them a little despondent from time to time. They say, 'When we do something good, it's not going to get reported. When we do something that's wrong, even if it's something that's chickenshit, the media will make a big deal out of it.' Their working assumption is that it's going to be awfully goddam hard to tell a good story."

For her part, Hillary saw the problem increasingly in fundamental terms. "[We need to] figure out a way," she told me in my Illinois interview on February 15, 1995, "to provide information to people that enables them to participate in the decision-making, but also rebuilds their confidence in their decision-makers, because there's no way we can have a virtual democracy of 250-plus million people to decide every issue that breaks twenty-four hours a day in the world. So we both have to expand democracy and rebuild trust in those whom we've asked to lead us. . . . It is very troubling to me that we have had a continuing erosion in the trust placed in our public leaders, often on matters that have nothing to do with public issues or the public good, however one were to define it. . . . I'm troubled by the negative, confrontational nature of every encounter over the exchange of information regarding issues and government. I'm troubled by the tendency to inflame, as opposed to inform, the electorate, and not because of who the President is. This is a trend that has been developing over time. . . . We all [have to] figure out how we're going to sustain a democracy in the information-overload age. . . . I'm concerned about who will enter public life, who will stay in public life, the quality of decisions that are made, the extraordinary role that big-monied interests will play because they can marshal information-driven campaigns that permeate the atmosphere with, frankly, misinformation or, if not wrong information, certainly inaccurate because [it is] incomplete. . . . These are really big, important questions, and ones that I worry about a lot."

13

The Arrival of Mike McCurry, and the Newt Factor

On January 5, 1995, President Clinton showed up in the media briefing room to announce that Mike McCurry would be his new press secretary. McCurry had proved himself an articulate and unflappable chief spokesman for secretary of state Warren Christopher, and the choice was greeted warmly by most White House reporters. The forty-year-old veteran of Democratic politics seemed to have the brains, access, savvy, and respect for journalists to improve the unhealthy relationship between the press corps and the White House.

McCurry also had a playful side. "I want to have some fun around here," he said at his first briefing. Turning to his wife, Debra, who was pregnant with their third child, he joked that the President had agreed to give him a break from the press secretary's hectic routine on occasion. "He's promised us at least one conjugal visit a month, but probably no more than that. We won't need one for a while, as you can tell."

McCurry was interested in improving the relationship in fundamental ways. First, he started out with a deeper understanding of the Washington press corps than either George Stephanopoulos or

Dee Dee Myers, his two younger and less experienced predecessors as chief White House spokesman. He had worked not only as chief spokesman for Clinton's State Department, but had served as director of communications for the Democratic National Committee from 1988 to 1990 and as a spokesman for three defeated Democratic presidential candidates: Nebraska senator Bob Kerrey, who had run against Clinton in 1992, former Arizona governor Bruce Babbitt in 1988, and Ohio senator John Glenn in 1984.

McCurry told friends there were several things he needed to do as swiftly as possible: establish his access to Clinton's inner circle; bring his own people onto the communications staff; and let the press corps know that he wanted to work with them, not treat them as enemies. Later he told me he was surprised at "the level of complaints about some of the basic ways in which the press operation functioned, the complaints about things that were really pretty basic, like returning phone calls and putting out accurate schedule information. The complaints were about things that should not have been given a second thought. That was pretty dispiriting."

During his first week on the job, McCurry convened the press and communications staffs and declared that one of their jobs was to serve the media in addition to serving the President. It was a big departure from the Stephanopoulos-Myers regime, when the press staff felt that their goal was to circumvent and contain reporters. Yet no one at that first meeting said a word about McCurry's new marching orders because, even though no one was sure how well his dance with the wolves would work, everyone knew that the old ways were a failure.

One aide said that McCurry had about a month to demonstrate that he alone—not spokesmen for cabinet secretaries, not outside political strategists, not other White House officials—was in charge of the administration's public relations. "He has to make it clear that the press secretary makes the final decisions," the aide said. "He has to get to the point where no one will challenge him."

McCurry managed to do all this within a few weeks. Even though he was still spending part of his time at the State Department until his successor could take over, he began showing up at chief of staff Panetta's 7:30 A.M. senior staff meetings. His goal was twofold: to include himself from the start in White House decision-making, and to show everyone on the senior staff that he was a member of the inner circle.

Realizing the depth of the Clintons' distrust of the media, McCurry resolved first of all to generate some goodwill within the White House press corps. If he could produce a few positive stories and improve the overall atmosphere, he reasoned, then the Clintons might grant more access and members of the White House staff might reduce their animosity. As part of this peacemaking effort, he tried to bring more of the press corps into public events involving the President rather than limiting coverage to tiny pools of reporters. His goal was to reduce journalists' cabin fever, a consequence of their being trapped in their small warren of cubicles and work spaces for hours on end with little to do but wait for official events and complain. "That is a petri dish for the culture of cynicism," McCurry said, "because everyone sits around with nothing to do all day long except to speculate on how venal we all are . . . part of it is the psychology of being in a mass. Everyone sits there and they talk to each other."

McCurry didn't know the half of it. Bored and bottled up in their maze, and unable to go anywhere in the White House complex without an appointment and a government escort, many press regulars spent hours cooking up bizarre but fascinating theories to explain government actions, based on little or no information. This is what every press corps does on every major journalistic beat, whether it is the White House, a statehouse, or the Pentagon, but the political consequences are always greater at the White House because the perception of the presidency is at stake.

As press secretary, McCurry believed his two most effective weapons were candor and humor. "Humor you use to deflect the ugly and to take the rough edges off," he told me in late March 1995, "but candor is what you do to enhance credibility and win confidence and respect."

A big surprise for the new press secretary was that no one had informed the President about how the press corps worked. One sore point among reporters was that Clinton seemed cavalier about letting his staff and the media know about his personal schedule. Reporters and aides would hang around the White House all day and evening, including weekends, because no one knew the President's plans for jogging, going out to dinner, playing golf, or other social activities. Sometimes he left the White House and sometimes he didn't. Not knowing in advance made for an enormous waste of time for everyone dependent on his schedule. Sometimes reporters would go home for the day and begin eating dinner with their families, only to be called back when the President left on an outing that he had known about all along but had neglected to mention. This created hard feelings, and some journalists felt that Clinton's lack of consideration stemmed from a desire to make their lives as difficult as possible.

"Is that how they do it?" Clinton asked in astonishment when McCurry explained the press corps' modus operandi.

"Yeah," the new press secretary replied. "They all sit around, and if you're going to stay in and no one tells them you're going to stay in, they hang around here all day long."

From then on, Clinton promised, he would call McCurry to coordinate his schedule with the press corps more closely.

While McCurry prepared to take the job as White House press secretary in the late fall of 1994, he met with Marlin Fitzwater and heard Marlin's views firsthand. But unlike Stephanopoulos and Myers, McCurry took Fitzwater's comments—and similar critiques by many other Washington veterans—to heart. One of Fitzwater's points was that a President can override the mainstream media on occasion, such as with Oval Office speeches directly to the country, but that he must find a way to deal with the journalists who cover him on a regular basis.

Fitzwater also explained that Clinton wasn't alone in misunderstanding the press, and that every President does so in one way or another. For all his experience in politics and his reputation as the Great Communicator, Reagan was always "mystified" by reporters, Marlin said. He never knew quite what to make of those boisterous, unruly people who shouted questions at him from a distance and constantly tried to trip him up or otherwise embarrass him. Reagan never knew many reporters by name, but the system worked because his aides understood the press and took the time to feed the beast.

By contrast, George Bush knew the members of the press corps as individuals. This helped him for a while, until it became clear that he had no domestic agenda and no particular plan for a second term.

No amount of schmoozing with reporters could change that basic flaw in his presidency. And because Bush also defined journalists according to his perceptions of the ideology of their news organizations, most of which he considered liberal, he thought of most reporters as liberals who never could warm up to a conservative President. In the end, this simplistic view led him to misperceive the cause of his political problems as ideological bias by the media.

Fitzwater's comments helped to confirm McCurry's view that the hard feelings Clinton harbored toward the media were not unique, and that the press was not out to "get" him as an individual. Above all, McCurry understood that if journalists didn't know the Clintons, they would be willing to believe almost anything about them.

MY WIFE, BARCLAY, and I threw a get-acquainted reception for the new press secretary at our home in suburban Bethesda on January 15, 1995, the day before he was scheduled to formally begin his duties. About fifty of the White House regulars attended, the core of the press corps, and McCurry spent two hours casually chatting with small knots of journalists. His goal, he told me later, was to make a fresh start.

Our party was an effective groundbreaker. McCurry pronounced it a success, as did virtually all the reporters, who felt that at last someone from the White House seemed interested in getting to know them as human beings. Unfortunately, when I had offered to host a similar reception for both Stephanopoulos and Myers two years earlier, neither of them showed any interest.

THE WHITE HOUSE got some breathing room in early 1995 from a strange quarter: House Speaker Newt Gingrich, the bête noir of liberal Democrats for many years. Gingrich and the resurgent congressional Republicans regularly got into trouble with the media, making outrageous statements, embarrassing themselves with flippant remarks, and pushing for extreme policies. It diverted attention away from the White House, which was just what Clinton needed and just what his advisers had hoped.

The week that McCurry was named press secretary, Gingrich got into a major dust-up with then-CBS correspondent Connie Chung over her taped interview with his mother. When Mrs. Gingrich revealed on camera that the Speaker had spoken privately to her about Hillary Clinton, Chung whispered, "You can tell me, just between you and me," and Mrs. Gingrich blurted out, "She's a bitch." It was a big story, and not only because it apparently revealed Congressman Gingrich's real feelings about the First Lady. It immediately became a media-ethics issue when Gingrich blasted Chung for misleading his mother and luring her into making the remark.

Hillary Clinton was gracious. She wrote the Speaker a private note saying she understood how the media twisted things, and invited Gingrich and his mother to the White House for tea. But later that week the Speaker was still fuming, and after meeting with the President and some congressional Republicans, he could not resist taking some verbal shots at reporters outside the White House. They were peppering him with questions about issues on which he and the President had disagreed, but Gingrich wanted to control the agenda and talk only about areas of agreement. Echoing the President's complaints about a cynical press, the GOP firebrand snapped: "There is no point in you all being destructive. Now, if the leaders of the United States can get together in a positive way, it would be nice for the [news media] to report accurately that it was a positive meeting and not to rush off and immediately try to find some way to get a cat fight started. . . . It would be very helpful for you to focus on the positive."

Of course this was just what the Clintons had been saying, and if anything, Gingrich had been experiencing a worse time with the press than the President had at the beginning of his administration. For months the Washington press corps had given Gingrich almost totally negative coverage. Even before the November 1994 midterm elections, mainstream media pundits had overwhelmingly panned the "Contract with America," the centerpiece of his agenda for change. This "Contract" was a promise, signed by scores of Republican House candidates at Gingrich's urging, stating that if elected they would try to force an immediate vote in 1995 on a number of longtime GOP initiatives, including a constitutional amendment to balance the budget and a measure to impose term limits on members of Congress. Media pundits tended to oppose these ideas as too restrictive on representative government.

As the House passed one item in the Contract after another, the press refused to give Gingrich and his Republicans much credit for success because the Senate was not eager to endorse many of those initiatives. Gingrich fumed. "An awful lot of reporters just don't get it yet, and so they're sort of floundering around," he told *U.S. News* on March 29, 1995. "I think they are culturally liberal in a broad sense, and I think that it's silly for them to deny it. And I think they are pathologically negative and cynical without regard to party or ideology. That is, they bite Clinton, they bite me, they bite anybody. Dick Armey [the House majority leader] had the best line; he said, 'A lot of reporters think they have to cover blood, and if nobody's bleeding they'll cut somebody.' So what you get is . . . unendingly negative coverage, and that's bad for the country because, in fact, it's not true of the world, it's not the way the world works."

Gingrich's overall point was well taken: The press was not giving him any breaks. But it wasn't because they were too liberal, as the Speaker contended; the real reason was because he had assumed power and the press corps' watchdog instinct had kicked in. It was time to hold the newly resurgent Republicans to account, and journalists had launched a barrage of critical stories designed to dissect the Speaker's conservative agenda, to determine if it would work, and to explain what Newt Gingrich was all about. He was widely portrayed as perhaps the most powerful Speaker in history, and reporters and editors assumed that the American people were desperate to know everything they could about him, ranging from his messy divorce from his first wife to his ruthless campaign of vilification in the mid-1980s, which had helped to force Democratic House Speaker Jim Wright to resign.

The biggest media feeding frenzy in December and January of 1995 was a $4.5 million book deal that Gingrich had negotiated with HarperCollins, a subsidiary of the News Corporation, which was owned by media mogul Rupert Murdoch. The press focused on two negative storylines: first, that Gingrich was cashing in on his position as Speaker; second, that Gingrich was too cozy with Murdoch, who was defending the Fox television network, which he owned, against a legal challenge from NBC and the Federal Communications Commission. Democrats demanded that the Speaker drop the book project, and while he did agree to give up the $4.5 million advance, the Speaker insisted it was perfectly proper for him to keep royalties from the book, a series of philosophical treatises on conservative politics.

In an hour-long speech on January 20, Gingrich called criticism of his book contract "grotesque and disgusting" and said that opponents, including the media, were out to destroy him. "I am a genuine revolutionary," Gingrich declared. "They are genuine reactionaries. We are going to change the world. They are going to do everything they can to stop us. They will use any tool. There is no grotesquerie, no distortion, no dishonesty too great for them to come after us." The Speaker said he and his wife had been ethically "scrupulous," and added, "Then to have the news media of this city used as a tool of the Democratic party, to just go out again and again and again in a one-sided way, is I think a despicable comment on how sick this city [has become]."

Actually the Speaker only got it partly right. The media were indeed focusing intently on his book deal and political views, but they didn't need the Democratic party to help them along. Most reporters and editors believed it was their job. Moreover, Gingrich was one of most quotable politicians in Washington, which made it easy to report about him. A few days after Congress convened that January, reporters publicized transcripts of a Gingrich college lecture in which he made some bizarre comments about men and women in the military. He stated matter-of-factly that women have a tough time in the infantry because they get "infections" if they squat in ditches for a month at a time. In contrast, males make good soldiers because they love to roll around in those ditches like "piglets," asserted Gingrich, who had never served in the military. It was colorful language and made for a good story.

THE FOCUS OF journalists on the Republican majority amounted to a sea change for the White House. No longer was Bill Clinton the big news every day. No longer did the press corps feel it necessary to scrutinize his every thought, word, and deed. There was a new game in town, the Republicans, and reporters were playing down the President.

"People have begun to see that there is not just one human being running this country," said Brian Lamb, president of the Cable-Satellite Public Affairs Network (C-SPAN), which carries the proceedings of Congress on live television every day. ". . . You have a Speaker now who is so active and activist and of the other party, and he has equal access on the television screen . . . equal access, that's what's different."

In the short term, the television networks were giving Clinton some of the best coverage of his presidency, according to a study by the Center for Media and Public Affairs in Washington, while Gingrich was assailed over a variety of issues, including his support for school prayer, his draconian proposals for welfare reform—such as the expanded use of orphanages—and his book contract. The Center found that ABC, CBS, and NBC had run 618 political stories on their evening newscasts from November 9, 1994, through December 31, 1994, and the statements by news sources about the House Speaker were overwhelmingly negative. "TV news criticism shifted from the President to the new House Speaker late in the year," the Center found. "In November, Gingrich's coverage was more favorable than Clinton's (45 percent to 34 percent positive). But in December, Clinton bested Gingrich by 42 percent to 33 percent good press."

For his part, McCurry began a round of private, off-the-record sessions with White House correspondents to solicit their views on what could be done to improve the working atmosphere. These conversations reinforced his desire to get back to basics—that is, to require the press staff to behave courteously, not dismissively or rudely, toward reporters; to return journalists' phone calls before their deadlines; and to produce advance texts of speeches so reporters could cover the President's remarks in a timely manner.

McCurry was told that many of the White House staff had stopped talking to reporters because they were afraid that other White House officials would accuse them of leaking negative stories. The result was that very little information was flowing to the press about what the administration was doing and planning. McCurry learned that even some of the White House's best media spokesmen, ranging from domestic policy advisers Bruce Reed and Bill Galston to national-security speechwriter Bob Boorstin, had become isolated from reporters. It appeared that the Clintonites were paralyzed.

Through most of December and January, the President still agonized over where he had gone wrong and why the voters had supported so many Republicans in November's midterm elections. He sought guidance from a wide range of people, including Democratic governor Howard Dean of Vermont, a dozen defeated or retiring Democratic members of the House, more than twenty retired generals and admirals, a variety of Arkansas friends, several presidential historians, philosophers, and religious leaders, and motivational gurus Anthony Robbins and Stephen R. Covey. He had come to see the election as "an indictment of the political process in Washington, the name-calling and the game-playing," a Clinton friend told me at the time, rather than a repudiation of his party, policies, or presidency.

Yet a *U.S. News* poll in January 1995 found that only 40 percent of the voters approved of Clinton's job performance, a substantial decline from 48 percent the previous October. Forty-two percent, including one quarter of Democrats and more than 37 percent of independents, thought Clinton should not run for reelection. The decline seemed more related to popular excitement over the bold new directions taken by the congressional Republicans than to anything Clinton had done or failed to do. What all this meant was that there was a real opportunity for the President to reinvent himself, and the White House was starting to sense it. As I wrote in *U.S. News*, "In an odd way, Clinton's lifelong instinct for accommodation may work to his advantage for the next two years. 'When the Democrats controlled Congress, his willingness to accommodate was always perceived as a sign of weakness,' says an old friend. 'Now, with the Republicans in charge, it will be seen as an asset. His cooperation will be the key to whether anything gets done.' Clinton understands this."

By reason of their new majority in Congress, the Republicans controlled the national agenda, and they were obliging the President for the first time to limit his priorities and pick a few issues on which to concentrate. In other words, the GOP was forcing him into a self-discipline he could not muster on his own.

In an interview on January 20, 1995, four days before his State of the Union address, Clinton told me that above all he wanted to emphasize conciliation and goodwill, and spent forty-five minutes outlining his plans for the next two years. He would resurrect the New Covenant theme of his 1992 campaign, arguing that government should provide opportunity but that individual citizens were responsible for their own success and for rebuilding a sense of community. He would urge a new spirit of comity with the Republicans. "There are some real opportunities for working together," he said, listing among them deficit reduction, a middle-class tax cut, welfare reform, health-care reform, and reducing "the size and regulatory reach of the federal government." Of course, he was well aware that this was the approach favored by the public. Our *U.S. News* poll found that 54 percent of the voters felt that the President ought to cooperate with the Republicans rather than fight them.

Yet while Clinton was talking compromise, his strategists were planning for the savage partisan warfare that nearly all of them expected within six to nine months. They had developed a list of a dozen issues on which the President could fight the opposition— places where he would draw lines in the sand and, his aides hoped, make a stand on principle. One of them was the administration's national-service program, enacted in 1993, in which college students received nearly $5,000 annually from the government in exchange for work in their communities. (Gingrich said that he opposed the program as "coerced voluntarism.") The White House also hoped the Republicans would try to roll back the popular ban on assault weapons that Congress had enacted in 1994. Clinton told his aides that he would veto it, but they weren't sure that he would stick to his threat.

As usual, what was most on the President's mind were rambling philosophical theories about changes in American culture. Nearly every weekend he would convene academics, philosophers, friends, or political activists at Camp David or the White House residence for freewheeling discussions about where our society was headed. Participants told me they resembled nothing so much as graduate-school seminars in philosophy or public affairs. There was never any clear statement from the President about what he made of all the highfalutin talk, or what he could do about the deterioration he saw in American values exemplified by the breakdown of the family, the rise in teenage pregnancies, and citizens' distrust in government.

In our January 20 interview, Clinton said, "Most politicians, contrary to public belief, are honest people, and most of them try to do what they say they're going to do, and most of them believe what they say. I know that's not the perception, but that's true, including my strongest opponents in the Congress. Most of them are honest, most of them believe what they say, and most of them try to do it. But there is a tendency in the modern world to treat citizens as if they are just consumers of our policies. You know, they will receive the benefits of economic reform, of political reform or whatever. But in a democracy they're partners." He added, "There are all these pressures that will tend to let us be alone more and isolate us more. A lot of the society . . . will be on the Internet and do E-mail and we can work at home and . . . isolate ourselves from one another even more. But in the end, unless we are citizens, unless we have certain networks in our local community, unless there's a certain level of trust that we have with our neighbors, unless we're constantly struggling to come in contact with people who are different from us, and listen to them and learn from them and make sure they understand us, it's going to be very difficult for what we do here in Washington to explode in a positive way across the country. So I've been very worried about that. . . ."

The President went on to talk about his visit to Rio Linda, California, that week to inspect damage from a catastrophic flood. People had been united in their adversity, he said, eager to work together and optimistic about the future. "Now, how do we recapture at least a smidgeon of that," he asked, "enough of that on a daily basis to be united as a country and hopeful as a people and alive to the pain and the frustration and the difficulty of people who are different from us so that we've got enough glue holding us together to be real citizens, to generate energy, to do things together so that we're more than just consumers? . . . I think that's the great question facing us, really."

It was a heartfelt summary of Clinton's aspirations and altruism. When the interview was over, McCurry came up to me in a corridor near the Oval Office and said he had been impressed by our concluding discussion. He said he would talk to the President's speechwriters, send them a transcript, and try to have it included in the State of the Union address the following Tuesday night. This is what Bill Clinton is all about, McCurry said excitedly; this is what the country needs to hear from him.

My reaction was quite different. If Americans knew anything about Bill Clinton, it was that he was a caring, empathetic individual, a man known for the mantra "I feel your pain." His riff on communitarianism struck me as too much like a seminar at a divinity school or a soul-searching monologue at the annual Renaissance Weekend gabfests of elite leaders that the President was so fond of. Bill Clinton seemed to be a smart, hardworking, goodhearted fellow but someone on a personal and political quest for individual and national self-fulfillment. He was in his wonder years, still asking questions, but his country wanted answers. The interview left me with the impression of a man out of sync with his times.

At the same time, Clinton couldn't be written off. Despite his flaws and his relatively low standing in the polls, the White House had a unique opportunity to reinvent Bill Clinton yet again, this time by encouraging the media to portray him as a moderating force in Washington, an indispensable counterweight to Republican extremism.

14

State of the Union

O N JANUARY 24, 1995, Bill Clinton gave one of the longest State of the Union addresses in history. Typically, the speech rambled from one topic to another and had no central theme beyond his by-now familiar idea of "reinventing government."

"I think we all agree that we have to change the way the government works," the President said. "Let's make it smaller, less costly and smarter; leaner and not meaner." He went on to talk about an extraordinary range of topics, all designed to show that he was a common-sense centrist, not a liberal. He pledged to reduce taxes for the middle class, overhaul the welfare system, reform the health-care system in an at least incremental way, and resist attempts to "explode" the deficit. He promised to control illegal immigration, campaign against teenage pregnancy, push for campaign-finance and lobbying reform, and "reinvent government." At the end of his address, he repeated a theme that he had ruminated on during our interview the previous Friday and that I had published in *U.S. News:* Americans were becoming too solitary and insular and needed to be more active citizens.

Opinion-makers generally panned the eighty-two-minute speech as undisciplined, self-indulgent, and unfocused. *The Washington Post* editorialized: "He is a man who likes to speak, and for 82 minutes he jumped from issue to issue, sketching out not only his vision of what the federal government should be doing but the responsibility all Americans have 'to give something back to their communities and their country in return.' These were the themes that made him a successful candidate in 1992. But in speaking about so much for so long, Clinton may have sacrificed his chance to do what many politicians and presidential scholars say he needed to do above all: explain to a skeptical public in clear and simple terms where he intends to take the nation as President."

R. W. Apple wrote in *The New York Times*: "The State of the Union Message that the President delivered tonight was notably short on demands for action and long on appeals for comity, a demonstration of just how much he has been weakened in the last 12 months." *Washington Post* columnist David Broder wrote on January 26: "If self-discipline is the requisite of leadership—and it is—then President Clinton's State of the Union address dramatized his failure. It was a speech about everything, and therefore about nothing. It was a huge missed opportunity—one he will regret."

It turned out, however, that the elite opinion of the press was out of sync with the country. White House polls and focus groups found that nearly two thirds of the voters were favorably impressed with the address, and that Clinton's viewing audience actually went up from 45 to 50 percent of adults by the end of his speech. His job approval also benefited. An ABC News–*Washington Post* survey conducted on January 26–29 found that 54 percent of the voters approved of the way Clinton was handling his job as President, a nine-percentage-point increase from three weeks earlier.

White House advisers said that this was one more case of media pundits not giving the President the credit he deserved. Pollster Stan Greenberg told me the week after the address that viewers were particularly impressed with the President's desire to reform welfare, cut spending, and make government more efficient. No matter what the media said, the American public was not ready to tune Clinton out and declare his administration a failure. "The public needs and wants the President to play a role," Greenberg said.

"The State of the Union was a strong reminder that [he] will play a role. They can trust the President to arbitrate—to join the Republicans when they're right, coax them in the right direction, and stop them when they go too far." But, Greenberg added, "the key is following up on the themes."

Even if Bill Clinton had never been good at that, most of America was willing to give him a second look. Voters clearly were paying close attention to the new political dynamic in Washington, and what they were seeing on Capitol Hill as reflected in the press was not pretty. Frustrated Democrats in the House of Representatives, enduring minority status for the first time in forty years, were resorting to delay and obstructionism, precisely the same tactics that Republicans had used when they were in the minority. For their part, twenty Republicans walked out before the President had finished his speech. The next day, Representative Robert Dornan of California attacked Clinton's failure to serve in the military during the Vietnam War and accused him of "giving aid and comfort to the enemy."

"The opposition party is very ambivalent about how to treat [Clinton]," said UPI's Helen Thomas. ". . . Should you treat him with respect today or is today the day you slap him around?" She referred to Helms's remark about the President's need for a bodyguard in North Carolina as particularly harsh. "Even at the height of Watergate, I assure you I never heard that kind of thing," said Thomas, who has covered eight Presidents, starting with John F. Kennedy in the early 1960s.

Things would get worse for the GOP. Three days after the State of the Union speech, House majority leader Dick Armey of Texas called Massachusetts Democratic representative Barney Frank, an open homosexual, "Barney Fag" in an interview with radio reporters. "Newt's always able to handle a harangue going on around him better than I am," Armey said. "I like peace and quiet. And I don't need to listen to Barney Fag, Barney Frank, haranguing in my ear because I made a few bucks on a book I worked on. I just don't want to listen to it." Frank said he accepted Armey's apology for the remark but added that it sounded, unfortunately, as if the GOP leader had been speaking from his heart. The story received prominent attention on the television networks, on radio stations, and in newspapers across the country. Trying to contain the furor, Armey described his remark as "a regrettable unintentional mispronunciation" of Frank's name. He then proceeded to do what public officials so often attempt when they get into trouble: attack the news media for carrying the story. It was a particularly bizarre defense because Armey had made the comment with full knowledge that radio reporters were tape-recording every word.

The furor quickly died down, but it showed how poisonous the atmosphere had become in Washington, and that as the messenger of bad news, the press was being blamed for problems that politicians were creating.

Still, all this was good news for the White House. Reporters were focusing even more intently on Congress, where the Republicans were serving up a steady diet of juicy gaffes and, more important, a full menu of serious policy debates. Every day, newspapers, magazines, and television newscasts were filled with stories about audacious Republican efforts to remove welfare as a perpetual entitlement for poor people, pass a constitutional amendment to require a balanced federal budget, impose term limits on members of Congress, and return vast amounts of power from Washington to states and municipalities. It was a heady time for the press; change was in the air and there were some fascinating Republicans to cover, including Gingrich, Armey, Helms, Dornan, and Senate majority leader Bob Dole, who was preparing to run for President.

In late January, the White House developed a plan based on this new environment. Clinton would try to remain above the daily Sturm und Drang of Capitol Hill and carefully pick his fights with the GOP in an effort to create "defining moments" for his presidency. The idea was to make Clinton look like a mainstream leader and cast the Republicans as right-wing radicals or incompetents. But White House officials were plotting an even longer-range strategy. Some senior advisers expected that eventually Congress would approve a series of draconian measures, such as forcing the needy off welfare without a safety net and imposing cuts in the growth of Medicare that would hurt the elderly. These advisers expected the GOP to include such measures in a variety of appropriations bills needed to keep government programs running or in a stopgap spending bill and they were urging Clinton to veto them to show that he had the courage of his convictions. It remained to be seen how far the President would go, but at least the Clintonites had finally adopted a political game plan, even though it was forced on them by the GOP landslide and the emerging press attention on the resurgent Republicans.

The new circumstances were forcing Bill Clinton to change a bit, not only in terms of limiting policy initiatives that could not pass, but in trying to appear more dignified as a contrast to GOP antics. He proudly told a friend, for example, that he had stopped answering questions from reporters at the end of his morning jogs. Aides had always cringed when they saw the President of the United States on TV—sweaty, out of breath, and wearing skimpy shorts—routinely responding to queries about everything from Russia policy to health-care reform. Finally the President had gotten the point and stopped the practice.

THEN, JUST AS Clinton seemed to be on another upswing, he suffered another setback. First, the character issue came back to haunt him. In late January 1995, *The Washington Post* began printing excerpts from *First in His Class,* a book by *Post* reporter David Maraniss, who had covered Clinton's 1992 campaign. A biography of Clinton before he became President, the book portrayed a well-intentioned, often high-minded public servant with a flawed personal life and a history of indecision on matters large and small. There were two important revelations. One was that Clinton had decided against running for President in 1988 after longtime confidante Betsey Wright, at the time his chief of staff, compiled a list of names of women with whom he allegedly had affairs and asked him to tell her the truth about each one. Wright "was convinced that some state troopers were soliciting women for him and he for them," the book said. The governor and his chief of staff discussed each woman and speculated on whether she might go public. In the end, Wright suggested that Clinton should not enter the race, in order to spare his wife and daughter any pain.

In a written statement after disclosure of these passages in the book, Wright said Maraniss may have misunderstood her comments. "My recommendation that the governor not run for President in 1988 was based on my fear that in the climate of Gary Hart that liars and gold-diggers would come out of the woodwork," Wright said. "What I learned from my conversation with the governor was that the rumors were nothing in reality. My concern was for the impact that the rumors would have on Chelsea and Hillary."

The second disclosure in the book concerned the President's avoiding military service during the Vietnam War. Maraniss wrote that as a congressional candidate in 1974, Clinton arranged to have destroyed what he thought was the original letter he had written five years earlier to thank army colonel Eugene J. Holmes, director of the University of Arkansas ROTC program, for "saving" him from the draft. A copy was retained, however, and it damaged Clinton's reputation for veracity during his 1992 presidential campaign.

The same week that the *Post* published a story about Maraniss's book, the President gave an interview with religion reporters in which he drew a distinction between "reputation and character." He said he had "increasingly less control" over his reputation, but "full control" over his character. "That's between me and God," he said. He added that he found strength in God's unconditional love, and said he was a sinner but had suffered for it. He told reporters he found solace in reading about God's forgiveness in Psalms, but also said, "It takes away from my ability to be President . . . to focus on the American people, if I have to spend all my time trying to answer charges about what people say that I did years ago."

This was a justification Clinton had used many times before when he was in political hot water because of his personal life. It was the old argument: The American people and the press should judge him only on his public life—the policies he adopted, the stands he took, the hard work he had invested in being governor and President. Like most politicians, Clinton's first instinct was to hide his troubles. If this didn't work, he would use evasions and half-truths to fudge his transgressions. If that too failed, he would argue that he should be judged only on the parts of his public record that he felt most comfortable defending. All of this dissembling only added to the impression that he was not the moral exemplar that most voters wanted in their national leader.

Maraniss's book deepened the impression among the political and media cognoscenti that this President could never put his past behind him and that new revelations about his transgressions might erupt at any time. The late-night talk-show hosts continued to have a field day with him, reinforcing Clinton's lack of stature in the popular culture.

IN POLICY TERMS, Clinton's strategy of creating "defining moments" was having mixed success. One positive initiative was his economic bailout of Mexico, where the peso was declining precipitously in value and the government was in crisis. The administration proposed a $40 billion legislative package consisting largely of loans and loan guarantees, but Congress balked. In a series of January consultations with congressional leaders, Clinton was told it would take several weeks to bring the package to a vote, and even then there was no guarantee of passage. But Treasury secretary Robert Rubin warned that there was no time to lose; if Mexico's economy collapsed, American investors would lose billions of dollars. So, on January 31, 1995, Clinton withdrew the legislative package and unilaterally provided Mexico with $20 billion in U.S. loans and guarantees backed by a special fund in the Treasury, along with several billion dollars in other loan packages through international financial organizations. His unilateral action was widely hailed in the media and on Capitol Hill as precisely the kind of bold decision-making that Americans expect of their President.

Less successful was Clinton's effort to end the baseball strike that had halted the major-league season prematurely in 1994 and was threatening to spoil the 1995 season as well. Spring training was scheduled to begin in less than two weeks when the President summoned baseball owners and players' representatives to the White House in early February 1995. Some advisers saw Clinton's chance to enter the pantheon of bold presidential leaders. After all, Ronald Reagan had shown his decisiveness in a labor dispute by firing 11,400 striking air-traffic controllers in 1981, John Kennedy had used the bully pulpit to intimidate steel companies into rescinding price increases in 1962, and Theodore Roosevelt had used the prestige of his office to mediate an end to the Russo-Japanese War in 1905—an action that earned him the Nobel Peace Prize in 1906.

Clinton worked out a game plan with Vice-President Al Gore for ending the strike. After the owners and players took their seats in the Roosevelt Room for a last-ditch bargaining session prior to the 1995 season (in plain sight of Roosevelt's Nobel Prize on a side table), Gore led each side through a series of detailed, lawyerly questions and answers to establish their differences and illustrate the areas where they needed to compromise. Then the President entered the room and tried to send them on a guilt trip, reminding everyone that thousands of Americans, including hot-dog vendors and other small-time concessionaires, relied on baseball for their livelihoods. "Most of all," he said, "the fans want you to play ball."

When the owners left the room for a private caucus in the President's study, Clinton schmoozed with the players, but his efforts failed. At 10:35 P.M., after both sides had met for five and a half hours, a gloomy President shook his head sadly and gave up. "Both of you have a lot at stake," he told the owners and players, "and I'm afraid both of you are going to wind up losers."

Of course it was Bill Clinton who was the immediate loser. "The President of the United States said, 'Play ball,' and these guys dissed him," said a senior Clinton adviser. Yet over the long run, White House strategists argued, his bid to end the strike would prove politically beneficial. "Voters will give him credit for trying," said another Clinton adviser. "That's more than the Republicans were willing to do." Indeed, Senate majority leader Dole and House Speaker Gingrich had both said Congress had no business getting involved. White House political adviser Paul Begala said, "Any red-blooded American who becomes President wants to make sure baseball continues. It's what a President does. He's the keeper of the American dream and a part of that dream is the national pastime."

Adding to Clinton's difficulties was another bungled personnel appointment. Dr. Henry Foster, Jr., had seemed like the perfect choice for surgeon general. He was a distinguished obstetrician-gynecologist from Tennessee who had operated a successful program to reduce teen pregnancies. As a high-achieving black man, he was an excellent role model for young people and seemed to be a noncontroversial figure, and the White House was eager to bring him on board after the stormy tenure of Joycelyn Elders, an Arkansas physician whose liberal views had led Clinton to demand her resignation.

Incredibly, the White House and the Department of Health and Human Services had failed to research thoroughly Foster's background on abortion, the one topic sure to come up in his confirmation hearings. White House officials said later they didn't think many Republican senators would raise the issue because it was so controversial, and they were correct about that. But the White House badly miscalculated the opposition from anti-abortion groups that were powerful forces in the Republican party, and these groups pushed the issue front and center. First Foster told the White House casually that he could remember performing only one abortion, and the administration put out this information as fact. Then he said he had performed fewer than a dozen abortions, and thereafter he put the number at more like thirty-nine. Later still, he admitted that additional abortions were performed under his supervision as part of the testing of a vaginal suppository that ended pregnancies. Republican senators said that the White House had misled them, anti-abortion groups were up in arms, and the White House got another spate of stories about its ineptitude. In the end, Foster's nomination died in the Senate.

15

Upswing

Despite such setbacks, Bill Clinton's teeter-totter presidency began to look up in the late winter and early spring of 1995. Not only were his job-approval ratings consistently above 50 percent for the first time in months but, not coincidentally, his media relations were much improved.

There were still cases of presidential pique. During his visit to Ottawa, Canada, on February 23–24, Clinton jousted with CBS correspondent Rita Braver over his diminished power. At a joint press conference with Canadian prime minister Jean Chretien, Braver asked Clinton about press speculation in Canada that he had been reduced to a titular head of state. Clinton tried to mask his irritation with a laugh, but he was clearly miffed. "Unless I miss my guess," he said, "a bill doesn't become law unless I sign it or it passes over my veto. So I don't consider myself a titular head of state, and until there is some evidence to the contrary, you shouldn't either." The White House staff was gleeful at the President's renewed zest for combat. Back in Washington, deputy chief of staff Harold Ickes was watching on television. "He really laid her out!" he exclaimed happily.

At last, Clinton seemed to have a grip on his presidency, and a big part of his political strategy for dealing with the Republicans involved the news media. White House officials called it the "rope-a-dope," a phrase coined by former heavyweight boxing champion Muhammad Ali, who would lie against the ropes, cover his head, and allow an opponent to pummel him. Then he would come alive in later rounds and knock out his exhausted foe. This was what Clinton had in mind.

The strategy was flawed. It was uncertain, for example, whether the President had the discipline and political skill to survive a pummeling by the Republicans, just as it was doubtful that the GOP would exhaust itself in the effort. But the White House plan did make some sense. The Republicans' move toward extreme positions was indeed costing them support in the polls. They had suggested cutting back the popular school-lunch program, and their proposals for slashing federal welfare—including the automatic denial of benefits to unmarried adolescent women who had additional children—seemed reactionary. "The great irony is that Bill Clinton, who was elected to bring fundamental change, could be reelected to check it," said Al From, president of the centrist Democratic Leadership Council. "People may want to have different parties in charge of Congress and the presidency to keep things from going off the deep end."

The rope-a-dope strategy had another advantage: The news media would naturally do much of the White House's work for it by focusing on the excesses, flaws, and foibles of the GOP leadership. Clinton told aides that the Republicans would be unable to deliver on their promises, a view seemingly verified when, in early March, the Senate failed by one vote to approve a constitutional amendment to require a balanced federal budget, which had been a key part of the GOP agenda. The media also continued to savage the GOP for extremism, and the White House deftly played the blame game. In early May 1995, Vice-President Gore and chief of staff Panetta attacked the Republicans for trying to make massive cuts in the growth of Medicare and Medicaid, the health-care programs for millions of elderly, disabled, and poor people, and at the same time give a tax cut to the rich. To the GOP's chagrin, their comments got extensive press coverage and the Clintonites kept up the pressure. The marginalized White House was playing defense but doing it effectively.

ANOTHER MAJOR TREND during that period was Clinton's deepening disenchantment with his White House staff. The media were focusing on the periphery of the story—but only the periphery, as *The New York Times, Time, The Washington Post,* and other publications did pieces on who was up and who was down. Panetta was described as losing influence to his deputy Harold Ickes, a former New York lawyer closely allied to labor unions, the liberal wing of the party, and Hillary Rodham Clinton.

The press's perception of staff turmoil was correct only up to a point. Ickes was indeed in the ascendancy, but it was not because he was elbowing Panetta aside. Actually, the chief of staff had assigned Ickes the tasks of building a campaign and working out a preliminary strategy for 1996. The real news was the extent to which Bill Clinton was taking charge of his own presidency and teaming with Vice-President Gore to set policy and determine political strategy. As I reported in *U.S. News,* Clinton had lost faith in many of those around him. "You won't find a single person at the top level of this White House who hasn't been criticized by the President," said one aide who regularly felt the sting of Clinton's temper. As a result of his dissatisfaction, the President didn't want to rely on any of his advisers too heavily, so he began to widen his circle of informal counselors, which he had done previously when he was in political trouble at various points in his public career.

Among those the President began talking to with increasing frequency starting in March 1995 was Dick Morris, a GOP-oriented political consultant from Connecticut who had helped revive Clinton's career after he lost his bid for reelection as Arkansas governor in 1980. At first Morris was used mainly to sharpen Clinton's rhetoric and to find ways to attack his adversaries. In succeeding months, his role increased and he began meeting every Thursday night with the President and Mrs. Clinton. By early summer 1995, Morris was meeting weekly not only with the President, but with a larger group including Gore, Panetta, Ickes, and deputy chief of staff Erskine Bowles, and he offered advice on everything from speeches to legislative strategy, issue development, and how to position Clinton for 1996.

The President also brought back media consultant Frank Greer, who had been an important adviser early in the 1992 presidential campaign but had been eclipsed by Mandy Grunwald. Now, after the 1994 midterm elections disaster, Grunwald was out of favor and Greer's star was rising. Other members of the emerging 1996 team were media consultant Robert Squier and Democratic strategist Ann Lewis.

Most important, Clinton turned increasingly to Gore, a fellow baby boomer who always seemed to have a commonsense view and who above all was loyal and discreet. Unlike most previous White House operations, the Vice-President's staff was not in conflict with the President's. Clinton and Gore seemed so close that their advisers saw no rivalry between them, and the President included Gore in so many decisions that the Vice-President's staff had none of the usual gripes about being excluded from policy-making.

Clinton and Gore had surprised their White House aides with a variety of joint decisions after the November 1994 elections. They decided abruptly to proceed with an administration proposal for a middle-class tax cut, overruling economic advisers who wanted above all to cut the deficit. They also agreed to again emphasize Gore's plan to "reinvent government" by reducing wasteful bureaucracy and useless programs. The President thought these two initiatives were political winners, and he relied more and more on what he called the "political synergy" he had with Gore.

In a series of private meetings during the winter of 1994–95, the two men decided to shore up Clinton's base among union workers, many of whom were still upset over administration support for two major free-trade agreements in 1994, the North American Free Trade Agreement and the Global Agreement on Tariffs and Trade. In February 1995, they gave organized labor a big victory: Gore announced at a union convention in Bal Harbour, Florida, that the President would sign an executive order forbidding government agencies from contracting with companies that permanently replaced striking workers. Clinton and Gore also surprised many White House aides when they endorsed an increase in the minimum wage from $4.25 per hour to $5.15 per hour. Both moves were concessions to organized labor designed to bring them back into the fold well before the 1996 election.

Gore and Clinton also came to believe that the public's anti-government fervor would burn itself out and that voters would eventually reject Washington-bashing, partly because the Republicans would go too far and take away programs popular with the middle class.

AS A DEFENSE mechanism, by the spring of 1995 the President had begun to tune out media criticism, especially on television. He was simply too frustrated by what he considered journalists' unfair stereotyping of him as an indecisive incompetent with a weak character. "He decided that the only way to really deal with it was to ignore it," said a senior adviser. The President would tune in to CNN periodically during the day in the Oval Office to learn what was being reported, but he stopped watching the nightly news on ABC, CBS, and NBC, except when aides told him there was something he had to see. Then generally he would ask for a videotape that he could view at leisure. He preferred morning-after written summaries of the network news prepared by senior adviser Stephanopoulos.

As for the print press, each morning Stephanopoulos would give Clinton articles he thought the President should read in their entirety—mostly from *The Washington Post, The New York Times, The Wall Street Journal,* the *Los Angeles Times,* and *USA Today*—and a cross section of stories from such regional papers as *The Boston Globe, The Chicago Tribune, The Dallas Morning News, The Oregonian, The Orlando Sentinel* and *The Philadelphia Enquirer.* On Mondays, the President would read *Newsweek, Time,* and *U.S. News & World Report.* The negative coverage irritated him, but if he limited himself to small doses of it, at least he could keep his anger from boiling over.

ON APRIL 19, 1995, press secretary McCurry interrupted the President's meeting with Turkish prime minister Tansu Ciller to impart some bad news. There had been a large explosion at the Alfred P.

Murrah Federal Building in Oklahoma City, and many people were feared dead.

The White House went into action. A federal relief effort was quickly organized in coordination with state and local authorities, and Clinton rose to the occasion. He was neither as inspirational nor as comforting as Ronald Reagan had been in similar situations, but his expressions of sympathy seemed genuine and deeply held.

In the first hours of the crisis, there was media speculation that the FBI was looking for two or three "Middle-Eastern-looking" men in connection with the bombing, which turned out to be untrue. Clinton was informed of the report and told aides privately that he was worried about a possible backlash against Arab Americans or Arab nationals in the United States. As a result, he warned the country not to jump to conclusions about whom to blame. He simply condemned the evil act and promised that the offenders would be captured and that he would ask for the death penalty.

The White House realized that Americans wanted their leader to serve as a voice of strength in this time of need, and the President continued to strike the right notes. He declared a national day of mourning for the Sunday after the attack. After the arrest of suspect Timothy McVeigh, who had connections to paramilitary groups, Clinton denounced organizations that advocated violence against the government and promised to ask Congress for new legislation expanding federal power to infiltrate and keep track of groups suspected of plotting terrorist attacks.

Moreover, the media were finally convinced that the President had something important to say to the nation. Unlike his press conference several days before the bombing, all three broadcast networks gave extensive coverage to his address at memorial services in Oklahoma City that Sunday. CBS's *60 Minutes* was suddenly eager to get Clinton on its show that night, and the White House agreed. The President used the occasion to make news by again attacking extremist paramilitary groups. "They have a right to believe whatever they want," he told CBS. "They have a right to say whatever they want. They have a right to keep and bear arms. They have a right to put on uniforms and go out on the weekends. They do *not* have the right to kill innocent Americans. They do not have the right to violate the laws, and they do not have the right to take the position that if somebody comes to arrest them for violating the law, they're perfectly justified in killing them."

The Washington press quickly began to speculate about whether the President had helped his chances for reelection, and opinion was divided. The truth was that his handling of the Oklahoma City tragedy gave him a boost. He was finally meeting the standard for dignity and efficient crisis management that Americans want from their President.

Clinton was again on an upswing, but no one could say how long it would last.

16

In Search of a Message

Even though Clinton was convinced that the field of GOP presidential candidates led by Senate majority leader Bob Dole was weak, he fretted. Only half the voters thought he was doing a good job, and he lacked a compelling message about what he would do in a second term. He spent much of the autumn of 1995 seething at how poorly his presidency was coming across, and began road-testing new themes for 1996.

Over the previous three years, Clinton had bounced from one message to another without finding one he was fully comfortable with. He was, by turns, a "new Democrat" seeking sensible solutions that didn't rely too much on government; an advocate of a "New Covenant" based on personal responsibility, community, and equal opportunity; the leader of a new generation ready to bring vigor and excitement to government in the manner of John F. Kennedy; and a social reformer pushing for a massive overhaul of the health-care system. After the GOP takeover of Congress, he had adopted a "triangulation strategy" developed by Dick Morris— meaning that he would try to position himself between ultraconservative Republicans and Democratic liberals. But Clinton didn't think "triangulation" was appropriately profound, so he rarely talked about the idea in public. Instead, he preferred a phrase suggested by his latest communications director, Donald Baer, a former editor at *U.S. News & World Report;* he would search for "common ground" with his opponents. At first the media liked the concept and the White House was delighted. Then, after Clinton failed to flesh out the theme with enough details, reporters began to lose interest. Every weakened President, after all, must seek "common ground" or face irrelevance.

Clinton told aides that if he couldn't penetrate the cloak of distortion that the press had wrapped around him as an individual, perhaps he could explain his problems in terms of historical forces beyond his control. What followed was bizarre.

Returning late on Friday night, September 22, from California after a five-day fund-raising trip across the country, the President strolled to the press compartment of *Air Force One* dressed in blue jeans, a casual shirt, and cowboy boots. He told the journalists on board that Americans were in a "funk" about the rapidly changing world and were worried about the twenty-first century. "What makes people insecure is when they feel like they're lost in the fun house," he said. "They're in a room where something can hit them from any direction any time. They always feel living life is like walking across a running river on slippery rocks and you can lose your footing at any time." He went on in this fashion for forty-five minutes in a combination of sermon, social-science lecture, and apologia.

When the story broke, journalists immediately began making comparisons to Jimmy Carter's infamous "malaise" speech on July 15, 1979, when he tried to blame the country for his own shortcomings. Many of Clinton's aides were furious with him. "I couldn't believe it," said one. "The economy is doing well and we're at peace, and he has to talk about how bad things are. What a downer. People want their President to be optimistic and cheery, like Reagan."

The following Tuesday, the President attempted some damage control. He told reporters that he didn't really mean that Americans were in a permanently sour mood and, in a typical obfuscation, argued that a "funk" is only temporary, while "malaise" would be long-term. Actually, he insisted, the country was basically optimistic, and he would do his best to keep it that way. It was the same old problem: The President was trying to have it both ways. As columnist Gloria Borger said in *U.S. News* after the incident: "At some point, voters are entitled to ask why the President hasn't learned his lesson. If they do, they might figure out that Clinton's *mea culpas* are not about honest accountability. They are about sweet-talking the voters into taking him back. . . . Maybe one reason Colin Powell has been hyped to a near-deity by the press is because he says what he thinks instead of thinking what to say."

Finding that all-important PR message increasingly guided decision-making at the White House in the autumn of 1995. At least three regular political meetings were held every week to map out communications strategy—what to say and how to say it. The most important occurred every Wednesday or Thursday at 8 P.M. in the White House residence with the President and Vice-President, Panetta, deputy chiefs of staff Ickes and Bowles, Gore's then-chief of staff Jack Quinn, and political consultant Morris. By early 1996, this meeting broadened to include pollsters Mark Penn and Doug Schoen, media consultant Robert Squier, Ron Klain, Quinn's successor as the Vice President's chief of staff, and other political strategists. There were also two weekly meetings—generally Tuesdays and Thursdays at 2 P.M.—in Room 180 of the Old Executive Office Building in which more than a dozen senior staffers planned political tactics, set the President's schedule, and discussed media strategy. This session, which Clinton did not attend, included Panetta, Ickes, Bowles, Morris, Quinn, Stephanopoulos, McCurry, communications director Baer, congressional liaison Pat Griffin, political director Doug Sosnik, presidential counselor Bill Curry, the First Lady's senior adviser, Melanne Verveer, and Democratic strategists Ann Lewis and Frank Greer. There was a fourth meeting on Thursday at 5 P.M. run by Panetta that included veteran Democratic strategists from around Washington, including Jody Powell, the former press secretary for President Carter, and occasionally Democratic pollsters Stan Greenberg and Geoff Garin.

But these sessions were largely designed to outflank congressional Republicans each day, and did little to address the larger problem of making a compelling argument for Clinton's reelection. That message, Clinton told friends, could not be set in stone until 1996 as the campaign evolved. It was the same theory of procrastination that had been used by George Bush and his team four years earlier, with dismal results.

ON FOREIGN POLICY, Clinton was having more success in fashioning a message. He hit on the theme of taking "risks for peace," and when his policies matched his rhetoric, he got substantial praise from the media. The high points included an Anglo-Irish agreement to stabilize Northern Ireland, peace accords in Bosnia, and futher progress toward stability in the Middle East. Clinton was instrumental in all three areas. Americans, however, showed little interest in the President's newfound deftness in global affairs.

CLINTON WASN'T THE only national figure searching for a message. On September 25, Texas billionaire Ross Perot made a surprise announcement on Cable News Network's *Larry King Live* that he would form a new national party that would field a presidential candidate in 1996. It was symptomatic of Perot's outsider image that he made his announcement not to a snarl of testy reporters at a press conference but in the non-threatening environs of Larry King's studio, where the Texan had announced his candidacy in 1992.

Perot said he hadn't decided whether he would run for his party's nomination, but said he would lead the effort to win a place on the ballot in all fifty states and the District of Columbia. Like Clinton's, his message was evolving, but he argued that most Americans were fed up with both the Democrats and the Republicans: "In a free society that is owned by the people, it is a sad commentary that almost two thirds of the people are not part of the political structure." Republicans feared, with good reason, that such a party would siphon off anti-Clinton voters from the GOP nominee—a point on which the media punditocracy agreed.

But many national journalists had turned against Perot since his first presidential run. His claims of conspiracies designed to bring him down, his harsh opposition to the North American Free Trade

Agreement, and his egotism and arrogance had antagonized opinion leaders. Within a week of his announcement, he fell off the front pages and dropped out of the nightly news because the media elite was tired of him. One of his biggest challenges in the coming campaign would be to insinuate himself back into the spotlight and force the media to take him and his party seriously.

THE HOTTEST POLITICAL story of autumn 1995 was Colin Powell. Propelled by a cross-country book tour to sell his memoirs in the early fall, the retired general rode a wave of media boosterism as he mulled whether to run for President as a Republican, as an independent, or not at all. More than anything else, it was the press that created the boom for Powell's candidacy, as the networks and the print media gave him coverage that was monumental in volume and often obsequious in content.

There were three reasons for this media frenzy. First, Powell was news; a non-politician would enliven an otherwise lackluster presidential race. Second, Powell offered a story line that the press found enticing; he was a high-achieving black man whose candidacy might heal some of the nation's racial divisions. Finally, many reporters, editors, and commentators believed that a Powell presidency would be good for the country. He was an American success story. Not only was he a unifying force, but he was an excellent role model, having risen from humble beginnings to become national security adviser to President Reagan and chairman of the Joint Chiefs of Staff under President Bush. He had led the military to victory in the Persian Gulf War, and his moderately conservative views, though sketchy, were not threatening to most voters.

For his part, Powell handled the media attention with poise and deftness, displaying the same traits that I remembered from his White House days. In an effort to demonstrate that he was a serious thinker, he gave bare-bones statements in support of affirmative-action programs and a woman's right to choose abortion, but he did little to clarify his views on most other domestic issues. His inner circle of advisers, led by former Reagan chief of staff Ken Duberstein and former State Department official Richard Armitage, decided that spelling out too many details would only alienate people, so he should delay such a reckoning as long as possible. In the meantime, Duberstein developed a portfolio of political talent, including pollsters, media strategists, and organizers, who would be available to the retired general if he decided to run.

Many questions remained about Colin Powell—such as how he had performed as a field commander in the Vietnam War and whether he had a role in the Iran-contra scandal. Just as important, no one could know how he would perform amid the pressures of a national campaign.

Still, Powellmania in the media did not abate, and the news-magazines led the way. *Newsweek*'s Howard Fineman offered "A Powell Scenario" explaining how he could win the White House, and Jonathan Alter wrote about him as a "force for good in American life." *U.S. News & World Report*'s John Walcott said his moderate views seemed to match the country's mood. "As trust in government and loyalty to the two leading political parties continue to fall," Walcott wrote, "Powell's stature is rising like a balloon riding the hot air over Washington." Jeffrey H. Birnbaum wrote in *Time*: "The general has become the nitroglycerin of the 1996 presidential contest. Virtually no one wants to jostle him out of fear that his popularity—and any slighting of his person—could prove explosive." A poll taken for *Time* and CNN in September found that if he were to run as an independent, Powell would win 33 percent of the vote, against Clinton's 30 percent and Bob Dole's 24 percent. A *U.S. News* poll in the same month found that 71 percent of the voters had a favorable view of him, projecting on him many of their hopes, dreams, and aspirations for a President.

No one, of course, could live up to the expectations created by the media that Powell was a combination of Dwight Eisenhower, Ronald Reagan, George Washington, and Bill Cosby, and it was inevitable that the beast would eventually turn on him if he entered the race.

With the approach of Powell's self-imposed Thanksgiving deadline for making a decision, his interest in running would ebb and flow. Powell told a friend it was a choice between the concerns of his wife and family, who were worried about his safety and did not want him to run, and his belief that many voters were counting on him to enter the race. Family won out, Powell said.

But that was only part of his calculation. Powell also realized that he lagged far behind his potential rivals in setting up a campaign. He had no fund-raising operation, no state-by-state field organizations, no public-relations or advertising team. His original theory had been that he could run as a man who was above politics, but he saw that such a message would be almost impossible to sell. His opponents and the media were sure to portray him, with considerable justification, as a conventional member of the Washington establishment who had played an insider's game for many years to insure his rise in the Army and in the government. He was hardly the apolitical outsider and agent of change that America seemed to be yearning for. Richard Armitage, his old friend from the State Department, echoed Powell's conclusion when he said, "People who think you can get a candidate who's above politics believe in a mirage." Powell decided not to run.

At 7 P.M. on Monday, November 6, Powell met to plan his announcement of noncandidacy with Armitage and Ken Duberstein in the library of his home in McLean, Virginia, a posh suburb of Washington. His wife, Alma, joined them about an hour later. They decided that Powell would work out his exit statement alone, but as the meeting broke up, Duberstein, not quite believing what was happening, said, "Is it over?" Powell answered, "It's over." Armitage added: "This is just the beginning of the next chapter of your life."

On November 8, Powell told a packed news conference in Alexandria, Virginia, that he lacked a burning desire to seek the presidency and announced his decision not to become a candidate.

FOR THE REMAINDER of the year, politics sank to new depths in the capital. Clinton and the Republican Congress were locked in a nasty battle over the budget that caused a six-day shutdown of portions of the government in November and a three-week interruption starting the week before Christmas. In one sense, it was politics as usual; such shutdowns had occurred several times before in recent years. But this time, the level of vitriol was especially intense, a harbinger of the 1996 campaign.

All sides battled to dominate the images conveyed by the news media, which tended, as usual, to focus on conflict rather than the substance of the issues in dispute. A favorite media image was of children playing in a sandbox. And the politicians made it so easy.

Gingrich offered himself as a perfect target when he complained to a large group of reporters that President Clinton had snubbed him on Air Force One during the November 5–7 trip to Jerusalem for the funeral of assassinated Israeli Prime Minister Yitzhak Rabin. Gingrich said the President never offered to talk to him or Senate Majority Leader Bob Dole about the budget during the twenty-five-hour round-trip flight. And Gingrich complained that he and Dole were forced to leave the plane through the rear door, along with the press and the lower-level staff, rather than through the front door used by the President and First Lady. Gingrich added that one reason he was taking such a hardline position against Clinton over a stopgap spending bill that could have averted a government shutdown was because of his pique over the alleged snub.

I was on the entire flight as a pooler for the press corps. And Gingrich was partly right; Clinton never made any overtures to discuss the budget impasse, even though he did find time to play a game of hearts for more than an hour with three other passengers and made small talk with several of the dignitaries, including the Speaker and majority leader. En route to Israel, I ran into the President, alone and wearing a sweatshirt and jeans, in a corridor of Air Force One. When he saw me, he grasped my arm and said somberly, "Glad you're here. He [Rabin] was a very great man." Clearly, Clinton was grieving, but he was not isolating himself. There were ample opportunities for Gingrich to take the initiative and suggest a serious budget meeting with the President, and the Speaker failed to do so.

Newt's snit was a terrific story. On November 16, the New York *Daily News* captured the idiocy of Gingrich's pique with a front-page caricature of the Speaker—in diapers, bawling, and holding a baby bottle—under the huge headline: "Cry Baby. Newt's Tantrum: He closed down the government because Clinton made him sit at back of plane." When Democrats began holding up the tabloid's front page and ridiculing the Speaker in speeches to the House, Gingrich's allies forced a vote that banned the offending edition from the House chamber.

Such stories overwhelmed substantive coverage of the underlying issues in the budget fight, such as the legitimate need to restrain the growth of Medicare and Medicaid spending and the appropriate level of tax cuts. As always, the media loved covering conflict, and the Washington politicians were supplying a steady diet of it. So the impression left with the public was of bickering-as-usual rather than an important policy debate over the role of the federal government in national life. This dynamic only intensified voter cynicism.

IN AN INTERVIEW at the end of 1995, McCurry summarized his first year as White House press secretary. He discerned a substantial improvement in the "level of respect" between reporters and his office—an accurate assessment. "There's a more cooperative attitude on the part of the staff, more of a sense of customer service," he told me. And even though McCurry was beginning to get noticeably miffed at individual reporters who baited him—ABC's Brit Hume led the list—McCurry said, "The biggest surprise has been how cooperative the journalists have been. I had expected far more confrontational briefings, a lot more acrimony. . . . There are times when you really do want to haul off and smack somebody, but I've resisted that. . . . The single biggest surprise for me being here at the end of a year is how much fun the job is."

For his own survival, McCurry had made a habit of referring the most troublesome questions to other administration spokesmen to avoid making mistakes and getting bogged down in technicalities. Whitewater, which was bubbling up again because of a newly aggressive congressional investigation into the affair, was a case in point. McCurry referred many media questions to the White House legal counsel's office or to the Clintons' private lawyer rather than being forced constantly on the defensive. His strategy helped distance the White House from the controversy.

Bill and Hillary Clinton remained conflicted. Above all, they were pleased that the press had mostly ignored their teenaged daughter and allowed Chelsea to live a relatively normal life. But they still doubted that the media could ever fully understand the Clinton presidency.

The President complained privately that journalists had bought into the Reagan model for communicating through stage management and tight scripting. Reporters would compliment McCurry and his aides when Clinton would come to the briefing room, make a brief announcement and leave abruptly without taking questions. That was considered "staying on message." Clinton despaired that, under such circumstances, his quest for knowledge, his love for discussion, and his eagerness to seek out different points of view would always be portrayed as indecisiveness and a lack of commitment to principle.

McCurry said, "The President on some days believes, 'If I could just sit down and have a straightforward discussion with reporters so they understood more of what my thinking was about, they would better appreciate what I'm trying to accomplish.' There are other days when he's just resigned to the fact that, 'I'm never going to get a fair break.' . . . He feels alternatively like, 'If I put more time into this relationship I could make it come out better,' and then on other occasions feels, 'I'm better off just sticking with a very disciplined approach.' "

There were other troubling signs that the institutional relationship between the White House and the press would fray even further. "The most horrible news of 1995 was that two more networks [ABC and NBC's cable-television operations] are considering 24-hour-a-day news broadcasts," McCurry told me. "That becomes a voracious animal with an insatiable appetite for headlines on the hour. The only way you can feed that is to comment on every single sparrow that falls from the tree. . . . To me, future Presidents are going to need two press secretaries, one for the day and one for the night."

17

The Media in
Transition

One factor that remained constant in Bill Clinton's White House was his ongoing critique of the press. When he was alone with friends or aides, he made a habit of attacking the press as overly cynical, negative, and simplistic, perversely absorbed with process, personality, and horse-race coverage. It seemed to be an obsession with him. The media, he claimed, were making it extremely difficult for him to govern.

He was by no means alone in this assessment. In fact, it is now a common refrain among media critics. Political scientist Thomas Patterson of Syracuse University argues that the news media unfairly treat all politicians as liars who don't keep their campaign promises, when in fact most politicians are actually public-spirited souls who are altruistic and high-minded. The media, Patterson argues, do presidential candidates a particular disservice by "burdening" them with negative news coverage. In his book *Out of Order,* he says negative news coverage of presidential campaigns has increased dramatically since 1960. "Of all evaluative references to Kennedy and Nixon in 1960, 75 percent were positive," according to Patterson. "In 1992, only 40 percent of reporters' evaluative references to Clinton and Bush were favorable."

Patterson attempts to show that negative press coverage is a big reason why Americans have grown to distrust their leaders. "News coverage has become a barrier between the candidates and the voters rather than a bridge connecting them," the Syracuse professor argues. "The press, as Frank Mankiewicz once said, 'poisons the well.' Election after election, the press tells the voters that the candidates are not worthy of the office they seek. 'I know a lot of people who are thinking about this election the same way they think about the Iran-Iraq war,' wrote Meg Greenfield in 1980. 'They desperately want it to be over, but they don't want anyone to win.' George Will said much the same thing in 1992: 'The congestion of debates may keep these guys off the streets for a few days. When they emerge from the debates, November—suddenly the loveliest word in the language—will be just around the corner.'

"Of course, a campaign is sometimes plagued by the candidates' deceit and pettiness," Patterson says, "and the media should inform the voters about it. But the press has gone way beyond that point."

As might be expected, President Clinton wholeheartedly endorses Patterson's theories, and he mentioned them to me during an interview in the summer of 1994; in addition, his staff has frequently pointed to Patterson's ideas to justify their media-bashing. But while Patterson's assessment is flawed—partly because he gives too much credit to politicians for high-mindedness—the problems he identifies are part of a much broader trend. Seismic shifts in the nature of the news business are sending tremors through the mainstream media, and part of the change is a move toward more sensationalized, trivialized coverage of public affairs, especially the presidency.

As discussed earlier, Presidents have been complaining about press bias and cynicism for more than two hundred years. Journalist James Deakin summarized the adversary theory more than a decade ago: "[Critics say] the journalists were not just hostile to conservative governments. They were hostile to *all* governments. The news media had become so habituated to criticism, so steeped in antagonism, so besotted with power that they were making it impossible for *anyone* to govern the United States. No President would get a fair chance; the moment he assumed office, the media would set about the task of destroying him. Automatically. Mindlessly."

It is true that the goals of the press and of government have always been different, and always will be. The government wants to sell its policies to the American people and to retain power. The media want to report those policies, assess whether they are working, and expose any abuses of power. Each side has powerful tools at its disposal. The government has a vast propaganda arsenal, a huge array of public-relations specialists in every department and agency, including the White House; but the press generally gets the last word, and conflict inevitably results.

Still, starting with my covering the Bush administration, I have gradually come to believe that the media's cult of conflict and criticism has gone too far.

Traditionally, the American public has had a love-hate attitude about the press. By the mid-1990s, however, there was no love left. In fact, much of the public had come to hate the media, to distrust its motives, and to tune out the news itself because it didn't seem relevant to their lives. Seventy-one percent of Americans believe the media "gets in the way of society solving its problems," according to one poll. They complain that the press is unnecessarily negative, adversarial, irresponsible, arrogant, out of touch, and insensitive to the people it covers. "The accusations that the press is a watchdog gone out of control are increasingly evident in our surveys," says Andrew Kohut, director of the Times Mirror Center for the People and the Press. "[People think] it's excessive even in the things they value the most, which is keeping the politicians honest. They appreciate the watchdog role, but they hate the way it practices its craft." Among the most despised tendencies are the perceived bias, "edge," attitude, and editorializing in news stories.

They have a point. A big problem is journalists' belief that the easiest way to stand out is not through more and better reporting, which is hard work, but by inserting attitude into their stories. Too often, journalists for national publications and television networks spice up their stories with their own opinions or with smart-aleck perspectives that mock everything and everyone. Too often, we try to impress political insiders, or one another, rather than providing the public with what it wants to know and what it should know.

Moreover, journalists increasingly place their highest emphasis on negativity rather than on balance. No longer is the goal to present all sides of a story. Now reporters are expected—even required—to place edge and opinion in their stories in order to separate themselves from the rest of the pack.

"The problem is economic," says Jack Farrell, White House correspondent of *The Boston Globe.* "The media are more fragmented these days, what with the rise of C-SPAN, CNN, local TV news, talk radio, TV talk shows, *Hard Copy,* the Internet newsgroups, et al. These new sources of competition have put tremendous pressure on the old media establishment—the three networks and dozen national print outlets that used to set the national agenda. The mainstream news corporations did well in the 1980s and got used to reaping big rewards on Wall Street. And much of the old media changed hands, passing from family ownership or stewardship into the control of operators with more of a concern about the bottom line. To secure ratings and circulation, these old outlets are going for juicier, more sensationalistic stories, which generally means that we will focus on the bad news, not the good. The days of selling papers or a nightly news broadcast via a reputation of judicious reliability and neutrality are over.

"The huge growth of the Washington press corps," Farrell adds, "in the years since Woodward and Bernstein became millionaires and folk heroes contributes to this phenomenon. More inexperienced reporters on the make results in more cheap shots as they strive for a reputation. Finally, the news cycle runs so quickly now that—for newspapers, at least—objectivity is becoming a liability. News from a 2 P.M. presidential press conference may be covered live on CNN and C-SPAN, digested by talk radio during drive time, highlighted by local news and then the network evening news, discussed on America Online, mentioned by the eleven o'clock news, chewed on by *Nightline,* and referred to by the morning talk shows before any of my readers sit down at the breakfast table and pick up the *Globe* the next morning. To make my story fresh, I have to look for an angle—and an angle, by definition, is subjective. And since the prevailing ethos of journalism is to be skeptical about sources of power, the angle is almost always critical."

The information glut is truly gargantuan. Readers and viewers can acquire information about government in an extraordinary number of ways. "When I hear somebody say that they're not getting the information, I say to them it's your fault," says Brian Lamb, president of C-SPAN. "It's all there and available."

C-SPAN, for example, potentially reaches the more than 60 million homes that have cable television. While the network doesn't conduct viewer surveys, it appears to have a devoted if small following of public-affairs junkies who watch its continual coverage of congressional floor debates, press conferences, committee hearings and other governmental proceedings, presidential speeches, academic conferences, and think-tank seminars.

Partly because of this information overload, Americans are not as interested in politics and government as they used to be. "We [C-SPAN] might be one of the reasons," Lamb says. "There's so much [coverage of public affairs] that people see so much of it. Familiarity sometimes breeds contempt, and that may be part of the problem. Politicians think they have to have constant exposure, and I think that's a huge mistake." As for the President, Lamb says, "the one given is that he can make a speech anywhere and we'll have it on and he can guarantee a certain group of people will be able to see it. Fifteen years ago that wasn't the case. He could give a speech and no one would see it [on television]."

When the Clintonites took office, they thought the country had an insatiable appetite for information about the White House. Jeff Eller, one of the new President's communications strategists, envisioned "BCTV"—Bill Clinton TV, a cable-television channel devoted to "all Bill, all the time." It would have been a disaster, of course; the President would have been horribly overexposed, and given his penchant for remarking on everything from his preferences in junk food to his underwear, he would have stumbled into one minefield after another.

Also changing the news business is "the CNN phenomenon." Editors and producers in Washington and New York are addicted to Cable News Network's around-the-clock coverage of news. Most editorial managers and reporters leave their televisions tuned to CNN all day so they won't miss any breaking stories; in fact, CNN has become the standard background noise in newsrooms all over the country. The problem starts when editorial managers turn away from the television thinking that if they've seen a story on CNN, the rest of the country must be familiar with it, too—even though the cable network has relatively few viewers at any given time. The result is that mainstream news organizations too often consider straight news to be old news, an assumption that determines the character of subsequent coverage of a news event. "The pressure has been on print reporters to advance the story and not regurgitate what editors think people have been watching all day," says Wolf Blitzer, the chief White House correspondent for CNN. When editors or producers decide to do a piece on reforms in the tax system, health care, welfare reform, or many other issues, they assume that readers or viewers already know the basics. Most of the time this is not true, but it produces coverage that is too often dominated by analysis of political maneuvering and policy esoterica, with a strong dose of edge or "voice" by the reporter. What ensues is the trend away from "objectivity," the straightforward recitation of events, as journalists try to set themselves apart from their competitors.

An ABC reporter says, "You can be wrong as long as you're negative and skeptical. But if you're going to say something remotely positive, you'd better be 150 percent right or you're going to be accused of rolling over. I was once told, 'Look, you're never going to get on the air with positive news; do you want to get on the air or not?' " Readers, viewers, and listeners are increasingly being told what to think, and this bothers more and more people—and more and more journalists.

"It is hard to remember now," says Carl Leubsdorf, Washington bureau chief of *The Dallas Morning News,* "but except for major events like the Watergate scandal, White House press coverage was much more low-key before the arrival a decade ago of Cable News Network and the onset of opinionated television programs like CNN's *Crossfire* and the syndicated *McLaughlin Group* that dissect each presidential step and misstep.

"In the 1970s, most television commentary resembled PBS's *Washington Week in Review,* then as now an analytical discussion by dispassionate reporters, rather than the opinions of columnists or politicians with a point of view . . . there was nothing like the multiplicity of polling that produces, several times each month, some new measure of the President's political temperature that becomes an integral part of the atmosphere. Today's more judgmental climate tends to exaggerate both success and failure—witness how George Bush went from near Superman status after the Persian Gulf War to political basketcase barely over a year later."

Kathleen Hall Jamieson of the University of Pennsylvania, who studied the media's coverage of health care in 1994, says the underlying assumption of many stories is that "everyone operates out of cynical self-interest." Marvin Kalb, a former NBC correspondent who analyzes media issues at the John F. Kennedy School of Government at Harvard University, said the result is "a mean-spiritedness to American journalism, a desire to tear down rather than build up. You cannot be positive today. You cannot even give a public official the benefit of the doubt. . . . The first White House correspondent who says something nice about the President is going to be withdrawn from the beat."

Not quite, but there is an element of truth in Kalb's hyperbole. When I did a positive story on White House chief of staff Panetta in the fall of 1994, several of my White House colleagues called to give me some ribbing. One said, "Hey, are you in Panetta's pocket or what?" He was only half-joking. Another said, "What a beat-sweetener! Now the rest of us will have to kiss up to Panetta, too." But my story had not been effusive. I had simply pointed out that while Panetta seemed to be introducing a central decision-making focus to the White House, it was far from clear whether Bill Clinton, a notorious micro-manager, would give him the authority he needed over the long term. I also noted that Panetta had suffered some embarrassments along the way. All in all, I thought I accurately portrayed the reality of the chief of staff's tenure up to that point, but there was definitely a price to be paid among my colleagues for being as positive as I was.

Journalists admit that the press has become more negative and confrontational, but they argue that they have no choice because government officials can no longer be believed. "They'll look you straight in the eye and tell you things they don't believe," said Joe Peyronnin, former vice-president of CBS News. "You just can't take anything at face value anymore."

A veteran White House correspondent says, "No White House is completely honest, and reporters don't expect it. But the antagonism to the press from the [Clinton] White House has been a problem, especially in the first two years. . . . [Dee Dee] Myers was so poorly grounded in Washington ways and what was really going on in her own shop that she often said things that weren't true. That takes a long time to overcome."

Bill Plante, who covers the White House for CBS News, says the networks began adding more edge to their coverage in the early to mid-1980s. "It happened during the Reagan administration," Plante says. "Early on, in '82, '83, because of pressures in our own business, the movement began to stop covering the White House the way we had for years and years, which was, 'The President today said . . . He went to Chicago . . . This is what he said in Chicago. . . . When I was covering the White House in the first Reagan term, we started to get pressure from the evening news to change the style of presentation. More voices. Go get an opposing voice, or at least an alternative voice. Do more graphics. Make it visually more interesting and easier to understand. . . . It was partly driven by the need to keep our stuff interesting and to hang on to our audience, which we haven't really done, but it was also partly driven by a desire not to let them do all the staging."

Television newspeople note that in the last decade 1985–1995, the growth of live coverage by CNN and C-SPAN has forced the three over-the-air networks to make their best film available to their affiliates immediately instead of holding it for the evening news. This means there is little new footage to be seen on the evening network shows because it's already been on local newscasts or CNN and C-SPAN. Hence, in order to be different, the producers and editors of the evening news on ABC, CBS, and NBC seek more attitude or edge.

"Edge? They love edge," says Plante. ". . . But what you really have to give them is some value added in terms of talking to somebody on the other side of the issue, somebody who gives you perspective—a think-tanker, an academic, an expert, somebody who brings a little bit more to the table than just 'Today the President said . . .' " He adds, "What they [White House officials] would like ideally is a sort of transmission belt. They put it in one side and it comes out the other, reproduced many times by all these different services with no spin other than theirs. Sorry. But they have a point in that it is told and retold so many times that at every step there is a temptation, perhaps even a necessity, to further analyze, further dissect, further discuss."

18

Downgrading the
White House Beat

The 1990s brought many fundamental changes to the White House press corps as part of the larger transformation of the news business—changes that are making the beat less glamorous, more tedious, and, considering expectations, more disappointing than ever before.

Chief among these is the diminution of the presidency itself. With the end of the Cold War, the constant tension between the United States and the Communist empire is over, and the fear of imminent nuclear war is gone. Since the President is no longer the final arbiter of an ultimate conflagration, it is natural that the White House is no longer the news epicenter of the free world. Just as important, cynical and self-absorbed Americans are losing trust in government activism. No longer can a President easily motivate and inspire the country to go on social crusades like the New Deal or the Great Society. Since the late 1994 Republican takeover of Congress, the talk in Washington has centered on devolving power and responsibility from the federal level to the states and local governments. There is, in short, a good chance that the imperial presidency is over.

Nothing has symbolized the marginalized White House more

than the media's treatment of new House Speaker Newt Gingrich as virtually an equal partner with Bill Clinton in governing the nation. From the moment of his elevation to the most powerful post in Congress, Gingrich has drawn a vast amount of press attention. He is always ready with a smart or provocative remark, and is a man of substance trying to bring about a conservative revolution in downsizing government. He spent years provoking fights with his Democratic opponents and never relented, exploiting reporters' impulses to cover conflict.

When the House Republicans completed their first hundred days in office, Gingrich asked for half an hour on prime-time television to address the nation, an extraordinary privilege up to then reserved only for Presidents. Surprisingly, CBS joined CNN and C-SPAN in giving him this time. (ABC and NBC refused.) In a relaxed but pointed style, Gingrich boiled everything down to a handful of ideas, just as Ronald Reagan might have done: House Republicans had kept their promise to vote on a series of proposals they called "Contract with America" (including a constitutional amendment requiring a balanced budget and a big tax break for many Americans, especially the affluent). He also claimed that the conservative revolution had just begun. "All of us together—Republicans and Democrats alike—must totally remake the federal government, to change the very way it thinks, the way it does business, the way it treats its citizens," Gingrich said.

President Clinton was speaking to the American Society of Newspaper Editors in Dallas on the same day; yet his remarks were relegated to secondary status in most media accounts. *The Washington Post,* for example, led the newspaper with a Gingrich story on page one and placed a piece about Clinton's address below coverage of the Speaker. The President attempted to set a middle-of-the-road tone as he pledged to work with the Republicans where possible but to veto any legislation he considered extreme. "I do not want a pile of vetoes. I want a pile of bills that will move this country into the future," Clinton said. "I don't want to see a big fight between the Republicans and Democrats. I want us to surprise everybody in America by rolling up our sleeves and joining hands and working together."

It was clear that Gingrich and the Republicans were dominating the nation's policy agenda and that Clinton was simply reacting to it. The presidency was a diminished office, and covering the White House became a diminished beat.

NO ONE HAS suffered more from the marginalized presidency than the networks' White House correspondents. Drawn to the beat because of its promise of major news stories and abundant time on the networks' twenty-two-minute evening newscasts, the reporters from ABC, CBS, and NBC have been frustrated. (To date, the reporters for CNN are relatively satisfied because their twenty-four-hour-news network still consumes White House news at a voracious rate, though for a much smaller audience.)

Day after day, the network correspondents sit in their tiny broadcast booths, reading *The Washington Post, The New York Times,* or *The Wall Street Journal,* sometimes making phone calls to administration officials to see if anything can be divined that is newsworthy, and commiserating among themselves about how so much of the action is on Capitol Hill. Just as frustrating, for most of 1995 the White House kept the President in the background, hoping the Republicans would come across as right-wing extremists while Clinton would seem newly moderate.

One example of the Congress-centered news environment was coverage of the GOP effort to shift responsibility for financing the school-lunch program from Washington to the states. The White House portrayed it as a "war on America's kids"; it was a catchy phrase, but it didn't help the networks' White House correspondents because the main story was on Capitol Hill and their reports were merely used as sidebars or inserts to the congressional pieces.

The network reporters would attend events scheduled by the White House each day—a string of minor speeches and presidential signings of uninteresting or unimportant bills. Then they would try to persuade their bosses, generally to no avail, to let them do full-blown stories. Often the White House would get a brief mention by the news anchors, who would then turn to reporters in the field who were handling more dramatic stories, such as the latest furor in Congress over one bill or another or the ongoing murder trial of O. J. Simpson in Los Angeles.

On April 11, 1995, Clinton met with President Benazir Bhutto of Pakistan at the White House, an event that five years earlier would have been the subject of intense coverage because of questions about Pakistan's political alignment with either the Eastern or Western blocs. But now most of the major media either ignored the meeting or made only brief references to it.

"White House correspondents for all the networks have always been the people you could turn to on a slow news day to do something with some *gravitas,* to get your show off to a dignified beginning," ABC's Brit Hume said that spring. "You could always make the case that what the President was doing was important because he was the President." But the Clinton administration, he added, "seems a spent force.... [My job now is] like being the Maytag repairman," referring to a popular TV commercial featuring a repairman sitting around with nothing to do. NBC's Jim Miklaszewski said, "I'm thinking of starting a suicide-prevention program."

THERE ARE OTHER signs of the declining importance of the presidency in the news business. One is the press corps' reduced commitment to a twenty-four-hour "body watch" that follows the President wherever he goes, a habit developed during the Cold War, when the President had to be ready to respond to a Soviet threat at any moment as a matter of national security. A key part of the strategic doctrine of mutually assured destruction was that the President had instantaneous access to the nuclear-launch codes that would send thousands of American bombers, missiles, and submarines on their way in case of a Soviet attack. "Covering the President every day is an outgrowth of the Cold War mentality," says Marlin Fitzwater. "It's from when nuclear missiles were only twenty minutes away and we had a hostile Soviet Union. The President needed to be in communication wherever he went." With the collapse of the Soviet empire, the geostrategic imperative for the body watch of the President ended.

But the biggest reason for the body watch was the ever-present fear among journalists that the President might be assassinated. Ever since John F. Kennedy was killed, older reporters have told rookies how some White House correspondents passed up JFK's motorcade in Dallas to have a beer or relax in their hotels, as a result of which they missed the biggest story of their lives. A generation of journalists has grown up promising themselves that such a fate would never befall them. For White House reporters, this meant that a small group of reporters, called a "pool," needed to be with the President whenever he was in public or in a place where there was a possibility of danger.

Nearly every President in modern times has experienced a potentially life-threatening problem. Several acts of violence have occurred around the White House during Bill Clinton's presidency, including a small plane crashing into the rear of the building and a gunman spraying the front of the White House with automatic-weapon fire, both in 1994. George Bush experienced atrial fibrillation. Ronald Reagan was almost assassinated in 1981, and later in his presidency suffered from colon cancer and skin cancer. Jimmy Carter collapsed from exhaustion while jogging. Gerald Ford survived an assassination attempt. Dwight Eisenhower suffered life-threatening heart problems. Clearly, tragedy can strike a President at any moment, and the news media owe it to the country to be vigilant.

Times and technology, however, have changed. Many daily newspaper reporters now acknowledge that the last thing they would need if the President got shot would be a "pool report" hastily put together by journalists at the scene, because everyone in America would be watching the coverage on television. Thus, as long as the networks remain committed to having a pool camera, crew, and reporter with the President wherever he goes, full-scale coverage by a van full of journalists seems unnecessary.

ABC's Brit Hume says, "There's a trend that started for economic reasons at the networks. . . . If the President of the United States went out to a restaurant at night for dinner, ABC News would routinely position one of its own cameras across the street to supplement the pool coverage. This was all because of the possibility that he might walk out of the place and get shot, and we'd have our own pictures. But the cost of doing that over and above just letting the pool cover things was so astronomical that when the networks began to look hard at ways to shave their news budgets, this was one of the first things that got examined. And of course . . . if you don't do it 100 percent of the time, it isn't worth very much, [so it] fell by the wayside."

ANOTHER IMPORTANT DEVELOPMENT that has dimmed the allure of the White House beat is the escalating cost of covering the presidency on the road. Many news organizations are cutting back. In the beginning, the Clinton White House never took this problem seriously. Ignorant of the news business, they seemed to think every organization had unlimited resources. Many Clinton advisers also thought that the White House travel office, which for many years arranged media travel, was too "pro-press"—an impression that contributed to the decision to fire the holdover travel-office employees in early 1993, causing a furor among reporters who considered the employees competent and hardworking.

The White House Correspondents' Association repeatedly warned press secretary Myers and other officials in 1994 that smaller and less affluent news organizations could soon be priced out of covering the President on the road. At first, they paid us little heed but the White House finally got the message in late November 1994, when Clinton announced he was going to Budapest December 5 to sign various nuclear nonproliferation agreements and to confer with European allies about security concerns. From the administration's viewpoint, this would be an occasion for the President to demonstrate his international leadership at a time when his popularity was sagging at home, but to most of the press corps it looked like a waste of money and time for a few photo opportunities. Clinton would fly for nine hours overnight, spend seven hours on the ground in Budapest, and then fly home. The initial cost estimate for the twenty-three journalists who signed up for the trip was $10,000 apiece for the prorated costs of a chartered jet. Food, transportation expenses on the ground, renting a media center, and phones would be extra. Reporters started backing out the week before the trip, and finally the White House canceled the air service. It was the first time in memory that any administration had canceled the press charter for an overseas trip because of lack of interest.

Stunned, Myers agreed to allow the reporters who still wanted to make the trip to travel not only with the small pool on *Air Force One,* which always accompanies the President, but to fill the seats on the backup jet, a specially equipped 747 that follows the President's in case it breaks down. This not only violated Defense Department regulations forbidding military aircraft from carrying civilian journalists but also established a precedent that the press corps could travel on the backup plane, which had always been forbidden in the past. If the backup plane was available at a reasonable cost (about a fourth of what the press charter would have required), why couldn't the press corps always use the backup? The White House said it would evaluate each situation as it arose, but it was clear that cost and the lack of news on Clinton's largely ceremonial trips were taking their toll, and fewer reporters would travel with the President in the foreseeable future.

Meanwhile, White House operations continued to irritate and anger the press regulars. Clinton made up his mind so late about his travel plans that his staff could rarely plan properly, which meant that arrangements for hotels and transportation were made too hastily by the overworked travel and press-advance offices. Frustrated that the rewards of their jobs were dwindling, reporters got ornery. Some complained that the press hotel in Hawaii during Clinton's four-day stop after his Asia trip in the fall of 1994 had been too far from the beach and didn't have adequate food service for late-working correspondents. The perks of covering the White House simply weren't what they used to be.

JUST AS IMPORTANT, many reporters were feeling a profound generational and political disappointment with Clinton and the presidency itself. Most of the White House press corps consists of journalists who have always thought of the Democrats as the insurgents, the apostles of openness, while the Republicans always seemed to be protecting special interests. Today those distinctions do not seem so clear.

For their part, the Democrats who took over the executive branch in January 1993 were offended that their longtime ally, the press, would question their values and potential for abuse of power. "Scratch any Democrat," press secretary McCurry says, "and you'll find someone who was an anti-war activist, an environmentalist, a civil-rights worker, a labor-union organizer. In some way or another they were grass-roots activists who always thought that the press was there to help you speak truth to power because we're fighting city hall, or we're going to take on the university administration, or we're gonna sit in, and the press will cover us and they like us. Given our pedigree as Democrats and our culture, the sense was that the press was our friend because they had been on our side as we tried to fight the power—and the Republicans were the power."

Both the Clintonites and the news media experienced a harsh awakening, for it turned out that there was little difference between the Democrats and the Republicans once they exercised power. "I believe," says Jack Farrell of *The Boston Globe,* "that the Clinton folks, as Ivy League baby-boom Democrats, entered the 1992 campaign expecting a break from their generational and educational colleagues in the press. And at first they got it; Clinton was soon anointed the front-runner. The economic pressures on the media, however, led to [excess] on the Gennifer Flowers and draft-evasion stories. *The Boston Globe,* for example, made an early resolve not to publish the Flowers allegations because they came from a supermarket tabloid. This resolve crumbled when CNN, local news, the networks, and the *Hard Copy* shows blanketed New England airtime with the story, so we dove in. Suddenly, the Clintons were treated to the experience of having their old media friends at their throats; it left a bitter taste of betrayal that hardened, after the election, into contempt.

"I don't think the Clinton White House is any less honest than other administrations," Farrell adds, "and its sins of credibility have been small compared to past Presidents, who conducted secret wars. The Ivy League baby-boomers of the press, however, have been surprised to see their generational colleagues in the White House acting like politicians, and so professed . . . 'shock' with the White House on the matter of honesty regarding Whitewater, Vince Foster, the travel office, and other early issues."

The depth of the press corps' resentment became vivid when I analyzed the survey I conducted of White House correspondents in early 1995. All the reporters who responded felt that the Clinton

White House was falling far short of the President's promise of ethical purity and a higher standard of honesty. "Clinton's tendency to try to have things both ways—on the one hand, but on the other hand—calls his credibility into doubt on a daily basis," said one White House reporter, who requested anonymity. A veteran wire-service reporter observed, "I think to the Clintonites truth is utterly beside the point. I cannot recall an administration like this one, although I'm told Nixon was even worse."

Stewart Powell of Hearst Newspapers, speaking of the first two years under Clinton, said, "The Clinton White House has been less credible than the Bush White House, in my opinion. During the first two years, Clinton aides rarely invoked the 'I have nothing for you on that' or 'no comment' to deal with a sensitive story. Instead, they either challenged the line of questioning, as Stephanopoulos did during the transition and the opening months, or they led you astray, as Dee Dee [Myers] did, probably inadvertently for lack of information." Another print reporter added, "Sometimes it has been difficult to distinguish between dishonesty and general incompetence. But the result for reporters is the same: You're not sure you can trust the information you've been given. This situation has improved with the arrival of Mike McCurry as press secretary."

IN THE EVERYDAY life of the White House press corps, nothing diminished the allure of the beat more than the constant foul-ups and petty humiliations that reporters endured because of the initial incompetence or inexperience of the Clinton press staff.

Network correspondents and producers were upset that the administration apparently had no policy for placing senior officials on the Sunday morning television talk shows such as *Meet the Press, Face the Nation,* and *This Week with David Brinkley.* These shows once set the tone for the start of each week in Washington, and gave the network White House reporters invaluable time with their sources on camera. Frequently, the administration could find no major policymakers who were willing or available to joust with journalists, according to network officials, with the result that the shows would turn to administration critics who wanted the TV exposure. Consequently, there was a lack of balance to these programs, and Clintonites would go ballistic because the shows were so critical of their policies. They argued that the networks frequently rejected officials offered by the White House because they were considered too dull and failed to draw big ratings.

One big problem, administration officials told me, was that senior officials were frequently unclear about what the President's policies were, so they didn't feel prepared to promote or defend them adequately. In addition, there was a paucity of officials who were comfortable on TV or who had a knack for the medium. Both secretary of state Warren Christopher and White House national security adviser Anthony Lake, the President's chief architects of foreign policy, came across as unimaginative and wooden in televised settings. On domestic affairs, the President and First Lady did well on television, but they were considered too important to place in the relatively pedestrian venue of the Sunday shows. Gore, Panetta, then-Treasury secretary Lloyd Bentsen, and White House economic adviser Laura D'Andrea Tyson were good television performers, but only in their areas of expertise.

Other administration figures, including domestic strategist Stephanopoulos, spokeswoman Myers, and political strategist Paul Begala, enjoyed appearing on television but seemed too young, arrogant, or flippant. For a while counselor David Gergen, a former commentator on public television, filled the bill, but some White House officials, such as Lake and Myers, considered him a self-promoter who was intruding on their turf, and eventually he was forced to cut back on his appearances.

For the press regulars, there were other manifestations of incompetence and inefficiency. The media quarters were a mess for months from ongoing renovations to remove asbestos from the ceiling. Dust collected everywhere, and technicians complained that before long their computers, cameras, and sound and video equipment would be affected. Reporters were unhappy with long waiting lines at the lone men's restroom. A renovation of the facilities had gained the men a new toilet bowl but cost them two urinals. New vending machines had been set up in the press area, but the installers had placed the main snack machine too close to a wall and the door could not be opened more than two feet. As a result, delivery personnel could only stock the machine with chips and candy two or three rows deep, and the machine would often be empty by noon.

Nothing ever seemed to run smoothly in Clinton's world. Take my experience one Thursday, my deadline day, during the winter of 1995. I had a full schedule: a telephone interview at 10 A.M. with Democratic economist Rob Shapiro; another phone interview at 11 A.M. with White House senior adviser Mack McLarty; lunch with travel office director Steve Riewirts; a 3 P.M. interview with Myers; a four o'clock appointment with communications director Mark Gearan; and a five o'clock interview with David Gergen. Then I had to return to my office and file my reports.

The Shapiro interview worked out smoothly, and we had a lively discussion on politics and policy. Significantly, Shapiro works for the Progressive Policy Institute, not the White House, which might explain why there were no glitches.

The McLarty interview had been offered by the press staff as a preview of the Summit of the Americas, which Clinton was planning to attend the following week in Miami. It was a good instinct on the press staff's part, except that it turned out that McLarty was holding a conference call with a different reporter every fifteen or twenty minutes. He had to change the time for our interview from 11 A.M. to 12:20, a direct conflict with my Riewirts lunch, which had already been postponed once before. I asked Matt Cooper, my colleague at *U.S. News*, to take care of the McLarty phone call while I rushed off to lunch with Riewirts. So far so good, except that McLarty, it turned out, had nothing newsworthy to say. Riewirts was helpful in providing insights into upcoming changes in travel-office procedures, but this was hardly newsworthy either.

I showed up at Myers's office ten minutes early and was told by her aide, David Leavey, that she was "running late." This, I had come to understand, often meant that you could wait around for hours and then she might cancel the appointment because she was still "in meetings." Still, I decided to hang around.

Down the hall from Myers's office, Matt Cooper and I were chatting when Gene Sperling, an economics adviser, rushed by with a huge sheaf of papers. When I asked what he was up to, he launched into a nearly incomprehensible attack on the Republicans for irresponsible proposals to cut taxes. He produced a two-page press release from Republican representative Bill Paxon of New York, flashed some sort of chart that Paxon was circulating, and said it was phony. Then Sperling's boss, Robert Rubin, appeared and Sperling left with him for "a meeting."

Carol Rasco, a Clinton domestic-policy adviser, walked by, stopped to mention that she had worked at a soup kitchen that day, and then left for "a meeting." Bill Galston, another domestic-policy adviser, passed us in the hall, returned a few minutes later saying he had forgotten something, swung past again wearing his raincoat, and left for "a meeting."

Dave Leavey stuck his head through a doorway from the private corridor outside the Oval Office and said Myers still wanted to do the interview. Before I could answer, there was a sudden commotion. Socks, the Clintons' black-and-white feline from Little Rock, made a break for freedom, slithering around Leavey's ankles and scrambling toward the press area. But he was tethered to a retractable leash, which jerked him backward. A young woman appeared, stroked Socks's back, and lured him away, closing the door behind her.

When I went off to check on Gergen's availability, I was told he had been called to "a meeting," then had to catch a plane to North Carolina to give a speech that evening. His assistant said that since I wanted to interview him in part for this book, and since it didn't sound as if I was on deadline, perhaps I could reschedule. I decided that the Gergen interview could wait, especially since I still had Gearan and Myers to interview for the current issue of *U.S. News.*

I dialed Gearan's office. His aide assured me he really wanted to see me but was in "a meeting." Could I call back?

It was 4:20. Myers was back from her meeting, eighty minutes late, and our interview proceeded, but she had little to say. As I was leaving, Mark Gearan walked in, looking sheepish. "Sorry," he said. "I can't see you today."

"Let me guess," I replied.

"A meeting," we said simultaneously.

All in all, it was another wasted day reporting on the White House, and one typical of the free flow of information in the Clinton era.

19

At the Core
of the Press Corps

There are many myths and misunderstandings about the White House press corps: that it is irredeemably liberal, arrogant, and elitist; pampered and lazy; overpaid and isolated. Based on personal experience from covering the White House for a decade, and on a survey I conducted of the media regulars in early 1995, it is clear that there is some truth to the stereotypes, but not nearly as much as media-bashers think.

At its heart, the mainstream White House press corps consists of six distinct constituencies—the TV networks, the big national daily newspapers, the wire services, the newsmagazines, the regional dailies, and the radio reporters—which are at odds with one another on many matters. When it comes to getting a competitive advantage, reporters will be at one another's throats in a nanosecond. For example, there is a constant complaint by the regional dailies that the elite national outfits, especially *The Washington Post* and *The New York Times,* are spoon-fed exclusive information while the regionals have to scramble for crumbs. In order to enhance their clout, the regional dailies long ago banded together in "tongs" to arrange interviews with senior officials who would not see them individually. Yet senior officials rarely break news with the regionals, because they get more impact from national organizations higher up the media chain. Nevertheless, members of the press corps have much in common in covering the individual who, despite the erosion of the presidency, is still the most powerful politician in the world.

What is it like covering the White House? Picture long stretches of boredom and tedium, often under cramped, uncomfortable conditions. Being escorted, or herded, everywhere by self-important young aides. Waiting, always waiting, for the Great Man. Baggage calls at 5 A.M. Eighteen-hour days. Cold coffee in press filing centers. Catching influenza in Indonesia, stomach flu in Moscow. Countless useless interviews. Long periods away from home. Being manipulated by everyone in sight. Trying to explain to Mom why the President didn't call on you at his last news conference. Still, it is punctuated by a handful of memorable moments and a few events of extraordinary significance.

During my decade at the White House, Communism has collapsed; the Soviet Union was unraveled; Eastern Europe was freed; unprecedented agreements were signed to reduce nuclear armaments; America won the Persian Gulf War; and power twice changed hands at the White House in the miracle of democracy. There was a conservative revolution at home. Ronald Reagan altered the terms of national debate. George Bush consolidated power for the Republicans, then lost his way. Bill Clinton promised to be a different kind of Democrat, but his fortunes sank in the GOP tide of 1994. It is such historic moments that a White House reporter lives for.

"The most rewarding aspect of the job is the scale at which you work," says Jack Farrell of *The Boston Globe*. "You're not trying to pry some [photographs] from a grieving family whose kid was just killed by a drunk driver. You're not writing about the local sewer commission. You are dealing with history every day. It's no accident that biographies, histories, and nonfiction books on politics pop up when the White House press corps settles into airplane seats and does some reading on a long plane trip. For a history junkie, the job is a delight."

There are still many complaints about the pace of the job and the difficulty of getting reliable information. A wire-service reporter says, "The sheer physical energy required when the President is traveling is difficult to sustain—late to bed, early to rise." A veteran print reporter adds, "The most difficult part is getting a real handle on what is going on and separating it from personalities that are more forceful than others. The least rewarding part is pointless pool duty at 6:45 A.M., not being able to really see the places we travel to, and not getting the access we should have to the people we write about all the time."

Getting timely access to key decision-makers is cited most often as the toughest part of covering the White House. "Piercing the White House curtain is a nightmare, the single hardest challenge I have ever met in ten years as a journalist," says Farrell. "Getting people to call you back and tell you stuff requires the patter and single-mindedness of [an] obnoxious door-to-door salesman. . . . The least rewarding aspect of the job, however, is the restraint placed on my reporting by the significance of the beat. Editors are never more insecure, and thus more likely to slip into the safety of pack journalism, than when it comes to White House coverage. The premium reporting is not on the edge of the wave but just a little way back, with perhaps a few gossipy tidbits thrown in to give a false appearance of trail-blazing. It is a straitjacket, and probably explains why wire-service reporters, trained in a formula, stay on for years while newspaper reporters, frustrated by the limits on their creativity, rotate more frequently, their career ticket punched."

This herd mentality is one of the most common complaints of the press corps. Twenty-four of the twenty-eight White House reporters who responded to my survey say that it is a serious problem. "All we need are the cow bells," says a print reporter. Doyle McManus of the *Los Angeles Times* adds: "Editors who insist that their correspondents match everything they've seen in *The New York Times* and *The Washington Post* are the herd bosses who force strays and outriders back into the pack whenever they can."

Stewart Powell of Hearst Newspapers says, "I liken White House coverage to being within a school of fish that darts, sometimes for no apparent reason, from one direction to another. We have a shared news judgment that we've developed individually over the years . . . that we practice together. But, much like a school of fish, if you are too far out of the pack, you get picked off by the competition—and questioned by editors. Institutionally, the news media covers the presidency too much and the executive branch too little. The daily drumbeat of CNN and C-SPAN only adds to the pressure to stay within the pack and the second-guessing of editors." A White House correspondent for a large national newspaper adds, "The herd instinct is not exaggerated. It is perhaps the most insidious problem of the beat."

THERE HAVE BEEN many cultural changes in the White House press corps over the years. For one thing, it is no longer much fun, and it has lost much of its eccentricity. Older journalists tell stories about frolicking, boozing, and womanizing (the press corps was almost exclusively male in the old days), especially when on the road. There were tales of reporters who passed out from drink and awoke to find that their stories had been written for them by sympathetic colleagues. There was the time several reporters placed a sheep in a colleague's room as a practical joke, and the occasion when Jim Naughton, then of *The New York Times,* showed up at a presidential press conference dressed in a chicken suit. There were virtually unlimited expense accounts, and reporters had no qualms about sating their appetites. Many of these hijinks were chronicled in Timothy Crouse's *The Boys on the Bus* two decades ago.

Today such antics are considered unprofessional and embarrassing. "Now the road is filled with a bunch of thirtysomething touchy-feely guys, tying up all the cellular-phone circuits trying to call home to talk baby talk to their wives and kids," says Maureen Dowd of *The New York Times.* The press corps is so busy and serious these days that it is rare for reporters to do more than duck out of a filing center for a quick dinner together or take a source out for a meal to get some new policy insights. Life on the road has become a grind.

Most of the perquisites the journalists receive are harmless, considering that many of them work sixteen-hour days. But if these perks get too outrageous, the press corps, like the politicians, gets nervous about appearances. When two hundred journalists took their seats on a Northwest Airlines charter to accompany the President to Europe and Moscow in January 1994, they received a special "welcome aboard" letter from the airline. As the jumbo jet took off, the reporters and photographers read a list of special features that Northwest was offering. A rumble of concern spread through the cabin as the corps read about the final treat: "Four specially trained masseuse's [sic] will travel with us from Geneva to Andrews [Air Force Base] to help soothe the aches and pains you've accumulated from the rigors of the trip." No one had ever heard of anything like this. Massages on the press plane! But most of the journalists were opposed to the idea. How would it look on our expense accounts? What if *The Washington Post* did a story on it? We'd appear to be pampered elitists. A representative of the airline was told thanks, but no thanks, and the masseuses never got on the plane.

Back in Washington there is even less conviviality, which used to be a staple of the profession. Most White House reporters, about two thirds of whom are middle-aged white males, are eager to return to their wives and families, and they rarely have time for one another outside work. Most news organizations also are pinching pennies, because holding down costs is an increasing concern. All of this discourages a climate of personal profligacy or an emphasis on fun and frolic.

DESPITE ITS MEMBERS' conservative personal habits, is the White House press corps too isolated from American life, as many critics suggest? Most White House reporters deny this, but in a contradiction, most admit that they devote too much coverage to matters that the American people don't care much about: inside stories of staff in-fighting; explanations of how the decision-making process works; endless speculative reports about who's up and who's down; and constant temperature readings of the President's popularity and reelection strategy.

"Yes, the press corps is preoccupied with 'inside baseball,' " says Doyle McManus of the *Los Angeles Times,* "but that's their job. And I'm often struck by readers' appetite for staff and process stories (how's Panetta doing, what really happens inside, etc.)."

But most White House reporters admit they dwell too often on esoterica. One says, "White House reporters, like political reporters, focus too much on strategy and process and too little on substance. That's because strategy and process is an easier, livelier, and more accessible story to do. It's also the predilection of editors. Substance stories are more difficult to [write], more difficult to make interesting, and more difficult to get good play for, unless there's a very strong news hook."

Despite this penchant for insider pieces, most White House reporters insist that they are not out of touch with everyday America.

A female reporter with a newspaper chain says: "The press corps is not too isolated from American life except that we live in Washington. We have children, mortgages, spouses; we go to school meetings and child soccer matches. The old days of reporters not being paid enough to live middle-class lives are gone. On the other hand, the [Sam] Donaldsons, [Andrea] Mitchells, [Brit] Humes, who get six-figure salaries, are the exceptions, not the rule."

Larry McQuillan of Reuters adds, "The typical White House reporter is a lot like everybody else. I ride the subway to work, eat at McDonald's, and stand in line at the grocery store. The handful of media elites who report about Washington are far outnumbered by working stiffs."

Not a single White House reporter favored imposing term limits on journalists' tenure as a way of forcing new blood into the press corps. A woman reporter for a major national publication voices a typical comment when she says, "I don't think that a news organization should place limits, but I surely wouldn't want to do this more than four years. I spend more time thinking about Bill Clinton than I do about my husband. It's weird."

Yet Stewart Powell of Hearst Newspapers says: "By definition, covering the White House means you're isolated from ordinary Americans. You may grab locals for reaction or comment at presidential events on the road, but that's a self-selected group—people who have chosen to come and hear the President or protest against him. The challenge is to take stories from inside the Beltway and translate them into useful insights for Americans beyond it."

Powell is right. Those who say the White House press corps isn't isolated from American life are fooling themselves. For one thing, our income levels are much higher than the national average. In my survey, no one in the White House press corps reported an individual income below $50,000 a year. Three said their income was between $51,000 and $75,000, nine said it was in the $76,000 to $100,000 range; two reported between $101,000 and $125,000, and one said it was above $126,000. The remainder declined to disclose their income, but my findings appear to reflect accurately the press corps as a whole.

The White House press corps also is overwhelmingly Democratic, confirming a stereotype often promoted by Republicans. Even though the survey was anonymous, many journalists declined to reveal their party affiliations, whom they voted for in recent presidential elections, and other data they regarded as too personal— even though they regularly pressure Presidents and other officials to make such disclosures. A few answered some personal questions but declined to respond to others. Those who did reply seemed to be representative of the larger group. Seven said they were Democrats, eleven were unaffiliated with either major party, and not a single respondent said he or she was a registered Republican (although some might have been but were not willing to say so).

Even more dramatic was the evidence of an overwhelming preference for Democrats in presidential elections. In 1992, nine respondents voted for Clinton, two for George Bush, and one for independent Ross Perot. Three said they had not voted for anyone, and one reporter wrote in the name of former Massachusetts senator Paul Tsongas.

In 1988, twelve voted for Democrat Michael Dukakis, only one voted for Bush, and three did not vote for a presidential candidate. In 1984, ten voted for Democrat Walter Mondale, no one admitted voting for Ronald Reagan, and four said they had not voted for a presidential candidate. In 1980, eight voted for Democratic incumbent Jimmy Carter, two voted for Ronald Reagan, four voted for independent candidate John Anderson, and three did not vote. In 1976, eleven voted for Carter and two for Republican incumbent Gerald Ford.

Many reporters said they were becoming more conservative as they grew older, and all respondents denied that their political views influenced their coverage. Nearly all the reporters—twenty of the twenty-six who answered this question about their political views—said they were moderates. Three said they were liberal on social issues and conservative on fiscal matters. Three said they were developing "libertarian" tendencies.

While the White House press corps is not an Ivy League crowd, as is often charged by press critics (there were only a handful of Ivy Leaguers when the survey was conducted in 1995), every respondent had a college education. Nor were the media regulars children of the wealthy: Most were sons and daughters of the middle class. They came from all over the country, although there was a slightly higher proportion of Northeasterners. Most of the respondents said they wanted to stay in journalism after their White House days were over.

THE WHITE HOUSE beat always produces its stars, drudges, mainstays, and bizarre characters, and today's press corps is no exception.

During my years on the beat, Helen Thomas of United Press International has been the doyenne of the press corps and one of the best-known media regulars—a no-nonsense woman known to millions as the reporter who closes each press conference with a "Thank you, Mr. President." But her workday illustrates the tedium that even the most famous White House reporters must endure to cover the presidency.

The only septuagenarian among the media regulars (she was born in 1920), Thomas has more energy than some reporters half her age. She generally arrives at her phone-booth-size cubicle behind the briefing room at about 5:45 A.M., and begins her days by browsing through *The Washington Post* and *The New York Times* as she sips coffee. She is often the first to arrive, although occasionally she joins a handful of sleepy-eyed photographers and less-known reporters from the networks stuck on the early-morning shift.

As the sun rises, Thomas phones her home office to find out what happened overnight and flips on a small portable television to watch the morning network news shows. If she learns that important people are about to leave meetings at the White House, she tries to intercept them with a few questions in front of the West Lobby.

"If one of the White House press-office people comes by and says the President's going jogging," Thomas says, "you drop everything, grab your notebook, get your coat, and start running." She usually tries to ask the President a few questions when he trots by, even though he generally refuses to answer.

For the rest of the day, Thomas patrols a small area where reporters are permitted to roam in the West Wing, lying in wait for press officers and other White House officials who happen by. For years the press secretary has held what White House officials call "the gaggle" for reporters at about 8:30 or 9 A.M., describing the day's schedule and answering questions about overnight developments. This routine is helpful to wire-service and TV reporters, and Helen Thomas is almost always there. There are also formally scheduled briefings in which administration officials step up to a podium in the media briefing room and spoon-feed "news" to the regulars. These events are also staples for Thomas throughout the day.

If there is a state dinner or other social event involving the President in the evening, Thomas often attends as a member of a rotating pool of reporters. Even though she is rarely an official guest, those attending frequently recognize her and seek her out as a celebrity. If there is no evening event to cover, she usually leaves work about 7 P.M. and dines at her favorite restaurant, a ten-minute cab ride away from the White House.

Over the years, some White House press regulars have come to resent Helen. By the early 1990s, UPI was in serious financial trouble and had relatively few clients, so Thomas's competitors began to question why she enjoyed celebrity status and why UPI was still treated as a major news organization. Moreover, Thomas rarely breaks big stories anymore and has few inside sources at the White House. (To my surprise, I learned that in recent years her phone calls have been only sporadically returned because UPI has become such a small factor in the news business. Her approach is mostly to report what officials tell her at press conferences and briefings.)

I must confess that I too considered Helen an anachronism until I got to know her and understand her perseverance. She started at the White House covering Jacqueline Kennedy in 1961 and, despite a bias against females covering hard news in those days, has never left the beat. She remains a hardworking journalistic purist, always quick to jump on Presidents and their advisers if she feels they are becoming too secretive. "They are paid to inform us," Helen says. "They are paid by us and all of the American people."

Thomas bemoans the decline in the collegiality of the press corps and says the culture of journalism has changed: "Everyone is so busy, and they don't spend time together in the evenings, even when they're on trips, which used to be the part where you would have your good friendships and go out to dinner. There's no such thing as going out to dinner. There's always one more [thing] to cover. . . . There's the whole electronic incursion. People can't get drunk, because they have to go on the air. Today there are no hangouts . . . no places where you can really gather. Everybody goes home or lives their own life."

BRIT HUME OF ABC is the TV journalist most feared by the Clintonites. They are cowed by his hard-edged manner and conservative proclivities, exemplified by his periodic articles for *The American Spectator,* a right-wing journal that regularly bashes the administration and that has published "exposés" of Bill Clinton's alleged adulteries as Arkansas governor. Unflappable and with a biting sense of humor, Hume rarely prepares detailed questions for Clinton's news conferences, preferring to jot down a few talking points as he sits in his customary front-row seat waiting for the questioning to begin.

"He was the most difficult reporter in the briefing room," former press secretary Myers says, the one who caused the most trouble. In fact, Myers holds Hume most responsible for the media's frenzy over Clinton's $200 haircut on *Air Force One* in early 1993 while the jet idled at Los Angeles International Airport. Hume viewed the incident as an example of Clinton's hypocrisy, his breaking faith with the everyman background he promoted in public.

Hume clearly enjoys the gamesmanship of his job, such as harassing the press secretary or throwing the opposition off balance. But despite his reputation as one of the White House's toughest antagonists, he is a thoughtful critic of his profession. "There is a definite style to the coverage of the modern presidency that has developed over the last twenty-five years," he told me, "and as a result there has been a certain premium on the negative. The level and the quality of scrutiny of the presidency transcend anything that we have previously seen. . . . There is relentless scrutiny, relentless skepticism bordering on cynicism."

When he started covering the White House during George Bush's administration in 1989, Hume noticed the greater interest that ABC had in the presidency compared with Congress, which he had covered for eleven years, or with any other beat in Washington. After Marlin Fitzwater's daily briefing, Hume would spend half an hour on the phone in his cubicle briefing the ABC Washington bureau in a conference call on everything that the press secretary had said. Reporters would flock to Fitzwater's briefings, as they had to those of his predecessor, Larry Speakes, during the Reagan years. "That's not true anymore," Hume says. Even more remarkable, television correspondents would regularly give live midday reports to their networks from the North Lawn on all kinds of news stories and crises, such as the U.S. invasion of Panama, the Iraqi invasion of Kuwait, George Bush's response to it, the Persian Gulf War, the breakup of the Soviet Union, and other major stories. "We were out there day after day after day," Brit recalls. "We never do that anymore. It's all changed."

Hume complained in 1995 of a growing sense that what President Clinton said or did was unimportant: "It used to be that you didn't want to stray very far from the White House because there was a possibility that news would put you on the air live immediately, and it could happen at any moment. That sense is almost entirely gone."

ANDREA MITCHELL OF NBC had a potential conflict of interest while she covered the White House. She maintained a personal relationship with Federal Reserve Board chairman Alan Greenspan, who probably has more impact on the economy than anyone else. Yet she reported on the administration's economic policies, which at least indirectly involved Greenspan's decisions as head of the independent agency that helps determine interest rates. Nevertheless, Mitchell leaned over backward to be tough on the Clintons. Her experience in covering the presidency is deep, and she is one of the most thoughtful journalists in Washington.

After covering the Reagan presidency, Capitol Hill, and then the first two years of the Clinton administration, Mitchell moved from the White House to the State Department at the start of 1995, but her insights on White House coverage are on the mark. Much of the Clinton White House's problem derived from its failure to tend to fundamentals, she says. "I don't care what the food is like on the press plane," she told me, "but I do care about whether we get an advance text of the President's State of the Union address or his health-care speech." If a reporter doesn't get an advance text, it is harder to focus on substance because there is no time for thought or context.

Clinton and his advisers got used to a campaign mentality where a few senior people, including Stephanopoulos and political adviser James Carville, controlled the candidate's time, steered him away from the media if they wished, and kept the Republican campaign on the defensive. But at the White House, decisions are required at a much more rapid pace, and events cannot be controlled. "Their problem is that they have constant meetings going on," Mitchell says, "and by the time they get to you, it's past your deadline."

In the beginning, the Clintonites tried to imitate Reagan's media advisers by focusing on the visual. But, Mitchell says, "we're past the day when we did a story just because it looks good. We've become more sophisticated." She pointed to a couple of Clinton media extravaganzas that flopped because the White House overemphasized the pictures. One was Clinton's much-photographed walk across the White House lawn with military leaders who had participated in the U.S. humanitarian mission to Somalia. The President walked briskly across the greensward, the long cuffs of his designer trousers dragging in the grass, as the soldiers, clad in desert fatigues that seemed out of place, strode step for step just behind him. It got on the news but looked contrived.

Another misplaced touch of Reaganism came during Clinton's June 1994 trip to Normandy to commemorate the D day invasion. At one point he broke away from his official party for a carefully choreographed "moment of solitude." By prearrangement, he bent down to the sand, arranged some seashells into a cross, folded his hands, and bowed his head in prayer. It was one more staged moment that offended many of the photographers on the scene and further damaged the President's credibility with the press corps, who felt manipulated.

WOLF BLITZER, THE bearded former Pentagon correspondent for *The Jerusalem Post* and now CNN's White House anchor, is the most willing of all the major network correspondents to indulge in instant analysis. He has to: CNN's twenty-four-hour news programming promises to update viewers whenever important events occur, and he has to fill the time. It's not an easy assignment, and Blitzer, at the mercy of his deadlines, is often used as a conduit by White House aides who want to plant rumors via CNN for their own purposes or to pump up the importance of a story. Many White House officials think that if that network carries a story, the rest of the press corps will play it up.

On May 11, 1994, the day before Clinton named federal judge Stephen Breyer of Boston to the Supreme Court, Blitzer was on the air live every hour giving updates on the selection process. In the early afternoon, he told CNN viewers that Clinton had narrowed the choice to interior secretary Bruce Babbitt, Arkansas judge Richard Arnold, and Breyer. These names had been in the major newspapers all week. At 4 P.M., Blitzer told his audience that Clinton apparently was moving strongly toward Arnold, an old friend. At 5 P.M., he said sources told him the President was now moving back toward Babbitt, his first choice, rather than caving in to Republican critics, who thought Babbitt was too liberal.

By the following afternoon, a Friday, competitive pressure was building in the press corps to get the Supreme Court scoop. Reporters waiting in the briefing room discerned profound significance in the smallest nuance. When photographers were told that a routine ceremony for women political leaders was being moved to the scenic South Lawn, many in the press corps jumped to the conclusion that Clinton was about to announce his Supreme Court decision—and to name a woman. It turned out that the ceremony was moved because it was a nice day and the President wanted to be outdoors.

In the middle of this pressure-cooker atmosphere, Blitzer had to file hourly reports. By 5 P.M., he and everyone else realized that no one at the White House knew what was going on except the Clintons and perhaps legal counsel Lloyd Cutler, chief of staff Mack McLarty, and senior adviser Stephanopoulos—and none of them was talking. Having reported that Babbitt and Arnold were the front-runners in the last twenty-four hours, Blitzer now heard the choice was going to be Breyer. He told his viewers that the judge had been the "safe" choice all along, and his sources were saying that the President was now leaning toward the Boston jurist. He had gotten it right this time. Clinton named Breyer to the court at 6 P.M.

The constant demand for updates on a twenty-four-hour network makes CNN particularly susceptible to errors in reporting rumors, and to being manipulated by White House sources who have only part of the story or have an ax to grind. Dee Dee Myers notes: "Wolf justifies it by saying he always hedges: 'Sources say it could be Breyer' or 'Breyer looks like he has the inside track.' But when you put that on the news, everybody goes crazy. . . . He would get a piece of information that may have been accurate in its narrowest context but distorted the bigger picture, and we were always fighting back and trying to [say] . . . 'Well, no, that's not the way it really happened.' Then people would say, 'Well, you gave it to Wolf.' "

Yet there is considerable truth to the argument that the White House uses CNN as a conduit. As journalist Tom Rosenstiel pointed out in *The New Republic* in August 1994, "CNN has become a means to communicate to the press corps without having to hold briefings or face reporters en masse. In times of trouble, White House Press Secretary Dee Dee Myers no longer even holds regular briefings." In the five months leading up to mid-August, Rosenstiel said, Myers briefed the White House press corps only twenty-nine times, and at the height of the Whitewater fuss in March, she did so only twice. To avoid tough questions, she simply gave information to Blitzer, who went on the air immediately with the "news" virtually unfiltered, serving as a bulletin board for the White House.

Myers says that there was no "conscious policy" to leak to Blitzer and CNN, although she admits that "occasionally" she would give him a story "just to get it out" immediately. Myers insists, "The reason that Wolf is successful, and particularly for a video wire service . . . is that he gets on the air so much, and he'll call you every five minutes . . . particularly if something is going on that he wants to be the first to break. . . . If your deadline is not until eight o'clock, then you're not going to call every five minutes starting at two o'clock. But Wolf does, or he'll come up to your office and call you two minutes later. . . . He is . . . relentless."

Blitzer loves to tell about "the night I broke the story that Nixon had died." It was straight, by-the-book, back-to-basics reporting, the kind of journalism that unfortunately is now less prized among the White House press corps and their bosses.

In the spring of 1994, Richard Nixon's health was failing badly. When the eighty-one-year-old former President checked into New York Hospital-Cornell Medical Center after suffering a massive stroke, it was clear that the end was near, and a large press stake-out formed outside the hospital. On the afternoon of Friday, April 22, Blitzer told his producers he was certain that before anyone made an official announcement, Nixon associates would call the White House with the news so that Clinton could put out an immediate statement honoring his fallen predecessor. It was a good hunch.

At 6:45 P.M., the White House put out a "full lid"—meaning that nothing else was expected to happen that day. The press regulars immediately began to leave, but Blitzer decided to make one more round of calls. At about 7:15 P.M., a senior White House official told him, "If I were you, I wouldn't leave yet. I'd stick around for a while." At 9 P.M., Blitzer noticed that several young aides in the press office were still on the job and that a senior communications adviser, David Dreyer, was prowling the halls. Blitzer told his desk editor, "I'm going to wait here till eleven o'clock tonight. If he's not dead by then, I'll go home."

At 10 P.M., Marty Kramer, Blitzer's producer at the White House, was chatting with Dreyer and several other young press aides when Dreyer's beeper went off and he left the room. (It turned out that Nixon had died at 9:08 P.M.) Blitzer started making another round of calls from his little booth in the basement, but turned up nothing. At around 10:10 P.M., Kramer phoned him with word that members of the White House technical communications staff, who set up broadcast facilities when the President gives a speech, were hovering about. "I think Clinton is getting ready to make a statement," Blitzer told his producer. "Nixon must be dead." But there was no sign of special activity at the hospital in New York.

Finally, Blitzer managed to reach a senior Clinton aide after another spate of phone calls. "Nixon is dead, isn't he?" Blitzer asked. The official wouldn't say, so Blitzer tried a bluff. "Look," he said, "I'm going out on the lawn now to announce that Nixon's dead and that the President will be making a statement shortly. You wouldn't let me make a total fool of myself, right? I'd look like an idiot, and it would be a career-ender if he's not dead." The official hesitated, then said, "No, I wouldn't let you do that." Blitzer said, "Then I'm going out to make the announcement." The official said, "Hey, it's your job, you gotta do what you gotta do."

Still, Blitzer was uncertain, and wasn't ready to risk his career on a possible misunderstanding. But at 10:20 P.M., he reached a second official, who confirmed that Nixon had died and that the family had notified President Clinton. Blitzer walked upstairs from his booth, peeked into the Rose Garden, and saw technicians getting lights and cables ready for a presidential statement. By this time Blitzer was the only reporter left at the White House. He walked to the North Lawn, where his camera was set up, making sure to keep his pace slow so that he wouldn't lose his breath. He heard a producer in his ear microphone asking nervously, "You sure you got this?" Blitzer replied, "I got it. Let's do it," and then went on live with the news: "President Clinton has been informed that Richard M. Nixon, the thirty-seventh President of the United States, is dead."

Some of his colleagues suspected that Blitzer had been spoon-fed this story by a White House official. Instead, it was the result of old-fashioned reporting.

This reminded me of when I broke the story of John Sununu's misuse of government aircraft in the Bush administration. Several of my colleagues later asked me who had leaked the story, as if it had just fallen into my lap.

BILL PLANTE OF CBS covered Ronald Reagan's White House, shifted to the State Department under George Bush, then returned to cover the Clinton White House in 1993. "The only thing that has changed is the ability of the White House to focus and present its case in the best possible light," Plante says. "That's the bottom line. I don't think that Reagan got off easy, which is what the Clintonites will tell you. He wasn't engaged, but nobody cared because the economy for his last six years was booming and voters knew what he wanted to do. He told them what he wanted to do, he did it, and then he continued to maintain his presence in office at a level that the public liked until the last couple of years, when he got partially derailed by Iran-contra. But even then he was still on a roll, because he had the beginnings of the Soviet Union collapse working for his benefit."

Plante notes that Bush did well initially by showing a command of his government, a knowledge of the details of many issues, and especially by winning the Persian Gulf War. At first Bush enjoyed a good relationship with the press corps, but then, Plante adds, "in a stunning display of disconnectedness and inability to understand what . . . was bothering the electorate, [he] failed to understand their economic concerns and made himself vulnerable. He really snatched defeat from the jaws of victory, I think, with his attitude."

Plante argues that the media have not treated the Clintons unfairly. "They have made their own bed," he says, "by having a decision-making process that is disorganized at best, to put the most charitable face on it, or that is dominated by a President who can't make up his mind and who meddles in everything."

Asked whether the media are too negative, Plante says, "What's the alternative? We can't be cheerleaders, and if we're kinder and gentler, somebody else is going to get the story. Yes, there's a lessened civility in the public discourse, no question about it. Can we mend that single-handedly by changing our ways? I don't think so. . . . I make the argument that it's not because of us that Clinton is a national joke; it's his own doing. The stuff about womanizing, inability to make a decision, and waffling all the time isn't the press's fault. We may have amplified the signal, but we didn't originate it. I think the people in this White House find it hard to deal with the fact that the emperor doesn't have any clothes. It's much easier to shoot the messenger."

Yet Plante, who grew up in Chicago and worked in the CBS Chicago bureau for ten years, has some strong criticism of his profession. "Self-awareness is the most important thing," he says. "I watch a lot of our younger colleagues who did tend to go to a lot of the same Eastern schools . . . I like them, but they don't have a wide experience of the country."

This lack of experience, which is more of a problem in the overall national press corps than with White House journalists, manifests itself as a collective blind spot among many Washington editors and reporters to conservative views of abortion, feminism, and such important parts of the culture as the professional military and Christian conservatives.

As of the spring of 1995, Plante was looking forward to doing more political coverage of the Republican presidential candidates, because Clinton was no longer a big story. "The slide to irrelevancy came stunningly fast," he said.

EVERY PRESS CORPS has its hard-asses—the reporters who do a tough job day in and day out and don't care about being popular with either the White House or with their colleagues.

Ann Devroy of *The Washington Post* is probably the toughest reporter covering the White House today. She doesn't have the most ingratiating personality, but she has won the press corps' grudging respect for her dogged pursuit of news. Once she focuses on something, it is virtually impossible to call her off. She was the reporter who so rattled John Sununu, George Bush's hard-boiled chief of staff, that he berated her just before a ceremony in the Rose Garden by shouting, "Your stories are all lies! Everything you write is a lie!" She was also one of the reporters who gave the Clinton White House the hardest time during its first two years.

Devroy makes no apologies. She sees her job as that of a watchdog, and she is a reporter of the old school. Her manner is curt and often unfriendly, but she works diligently to cultivate a wide network of sources who want to play ball with *The Washington Post* as the country's foremost political newspaper and the hometown paper of the nation's capital. Anyone wanting to leak stories tends to turn to the *Post* because of the exposure it guarantees in Washington. Yet Devroy doesn't wait for leaks to drop into her lap. "The reason you have to respect her, even though she wasn't always civil," ex-press secretary Myers says, "was that when she was wrong, she took it very seriously. If you called her up and told her she got something wrong, she'd immediately say, 'Oh, my God, what was it? Explain to me why it's wrong.' Then she'd verify it, call you back, and say, 'Okay. You're right, it was wrong. What do I need to do? Do you want a correction?' There was a real commitment to accuracy, and a real willingness to demand accuracy from her sources and to demand it from herself. . . . People leaked to her because they always felt they would get a fair shake from her. I was certainly not one of her favorite people in the White House, and yet I gave her the story when I decided to leave because I figured she didn't have to prove to anybody that she was objective about me, and that I would get treated fairly by her, which I think I did."

"Devroy was always known for calling you at home late at night," says Marlin Fitzwater. ". . . She was hardworking and tenacious in pursuing a story. Just when I poured that first drink, the phone would ring and it would be her."

Ann Devroy would have been an excellent and influential reporter no matter what newspaper she worked for, but her influence was immeasurably increased because of her status as the lead White House reporter for *The Washington Post*. Every morning, virtually every person of importance in the federal government and in Washington journalism gets the *Post* on his or her doorstep. It is at once the capital's bulletin board, gossip sheet, and main source of news about politics and government. When there is a big Washington story, the *Post* will throw more resources than any other news organization into covering it.

"That makes the *Post* a feared publication," says Fitzwater, and so every White House staff member is schizophrenic about dealing

with it, worried about getting in trouble with higher-ups for talking out of school, yet concerned that a rival might be leaking information that needs to be countered. "The *Post* devotes a large
amount of its coverage to process, fights inside the White House,
internal intrigue, who's up and who's down," Fitzwater says.
"Presidents always resent that kind of coverage, and the White
House staff is always upset by it."

Yet the *Post* is the recipient of choice for leaked information.
Fitzwater says that an important story leaked to the *Post* will always be a prime topic of discussion at the White House briefing the
day it appears. The paper is also unrivaled in its ability to keep a
story alive; no other single media outlet comes close to having its
kind of impact in Washington.

RICHARD BENEDETTO, A veteran of *USA Today,* is another back-to-
basics reporter. His critique of both the White House press corps
and the Clinton administration is sharp. "A lot of journalists forget that the role of the press in a democratic society is not only to
point out those things to the public that need fixing," he says. "The
ultimate goal is to make the system work better, not to tear it
down. A lot of people think they've done their job by just reporting how bad everything is, and that's all."

USA Today is a rarity in many ways. For one thing, it does not
generally allow the use of anonymous quotes, and it tries to be as
straightforward as it can in its reporting. This means that few
Washington insiders will leak to *USA Today.* "We don't do that
much 'inside-baseball,' " Benedetto says. ". . . I don't think it means
a helluva lot to the average reader out there, especially our readers
who are all over the country and are not tuned to inside-the-
Beltway, inner White House intrigue. . . . We try to stay away from
those [feuds]. . . . It's good for us to know [them] as we go through
the process of reporting and writing, but we just don't do many
[such] stories. . . ."

Benedetto, who grew up in a working-class family in Utica, New
York, recalls that years ago journalists had a better sense of
working-class and middle-class America. "It used to be that a journalist was able to read the public's mood very quickly because re-

porters were part of the public. . . . They got among the people. They knew what people were thinking [and] therefore they could immediately take the public pulse by instinct. Today journalists take their own pulse and think it's everybody else's." He recalls that just before George Bush began bombing Iraq in the Persian Gulf crisis, a prominent reporter told him that no one he knew supported the bombing and that it would be extremely unpopular with the voters. The famous journalist was flat wrong.

Benedetto, who has covered the White House and national politics since 1988, feels that the Clintons' keeping an arm's distance from journalists has raised questions about whether there is something in their personal relationship that they want to hide. He also suspects that the Clintons have not resolved their own identities. "They don't seem to be comfortable with who they are in public," he says. ". . . If they knew who they were, they wouldn't have to make themselves over so often."

SOME WHITE HOUSE reporters have had a problem separating their celebrity from their journalistic duties. Eleanor Clift is a prime example. I knew her in the 1980s, when she had covered the White House for *Newsweek* and then for the *Los Angeles Times*. She was a hard worker who started in a clerical job and eventually proved to be a top-flight journalist. But when she left the *Times* to return to *Newsweek,* she began to appear more frequently on television and to mix the roles of commentator and reporter. She achieved considerable celebrity from her appearances on *The McLaughlin Group,* a televised public-affairs discussion that resembles a rhetorical food fight. Gradually, she came to accept the role of "designated liberal" as her television persona, and found herself defending Clinton so strenuously on virtually all fronts that she was no longer a reporter but a pundit-cum-entertainer.

Clift embodied a troubling trend in the news media: the endless pursuit of celebrity, in which getting attention, rather than substantive reporting, is the ultimate goal. The more outrageous and provocative the commentary, the better the producers like it, even though the journalists aren't often discussing areas they specialize in. Further, a reporter who becomes known on television is in more demand on the lecture circuit. Regulars on talk shows like *Meet the Press* and *The McLaughlin Group* can collect thousands of dollars for each speech, with the money sometimes coming from special interests they might cover. Even in the pages of *Newsweek,* where ostensibly Clift tried to be a more even-handed White House correspondent, she was an apologist for the administration. Her interview with Hillary Rodham Clinton, printed on March 21, 1994, was fawning and self-indulgent. Clift quoted herself repeatedly in the question-and-answer format, and at one point said, "I guess the only thing I see comparable [between Whitewater and Watergate] is that a lot of people want to launch careers based on finding something."

In August 1994 *Newsweek* announced that Eleanor Clift would no longer cover the White House and would become a contributing editor. The move was overdue.

Another example of the perils of celebrity was Margaret Carlson of *Time.* While covering the White House at the start of the Clinton administration, Carlson, like Clift, felt no restraint about offering her liberal views on *The Capital Gang* and other television shows. As an offshoot of her celebrity, she also started making lucrative speeches around the country. She once said, "The less you know about something, the better off you are. . . . What's good TV and what's thoughtful analysis are different. That's been conceded by most producers and bookers. They're not looking for the most learned person; they're looking for the person who can sound learned without confusing the matter with too much knowledge. I'm one of the people without too much knowledge, [so] I'm perfect!"

"I was a much more thoughtful person before I went on TV," Carlson said on another occasion. "But I was offered speeches only *after* I went on TV. . . . My view is that I just got on the gravy train, so I don't want it to end."

Eventually, Carlson was made a *Time* columnist, a position from which she could freely give her opinions and not be expected to cover the White House "objectively."

FINALLY, THERE ARE members of the press corps whom most other reporters consider an embarrassment and would prefer that the public not know about. The best example was Naomi Nover, the widow of a *Denver Post* Washington correspondent. Although she had no discernible outlets for her freelance reporting, she insisted on carrying a White House press pass and going on virtually all foreign trips with the President, apparently at her own expense. Nover always wore a blue dress and pulled a luggage carrier piled with grapefruit and unknown materials wrapped in plastic bags. She was shunned by most of us. She died in April 1995 at the age of eighty-four after collapsing in the Senate press gallery while renewing her credentials.

20

What's Wrong with the Press

As we approach the end of the twentieth century, the traditional adversarial relationship between the media and the presidency has deteriorated into something ugly: a mutual cynicism that interferes with the ability and willingness of both sides to educate the country.

The White House doesn't reveal the unvarnished truth, or anything close to it. The press corps doesn't trust the presidency to do any more than spew out self-serving claptrap. The White House tries to manipulate reporters into putting a favorable spin on every event. Reporters engage in a game of "gotcha" as they attempt to embarrass, hector, or trick officials into making a gaffe or revealing some subliminal truth. Most Americans don't have confidence in either institution.

A big part of journalism's problem, of course, is the natural instinct of most people to blame the messenger for bad news. It has forever been thus. But since the 1960s, reporters have served America a steady diet of trends and events of such a fundamentally negative nature that we have undermined the country's faith in itself. There were Vietnam, Watergate, and the Iran-contra scandal.

There were reports of worsening crime, racial hatred, gender and ethnic bias, and the decay of the family. There was intensive coverage of inflation, recession, dire structural problems with the U.S. economy, and a drumbeat of warnings about the burgeoning federal deficit. There were stories about corruption at every level of government. There were exposés not only of politicians who abused their trust but of religious leaders who preyed on their flocks, of educators who failed to teach, of cops who were on the take, of entertainers and sports heroes who fell from grace.

Of course, the press has to report such stories, but they have taken their toll. The media are no longer seen as society's truth-sayers. In holding up a mirror to America, journalists too often have filtered out the good and embellished the bad, resulting in a distorted image. A negative picture emerges, but not a fully truthful one, because the positive side of issues has been neglected. It is understandable that Americans have come to associate the press with everything that has gone wrong. We have become the chroniclers of the country's failures while we have ignored its successes.

Within these larger developments, four major trends within the Washington media are undermining the credibility of journalism: 1) We have too much attitude; 2) we are too negative; 3) we rush to judgment about events, trends, and people; 4) we are losing contact with everyday America.

THE PROBLEM OF ATTITUDE

AS THE WHITE House has become increasingly preoccupied with public relations and "spin," the press corps has responded by reducing its straightforward reporting. Journalists say they simply cannot get much basic information from the White House because material is too often manufactured by the massive government public-relations machine. Just as important, many reporters and editors feel that with a twenty-four-hour news cycle, they need to offer more than straightforward reporting to hold readers' interest. Hence journalists focus increasingly on analysis and interpretation, and sometimes on outright opinion.

A two-month study of front-page stories in the *Los Angeles*

Times, New York Times, and *Washington Post* in 1993 by the *LA Times* found that half of the 1,332 stories that ran during that period were straight news; 40 percent were analytical or interpretive (80 percent of which were not labeled as analysis or interpretation); 5 percent were features; and another 5 percent were special projects.

Of course, this trend toward subjectivity and attitude in mainstream journalism was growing rapidly before Bill Clinton rose to power. Too many Washington-based journalists take their cues from Cable News Network, thinking that if they have seen a news report on CNN, everybody else in the country has viewed it too and that it is no longer news.

"The hard lead, the hard news, has been given over to CNN and the wire services," says White House press secretary Mike McCurry. "Nobody in print journalism can write a hard lead anymore because the presumption is, 'Our readers already know all about this because they saw it all on television or heard it on radio and it's been out there on the Internet all day long.' . . . I think this is flat-ass wrong. As the day goes on, the assumption is that all of these facts spewing out of the White House are instantly absorbed, so the story has to move on to the next chapter right away. It creates a hyperventilating quality to the press-White House relationship. Everybody is scrambling all the time—the press, to catch up with the headline; the White House, to get on top of the facts to try to get them out in an orderly way. . . . Nobody has a moment or two to reflect on whether any of it is important, what it means, or how it's going to add up."

Clinton and his aides argue, justifiably, that the country has never understood the range of his administration's accomplishments, such as his success in cutting the federal bureaucracy, reducing the growth of the federal deficit, and winning congressional passage of the North American Free Trade Agreement. The trend of news analysis over straight reporting is largely to blame for the President's long spells of unpopularity, say the Clintonites.

Journalists are deeply split on this question. A survey conducted by the *American Journalism Review* in the winter of 1995 found that only 54 percent of the readers who responded (presumably, most of them journalists) said that the President had been treated fairly, while 46 percent said he had not. My survey of White House correspondents in early 1995 found a similar split. The very fact that reporters are divided shows that there is a lack of even-handedness in assessing the presidency.

A case in point came in late October 1994. The President gave a speech in Cleveland declaring that the federal budget deficit for fiscal 1994 was $102 billion less than what had been projected two years earlier. Yet most of the press focused not on this good news but on a leaked White House memo suggesting that one conceivable option for the administration at some future date might be to cut deeply Medicare and Social Security, two extremely controversial possibilities. Among the three broadcast networks, only Rita Braver of CBS reported the decline in the deficit. Brit Hume of ABC said that Clinton had failed to "get back on the attack" against the Republicans because of the leaked memo. Andrea Mitchell of NBC noted that Clinton had suffered a setback in his campaign for Democrats in the midterm elections: "His game plan was in shambles because of the memo." It was a case of good news being overshadowed by the media's preoccupation with speculative analysis that had little basis in reality. No one could seriously believe that Clinton planned to go ahead with cuts in both Medicare and Social Security, which would have caused a calamity by alienating elderly voters, so legitimate good news was lost in a one-day frenzy over an ill-advised hypothesis.

The Center for Media and Public Affairs in Washington found that between Clinton's Inauguration in January 1993 and June 1994, the President was the target of 2,400 negative comments on the evening news shows of ABC, CBS, and NBC. Sixty-two percent of all evaluations of President Clinton by reporters and sources were negative. In contrast, only 51 percent of the evaluations of President George Bush were negative during a similar period four years earlier.

Another factor propelling the mainstream media toward subjectivity is competitiveness, also mentioned earlier. Reporters and their editors want to set themselves apart from their colleagues. Adding edge or attitude to a story is often the easiest way to do so, even though the best way is to improve the reporting. News analysis was once the province of a small group of veteran columnists; now even rookie reporters write analysis as a matter of course. "Reporting has been replaced by punditry," says George Stephanopoulos.

Adding to the problem is that the line is increasingly blurred between the mainstream news media and the rash of commentary-entertainment shows such as *The Capital Gang, The McLaughlin Group,* and trash-television programs ranging from *Geraldo* and *Jenny Jones* to *Hard Copy* and *Inside Edition.* All of the shows deal with the news, and the public often has trouble differentiating among the hosts. Who is a journalist, who is a commentator or a pundit, who is an entertainer, who is a political strategist? Is Rush Limbaugh entitled to the same credibility as CBS anchorman Dan Rather? Is conservative analyst George Will to be trusted as much as R. W. Apple, Washington bureau chief of *The New York Times*? Definitions are less clear than ever, and we would be wise to keep journalists separate from combatants in the political wars.

"No show has done a better job of lumping reporters and politicians together in one pea pod than *The Capital Gang* (Saturday evenings on CNN)," writes journalist James Wolcott. ". . . [The] buddy-buddy tone expresses a truth about Washington life. The political establishment and the opinion elite share the same stratosphere of money, status and education. They send their kids to the same private schools, dine at the same restaurants, bathe in the same sun-lamp glow of media attention. They're on easy terms with one another because they're all on the same side of the camera. People who appear regularly on TV really don't like wasting their time with . . . the peasants—who stay home and watch."

The view that there is too much subjectivity is widely shared by politicians in Washington and by a considerable number of journalists. Smart-aleck journalism and wise-ass punditry are crowding out thoughtful analysis and solid reporting. Editors should police their coverage more aggressively to make sure that their reporters and writers return to the basics of informing the country and move away from such self-indulgence.

Mark Gearan, Clinton's first White House communications director, says, "When we live with five hundred news channels, a proliferation of specialty-press magazines, a commercially pressured environment, when . . . 150 newspapers close in the seventies, when only one in four people watch TV news today, and one in ten watching the morning news, the commercial pressures that exist are huge."

Gearan points out that ABC, CBS, and NBC generally refuse to carry Clinton's press conferences live because they lose large amounts of money when they pre-empt their regular entertainment programming. "This is the hand we've been dealt," he says. Further, "There is no reward for gray [in opinions]. . . . Everything is black-and-white."

THE PROBLEM OF NEGATIVITY

THE MEDIA ARE not only are too subjective but are excessively negative, especially toward the President. Political scientist Kathleen Hall Jamieson is among the scholars who argue that journalists are undermining public confidence in our most important institutions. When the press does cover issues, she says, "more often than not it focuses on attack and counterattack, including dismissal of the status quo, which raises the anxiety. The status quo doesn't work, neither do any of the alternatives. That invites cynicism as well. But the press that is the carrier of the message is now inviting cynicism about everyone, including itself. You can't survive that way."

A Times Mirror poll conducted in July 1994 by the Roper Center at the University of Connecticut found that 71 percent of Americans believe that the news media "gets in the way of society solving its problems," while only 25 percent believe it helps society solve them. Thirty-six percent said the main reason that the press "gets in the way" is because of biased or slanted reporting; 30 percent accused it of "sensationalism." George Stephanopoulos was on the right track when he said, "There's been a tendency to move much more toward coverage of conflict and controversy in all areas of politics . . . In all areas of society there's been an increasing tendency to view every issue in terms of personality, and once you start viewing every issue in terms of personality, there's really no end. That leads to the fascination with Tonya Harding and O. J. Simpson. It's the same impulse that leads to the deifying and then demonizing of Presidents. . . . The world is too complex, and because [it is so complicated] and because you can't [absorb] everything, you can't understand the forces surrounding you and influencing your life, so personality becomes [a shorthand] way of understanding the world."

Journalist Paul Starobin argues that cynicism can sometimes yield coverage that is "great fun to read and selectively true, yet indulges in blithe contempt for the political scene. Take the withering oeuvre of Maureen Dowd, the veteran Washington-based *New York Times* reporter recently named to replace Anna Quindlen as a *Times* op-ed columnist. . . . Consider the now-famous lead, so delicious, yet so dismissive and reductive, of Dowd's front-pager last June [1994] on a trip by President Clinton to Oxford University: 'President Clinton returned today for a sentimental journey to the university where he didn't inhale, didn't get drafted, and didn't get a degree.' "

Starobin praises Dowd's witty, entertaining style, but adds, "Still, the Dowd formula can get pretty old. Her eye locks onto telltale marks of hypocrisy that are certainly not missing from the Washington scene, but are only one aspect of it."

Many politicians agree. When McCurry sent the President a copy of Starobin's piece, with the comment that the press was finally doing some healthy soul-searching, Clinton wrote back that Starobin's conclusion was "very wise." That conclusion read: "Today's generation of cynics, in journalism and elsewhere, seems afraid to believe. Perhaps after the Kennedy assassinations, Vietnam [and] Watergate, they built up a defensive wall, like disappointed lovers who vow never to fall in love again. Cynicism beckons as a seductive retreat from belief, but it is also a barren spot, one that deprives the soul of sustenance. It produces little that endures."

Reporters feel pressured by their editors and colleagues to have a harder edge, to take shots at those in power, and almost never to praise anyone in public office. Journalists are simply afraid of being labeled as shills for those in authority, and with good reason. Covering a beat like the White House, when you are dependent on the handouts of the government, can easily make a journalist into a house pet.

To citizens who wonder why the media are so negative, there is a simple answer: lies. Too many have been told over the years to justify much trust in government. Journalists have been conned and attacked too often by any number of officials at the White House, and by several Presidents, on Watergate, the Vietnam War, the Iran-contra scandal, and many other issues. Back in Nixon's administration, Vice-President Spiro Agnew made a crusade of attacking the news media, and few reporters who covered the 1964 Republican convention will ever forget the visceral hatred of Barry Goldwater's supporters for the press.

In the survey I conducted of reporters who cover the White House full-time, virtually everyone who responded said he or she had been lied to at some point in covering the beat. CBS's Bill Plante said that during the Reagan administration he got a tip that the United States was about to invade Grenada. Bringing along AP's Terry Hunt as a witness, Plante bearded Reagan spokesman Larry Speakes and presented him with the rumor. Speakes disappeared into his office, then returned twenty minutes later with a reply from White House national security adviser John Poindexter. "Not true," Speakes said. "No invasion. Knock it down hard. Poindexter says knock it down hard."

The next morning Plante arrived at the White House at 6 A.M. "It was quite clear when we got there," he recalled, "that something was going on. We had heads of Caribbean nations coming to the front gate." Of course the invasion was on, but Plante does not think such lies are unusual in any White House. "I think they all lie to us to some degree."

The trend toward negativity is similarly intensified by the experience of the presidential campaigns of the last twenty or thirty years. "I think the coverage reflects the nature of our politics," says commentator Tim Russert, host of NBC's Meet the Press. "Campaigns have become much more negative, not because of the media but because of the candidates. With the declining influence of parties and the growing importance of primaries, you can have seven or eight candidates all vying for the presidency, and it gets rough. Half their budgets go to television. By the time anyone is elected President of the United States, his negatives are upward of 40 percent [i.e., 40 percent of the voters have a negative view of him], largely inflicted by his opponents' negative television advertising.

[Admittedly], the media plays on that. We cover what we see [and] hear. The negative TV commercial has replaced in many ways the streetcorner stump speech of years ago.

"Secondly, the candidates have become very specific in their promises to the American people [in order] to curry votes, and our information-recall systems have become very good and very sophisticated. So when we try to keep a level of honesty . . . and accountability, the candidates squeal. They hate it. . . .

"Thirdly, I think the attitude of the press corps continues to change. . . . As television plays more and more of a role, print becomes less and less important. We live in a country now where three fourths of the American people admit that they get most of their news from television. Half the people in the country say they get *all* their news from television, and the medium has difficulty with complicated nuance. It is easier to cover conflict. I think what happens is that candidates play to this in a campaign, so we and they get conditioned, and then suddenly they start governing and wonder why it hasn't changed."

THE RUSH TO JUDGMENT

THE PRESS HAS become obsessed with snap judgments. Since so many reporters are chasing the same facts, they have turned more and more to searching for "insight scoops" to set themselves apart from their competitors. Who will have the definitive thought about Clinton and his relationship with women or how Clinton's abusive stepfather shaped the future President's psyche or how Clinton's Oxford background is constantly at war with his Arkansas roots? Many of these topics are interesting to explore, but we have gone overboard in such theorizing.

Former communications director Mark Gearan says that the tendency to make such judgments was particularly clear on the day Clinton ordered the bombing of Baghdad early in his presidency. Gearan was in national security adviser Anthony Lake's office when the planes went out at 6 P.M. At 7 P.M. *The Capital Gang* television program came on in Lake's office, and the two U.S. officials were aghast at what was being said. The first question examined what effect the bombing would have on the Clinton presidency. "It was a call for instant analysis and judgment even before the facts were known," Gearan recalled.

Another case in point came in September of 1994, when former President Jimmy Carter, Senator Sam Nunn, and retired general Colin Powell held a press conference announcing an accord designed to force the military junta in Haiti from power and to restore the civilian government of President Jean-Bertrand Aristide. Minutes after the announcement, a reporter called Gearan and said he had to do a story that night on whether the agreement represented effective diplomacy or a flawed political settlement doomed to failure. Of course, it was a ludicrously premature notion. Gearan said later, "That's the commercial pressure on reporters. . . . They have to analyze news [immediately]."

Accelerating the unfortunate trend toward quick judgments is the fact that the news cycle has speeded up exponentially. The time frame for judging a President has been telescoped. "We used to ask if [the President] had a good week," NBC's Andrea Mitchell says. "Now we ask, did he have a good Tuesday?" There is no breathing space for considered judgment and deliberation. Yet most citizens judge their Presidents over a much longer span of time, not in the day-to-day time frame developed by the press.

Dee Dee Myers says, "Decision-makers no longer have any room [in which] to make a decision. Compare the amount of time that Kennedy had to deal with the Cuban Missile Crisis or the Bay of Pigs to the amount of time Clinton had to deal with Somalia or Haiti. Our Haiti policy was undermined because CNN had pictures of a couple of barefoot thugs throwing rocks at an American ship. If it were not for those pictures, that policy would not have been perceived as being an utter failure. The truth was that the President couldn't send lightly armed UN soldiers into Haiti when the Haitians were breaking their [side] of the Governor's Island agreement. But the pictures overpowered the facts, and they came to define the Clinton administration's [policy as] retreat in the face of barefoot thugs."

Myers adds, "I don't know how Presidents, secretaries of state, and other decision-makers who are dealing with genuine crises are supposed to make decisions. Part of it is our fault. If Wolf Blitzer is out on the front lawn broadcasting what's going on in the Oval Office, it's because somebody is telling him. . . . There are so many reporters now who cover the beat that there's a lot of pressure on us to [say something], or [else they] will get their information from someplace else. . . . There are leakers who try to make themselves important [or] who are stupid, and then there are leakers who are trying to get the right set of facts out. . . . It creates [a] horrible competition for factoids and anecdotes, and right or wrong, it's likely to end up on the front page of the paper. I think there's plenty of culpability to go around."

Part of the problem is that editors far removed from covering the White House think they know the President and feel they have special insights. The "food-fight" television show mentality, in which politicians and pundits venture their opinions and the most glib and provocative ones prevail, occurs in editorial conferences every day. With no basis for their ideas, people speculate and postulate, and then reporters are sent out to chase down theories. Even if there is no backing for them, such theories often find their way into stories. "Your editors no longer rely on [reporters'] sense of nuance," Myers observes.

One of the first things that Mark Gearan discovered when he became communications director in January 1993 was a wet bar tucked away in his office. "I always thought this was a wonderful anachronistic symbol of the changing nature of modern communications," Gearan recalled later. "I [imagine] that in other times, the press folks would be invited in for after-deadline drinks with administration officials at the end of the news cycle. I used to wonder, when would I invite people in? Before the nightly news? After the nightly news? Before *Crossfire*? After *Crossfire*? Before *Nightline*? After *Nightline*? Before the morning shows? After the morning shows? There's no end to the news cycle, [and] if policymakers make decisions based on how they will immediately be judged, in many instances they are making bad public policy."

Much of what Mike McCurry did immediately after his arrival as press secretary in late 1994 was to attempt to slow down the news cycle. Otherwise, the constant temptation, he says, was to comply with the press's demands to push a story further and further.

"[What's] driving so much of the . . . adversarial relationship is technology . . . the instantaneous communication now available through the Internet and through twenty-four-hour news cycles," McCurry says. "Nowadays, the wires are [always] working, CNN is [always] working, people are working around the clock."

McCurry thinks that the White House relationship with the press is no longer dictated overwhelmingly by the need for televised images, as it was during the Reagan years. Now, there is a much more complicated process: controlling the President's activities and themes, leaping ahead of the media by trying to anticipate their rush to judgment, and coordinating everything with what people see on television and when they see it. "You can't merely control the picture and the message," McCurry says. "You have to also control the order in which these images and pictures are going to appear as everything goes faster and faster. [This] is . . . dangerous, and it worries me a great deal, because we are by definition limiting the President's access to the public now in order not to clutter up what gets through. . . . Information can go like a waterfall out of the White House, [but] unless we control it more effectively and try to put it out at a slower pace and in a more orderly way, nobody in the country will have any time to absorb what it is the President is trying to do."

LOSING TOUCH

PERHAPS REPORTERS' BIGGEST problem is that they are out of touch with the rest of the country. Until recently, voters believed that the media's keeping close tabs on those in power would promote good government and improve society. No more. "I've noticed a change in people's attitude toward the press," Helen Thomas says. "After the drumbeat against the press, people come up and say, 'Why don't you write the truth?' In the old days, they used to come up and say, 'You meet such interesting people in your profession!' "

We White House journalists no longer live like average Americans. We make more money than they do. We live in a world where national politics and government are the dominant themes in our lives, which is not true anywhere else in the country. We often eat at fancy restaurants on expense accounts. We visit exotic places, and our travel arrangements are made by the White House travel office. We rarely have our flights delayed by commercial-airline traffic, because *Air Force One* and the press plane get priority. We stay at luxury hotels. In our work lives we constantly look for inside information, and we tend to define people and events in terms of how they affect our small world.

Doug Stanglin, then the State Department correspondent for *U.S. News,* witnessed this isolation when he filled in for me on George Bush's visit to Gdansk, Poland, in 1989. The trip did not go smoothly. Stanglin and a few press-corps regulars were delayed in getting to their assigned seats when their U.S. escort failed to arrive on time at the site of the main event, where a monument was to be dedicated to protesters killed by police during the Communist regime. But when the reporters finally made their way to the monument and Bush spoke with Polish leader Lech Wałesa at his side, Stanglin was moved. As a former Warsaw bureau chief for *Newsweek,* he was keenly aware that the location, which was outside the shipyard where the reformist labor movement Solidarity had been founded, was hallowed ground in Poland. Turning to a White House correspondent for a large newspaper, he asked what she had thought about the occasion. She replied, "Worst advance work I've ever seen." Stanglin saw this as the typically jaded reaction of a White House reporter cut off from human feelings. He recalled later, "It showed a sense of isolation that the traveling White House press corps couldn't step back from what they were doing and see the larger context."

The Zoe Baird case demonstrated how isolated the press can be. When it was revealed in 1993 that Baird had hired an illegal alien as a nanny for her children, many opinion leaders in Washington, including most White House reporters, weren't sure that it was a problem for her nomination as attorney general. In the end, a firestorm of opposition from around the country torpedoed the nomination. "I think the American people thought it was more than a little odd that a $500,000-a-year corporate lawyer couldn't find a legal baby-sitter," one Clinton adviser told me. "That's about the best example of who is out of touch—all of us in the White House, to be sure, but also all of you in the media."

There is good reason for concern about the cultural chasm that exists between the public and the Washington press corps. A survey taken for *U.S. News* in the spring of 1995 found that 50 percent of Americans thought that the media were strongly or somewhat in conflict with ordinary citizens' goals, while only 40 percent thought the media were strongly or somewhat friendly to their goals. This was the worst approval rating of any group measured—lower than prime-time-television entertainment providers, welfare recipients, even lower than elected officials, whose goals were judged to be in conflict with those of ordinary citizens by only 36 percent. Even lawyers did better, with 45 percent of Americans saying attorneys' goals conflicted with the public's. Clearly, the media were seen as part of a strongly disliked governing elite. When asked about "the people running the country," 52 percent of those surveyed said that they had little or nothing in common with them.

A survey taken by the Times Mirror Center for the People and the Press in the spring of 1995 came up with similar evidence of the divide between the mainstream media and the public. More than half of the public said that homosexuality should be discouraged, for example, while eight out of ten national journalists said that it should be accepted. Two out of five Americans said they attended church or synagogue regularly, compared with only one out of five national journalists. Thirty-nine percent of Americans said they were politically conservative, compared with only 5 percent of national journalists (nearly two thirds of the national journalists identified themselves as moderates, and 22 percent said they were liberals). When the Times Mirror survey asked if news coverage had improved, 37 percent of those questioned said no, and an additional 15 percent volunteered their own criticisms of news coverage, while 15 percent gave no answer.

More than half of the public agreed that the press was too cynical and negative in covering Congress, while eight out of ten national journalists disagreed. Two thirds of the public believed that the media had overplayed Bill Clinton's character problems, while two thirds of the journalists rejected this premise.

This cultural disconnection shows why journalists should take pains to move away periodically from government beats and gain fresh perspectives on the rest of the country. This means doing the kinds of stories that could provide insight into everyday American life—say, on crime, on trends in raising a family, or on how average couples make ends meet.

Joann Byrd, then the ombudsman for *The Washington Post*, wrote on November 27, 1994: "Cynicism is hardly reserved for . . . government bodies. If letters and calls to the ombudsman are a gauge, readers, listeners and viewers of the nation's media are, in the extreme, suspicious of news judgments. More and more people are convinced that there's something nefarious behind every news decision that seems to them wrong or cockeyed. People . . . see too many choices being made that don't square with what they would have done, with what they expected or with what they presume would be the fair thing to do.

"When it's the news media, people don't perceive a 'culture of influence by money' (though when all else fails the presumption is that this bad call was made to sell newspapers). The media are viewed more often as operating in a culture of influence by bias or connection. News decisions seem to result from the ideologies, associations and interests of people making those judgments. It is a measure of the breadth and depth of this skepticism about the press that people give newspapers no room for dumb mistakes."

I have often seen this cynicism toward the press in questions from audiences after I give a speech, in call-ins on radio and television talk shows, and in letters and phone calls to *U.S. News*. The left-wingers say that the media are too hard on Bill Clinton, and the right-wingers say we are too easy on him. What is most bothersome are the middle-of-the-roaders, the average citizens, who simply don't trust us. The irony is that we in journalism, who have adopted a studiously skeptical or cynical view of the world as part of our professional outlook, are now suffering from the same negativity because it has been turned on us.

The answer, I believe, is to return to straightforward, factual reporting wherever possible, with less editorializing or analysis by the writer. Often journalists don't give the public enough credit for being able to figure out the meaning of stories for themselves without our guidance.

We should go back to first principles, which means, above all, making sure that our stories are accurate. Friends who are casual consumers of the news often say that when they read in a newspaper or see on television a piece on something they know about— say, a decision made by their business or agency, a traffic accident, or a water-pipe break—key elements are wrong, whether it's a name, a street, or a part of the larger story. I've had the same experience. When I've been quoted or paraphrased, there have been errors—nothing malicious or egregious, just mistakes. Whether it is sloppiness or simple deadline pressure that limits a reporter's ability to check facts, such basic mistakes tend to undermine public confidence in the news they read or watch. Rigorous standards have to be reinforced by editors.

A more fundamental problem is the failure of the press to explain itself to the country. "Journalists don't appreciate how mystifying news judgment is to people who don't do it," says *The Washington Post*'s Joann Byrd. ". . . The motivations [readers] assign are often wrong, and very discouraging: the biases, the friends and the private interests of journalists are not even close to being as influential as critics presume they are. But if people don't know a plausible alternative, why isn't it just as sensible to assume an inappropriate influence is at work in newspapers as [it is] in other big institutions?

"The public's cynicism about news judgment could be part of a general mood of distrust. But whether it is or not, it is nurtured by newspapers' not making their work transparent. And it thrives because of something now totally ironic: The other reason newspapers don't think to explain themselves is that journalists believe the public has an unshakable faith—a faith that news decisions are made solely in service to the public, and hence on the merits. And if we could count on that trust, there'd be no explaining to do."

FINALLY, THE PRESS must come to grips with the character issue, perhaps the most difficult ethical question facing the news business today. Should a President's private behavior be fair game? What should be off limits to the media? Should there be a statute of limitations on past indiscretions? Should a President be treated differently than a member of Congress, a governor, or a nongovernment celebrity? Journalists have not reached any consensus on these issues.

Some guidelines certainly are in order. First, the old standards no longer apply. Reporters simply cannot and should not enter into a conspiracy of silence to hide a President's indiscretions, sexual or otherwise, as they did to protect John F. Kennedy. If a President emphasizes family values and his commitment to his spouse, then his private sexual conduct is certainly relevant, if only on the level of hypocrisy. In addition, it is no longer enough to say that a politician's private life should enter the public domain only if it affects his or her job performance. The issue is not merely one of hypocrisy; the question of character is especially relevant where a President is concerned. At a time when political ideology is less predictable or definable than it has been at any point in the last fifty years, a President's character is an increasingly important factor to millions of Americans—not a majority, perhaps, but a substantial minority of the electorate. That is an important segment of the country—one that is more culturally conservative than many national journalists—whose needs must, in fairness, be served.

When Paula Corbin Jones made her allegations of sexual harassment against Bill Clinton in early 1994, the press was divided about how to handle the story. On February 11, she told a Washington press conference (organized by hard-line conservatives, including Clinton archenemy Cliff Jackson) that Clinton had propositioned her on May 8, 1991, when she was a clerk for a state agency in Arkansas and Clinton was governor.

A woman filing suit against the President for sexual harassment is explosive stuff. This was not an anonymous rumor of womanizing of the kind that had trailed Clinton for years, nor was it a woman selling her story of an affair with Clinton to a supermarket tabloid, as Gennifer Flowers had done during the 1992 campaign. Paula Jones was willing to come forward without payment, albeit with encouragement from Clinton's enemies, to file suit in a court of law.

At first the media were slow to react. CNN, CBS, and NBC carried no stories that night, though ABC had a sketchy thirty-second report. The next day, most major newspapers used brief wire-service stories on inside pages. *The New York Times* carried five paragraphs, written by a staff member, on page eight; *The Washington Post* did not mention it at all.

Three months later, however, Jones received extensive coverage when she filed her civil lawsuit. At this point most news executives felt that the story could not be ignored, and with good reason: The case was a matter of public record in the courts. Further, the President had hired Washington super-lawyer Robert Bennett to defend him.

In mid-May, an ABC News/*Washington Post* poll found that 17 percent of Americans believed Jones, while twice as many believed Clinton. About 43 percent considered the charges important, while 45 percent thought they were not. Clearly, a substantial portion of the country thought the charges were either true or worth knowing about.

Which is the point, of course. The media should not act as a priesthood censoring information that many voters consider essential to evaluating their President and his values. Voters should decide such matters. But the decision to cover the story of Paula Jones's lawsuit is only half of the question. Just as important is *how* media organizations cover it—as the lead story, as a brief stand-alone item inside the newspaper or late in the newscast, or as an insert in a larger story placing Clinton's character problems in perspective.

As discussed earlier, my own standard when dealing with such stories has three criteria: Is the allegation true? Is it relevant to a public official's duties or public life? How much do Americans care? I run through this checklist whenever I consider whether a particular character story is newsworthy. What is most important is to give voters as much information as possible and allow them to make up their own minds—and of course this is supposed to be the press's *raison d'être*.

Backlash

The backlash has already begun, and we journalists ignore it at our peril. Our penchant for the negative and the subjective, our rush to judgment, and our lack of contact with everyday America are causing the public to turn against us. Over the next decade, we could find ourselves isolated more than ever, with few defenders and many interests clamoring to rein us in, legally and in other ways.

"People don't think the media tell the truth," says Democratic pollster and Clinton adviser Geoff Garin. "People don't think *anybody* tells the truth anymore." His surveys show that fewer and fewer Americans follow the news day to day: "They don't feel an obligation to follow the news, because there's no utility to being informed. People feel completely powerless."

Newspaper reading is on a long, steady decline. From 1972 to 1989, Americans who read newspapers every day dropped from 69 percent to 50 percent. The dropoff was most pronounced among young people. Among those eighteen to twenty-three years old, daily readership dropped from 45 percent to 23 percent. Among those twenty-four to twenty-nine, the decline was from 48 percent to 26 percent. Among those thirty to thirty-five, the drop was from

72 to 40 percent. Only the most elderly Americans—those sixty-six and older—have remained faithful readers of daily newspapers, increasing from 72 percent in 1972 to 73 percent in 1989.

Americans no longer believe their voices are being heard or that an individual can make a difference. To citizens, the media seem to be part of the ruling elite. "In American politics, there's a tendency to be suspicious of power brokers, no matter who they are," says political science professor Darrell West of Brown University. "It used to be that this was the backroom politicians, and people were very upset with them. Now people have become more suspicious of the media. They see the media as part of the establishment, and that's not a great position to be in." Pollster Garin and many press analysts predict a surge in public journalism at the local and regional levels—civic-minded journalism that advocates making the community a better place, such as crusades to clean out drug-infested neighborhoods or find effective ways to reduce crime.

By and large, this is a good trend, but at the national level it is being resisted. Through such insensitivity, we in the media are so alienating the public and politicians that our special niche in society could be jeopardized.

In 1994, there was legislation before Congress to equate journalists with lobbyists as part of a comprehensive overhaul of ethics laws. The concept that journalists have no special place in society as tribunes of the public was shocking to reporters, but the White House Office of Government Ethics supported the idea. The legislation died in Congress that year, but not because anyone wanted to protect the media; in fact, few legislators were willing to stand up for the press, whether in subcommittee or committee or on the floor of the House or Senate.

As president of the White House Correspondents' Association, I had firsthand experience with this issue, and I learned that the old arguments about the press's protection by the First Amendment aren't as influential as they once were. Burned by negative coverage and sensing the anti-media backlash, many politicians are eager to take the fourth estate down a few pegs.

In July 1995, the Senate passed a nonbinding resolution by a vote of 60 to 39 that reporters who cover it be required to file financial-disclosure statements similar to those required of the legislators.

Senator Robert Byrd, a Democrat of West Virginia, argued that it is hypocritical for the press to delve into senators' financial affairs while exempting themselves from such scrutiny. Not a single senator spoke up to defend the media. There is little doubt that this is the beginning of a trend toward open warfare between politicians and the press.

Jody Powell, a public-relations consultant in Washington and former press secretary to President Jimmy Carter, says the public doesn't care anymore about protecting the press, because most Americans no longer think it informs them well. There is too much opinion and attitude in the news columns, Powell says, and citizens don't see much difference between the mainstream evening news and the infotainment shows such as *Hard Copy* or *Inside Edition*. Public life and the news environment are focused too much on failure, finding fault, and promoting conflict, he believes. "I wish everybody would take two steps back and say, 'Look what we are doing to ourselves.' " The environment of cynicism, Powell says, "has resulted in a downward spiral toward an ungovernable country, a society where leadership is virtually impossible, and the people who might be best equipped to [lead] aren't willing to even try because they're not willing to put themselves and their families through it all. Journalism has so greatly damaged its standing as a profession and in society that it becomes a target not merely for criticism and complaints but for legal changes that are a real threat to a free press. Journalists have hollered so much about the First Amendment that folks are inclined to view it as crying wolf. I think the day could come when there really *is* a threat, and then who's going to defend the legitimate rights of the press?"

IF WE DO not mend our ways, within a decade there will be a rollback of our protections. Libel laws could be weakened to clamp down on us, and laws governing access to information could be tightened to limit reporters' ability to cover news and to investigate abuses in government and the private sector. In the early 1990s, jury awards for libel had already spiraled upward as the public's trust of the media declined.

The press's precarious position might be compared to that of trial lawyers. As Powell says, the average citizen used to feel some bond with lawyers because they gave everyday people access to the judicial system. But over time, support for lawyers has eroded as they seemed to grow out of touch with middle America, and legislation has gained support to limit the amount of damages that attorneys can claim for their clients.

Public confidence in the press has been declining for a generation. In 1973, at the start of the Watergate scandal and amid deep disillusionment over the Vietnam War, 23 percent of our citizens said they had a great deal of confidence in the people running the press, 62 percent had some confidence, and 15 percent said they had hardly any. By 1989, George Bush's first year in office, only 17 percent had a great deal of confidence in the press, 55 percent had only some confidence, and the percentage who had hardly any confidence in the institution had risen to 27 percent.

By 1994, two years into Bill Clinton's presidency, the confidence level had plummeted even further. Only 10 percent were in the first category, 50 percent had only some confidence, and 40 percent had hardly any—a huge drop in esteem over twenty years.

This decline has paralleled the dwindling confidence in the President and the executive branch. Those who had a great deal of confidence in the President dropped from 30 percent to 21 percent between 1973 and 1989, and fell to 11 percent by 1994. Those who had only some confidence in the executive branch went up from 51 percent to 57 percent between 1973 and 1989, and increased to 63 percent by 1994. Those who had hardly any confidence in the presidency rose from 19 to 23 percent by 1989, and then increased to 37 percent by 1994.

Part of the reason for these figures is the public's cynicism toward *all* of our institutions, especially politics and government, and this is constantly fueled by the media. Writing in *The Washington Post* on October 15, 1994, Richard Harwood noted a surge of stories just before the midterm elections in 1994 about the cynical, angry mood of the electorate, and he wondered if the media were creating the negative mood they were describing.

The depth of this negative mood is remarkable. A study by the Times Mirror Center for the People and the Press suggests that the public has become less altruistic on social issues, more indifferent to the plight of blacks and poor people, and more resentful of immigrants. "The percentage of Americans thinking the government should take care of needy people fell by 12 percentage points between 1992 and 1994," the Times Mirror report said.

Kathleen Hall Jamieson, of the University of Pennsylvania, says, "Journalists are now creating the coverage that is going to lead to their own destruction. If you cover the world cynically and assume that everybody is Machiavellian and motivated by their own self-interest, you invite your readers and viewers to reject journalism as a mode of communication because it must be cynical, too."

Political consultants are beginning to find that attacks by the media on candidates have the same credibility as attacks by the candidates' political enemies—which is to say, little or none. Media critic Joann Byrd wrote in late 1994: "We haven't managed to get in touch with what people talk about over the dinner table. We strew our own opinions throughout what we advertise as straight news reports. We are fascinated with the minutiae of political campaigns and political strategies and write for others who are similarly fixated. We tire of readers' not understanding the true definition of news. In 1994, candidates and voters are circumventing the conventional media with every technology they can find. Candidates actively running against the media—Marion Barry [who won the mayor's office in Washington, D.C.] and Oliver North [who ultimately narrowly lost his bid for the U.S. Senate from Virginia], for instance—are getting cheers for their anti-press one-liners. Some voters are defiantly supporting candidates because they think the establishment media don't approve. Voters are, it seems, overthrowing the oligarchy and taking back the political process."

SOME THINGS CAN be done.

More than ever, journalists should stand apart from their sources and the special interests they cover, especially the rich and the powerful. Appearing too clubby only drives a wedge between us and the public, which is increasingly skeptical that we represent their interests against those of entrenched power. We need to return to the ideal of journalism that I remember from my days as a cub reporter: a higher calling, a way to inform, educate, and enlighten the country, not a way for individual journalists to become rich, famous, and powerful.

One change that would help is for journalists to voluntarily disclose the sources and amounts of their outside income from lecture fees and "honoraria"—the same standard we demand of politicians. Better yet, journalists should forgo most of these fees, or at least the ones that create the impression that we are too close to our sources or are in the news business only to make a buck. Sam Donaldson is said to command up to $30,000 for a speech, Cokie Roberts to draw more than $20,000, and CNN's Judy Woodruff $7,500, but no one knows for sure because they refuse to reveal the details of their moonlighting profits.

The perception problem is serious, and journalists can't afford to lose any more of their credibility. Taking money from groups with an interest in news coverage could easily become a conflict of interest. But even if there is no conflict, it is hypocritical for journalists to accept fees or favors from special interests when they criticize politicians for doing the same thing. "I think we ought not to be doing this," says former CBS and NBC correspondent Roger Mudd. "It poses so many difficulties. Journalists as a breed hold the politicians to a certain standard of conduct and a certain standard of the appearance of conduct. When it applies to us we frequently fail our own test."

In the end, we need to make a few sacrifices as a gesture of solidarity with and sensitivity to our readers, viewers, and listeners, and to distinguish ourselves from the elites we cover. Journalists who want to deliver speeches to important constituencies should see themselves as educators, not as entrepreneurs.

BUT THE SADDEST part of the news business in Washington, including the White House beat, is that we are losing contact with Middle America. Walter Cronkite, the former anchorman for CBS News, reminds us, "There was a day not far distant, just before World War II, when nearly all of us news people, although perhaps white collar by profession, earned blue-collar salaries. We were part of the 'common people.' We suffered the same budgetary restraints, the same bureaucratic indignities, waited in the same lines, suffered the same bad service. We could identify with the average man because we were him."

Many Washington journalists, and certainly all the leading ones, are now members of the elite because of their high salaries and extensive education. Few have had recent experience covering general assignments or everyday beats that would put them in contact with the life of Middle America. The day-to-day experience in Washington—hobnobbing with upper-middle-class people in politics, government, the consulting world, or academia—creates an elitist sensibility. This tends to mean that the mainstream media decision-makers are liberal or libertarian on such social issues as abortion, gay rights, and affirmative action but conservative on such fiscal issues as lowering taxes and cutting government expenditures.

Few journalists or news executives in Washington, New York, or other large cities saw the whole picture in assessing the North American Free Trade Agreement (NAFTA) in 1994. Thousands of working-class Americans feared that they would be thrown out of work by the treaty; yet the press gave short shrift to their legitimate concerns because NAFTA was thought to be good for the macroeconomy.

One of the easiest remedies for us is to break away from Washington regularly and write stories outside the Beltway. It is almost always insightful and refreshing, and it can restore our grounding in American life. The most illuminating experience I have had in recent years was covering the aftermath of the bombing at the Alfred P. Murrah Federal Building in Oklahoma City in April 1995. When the blast occurred, I was thirty miles away in Lexington, Oklahoma, on one of my periodic head-clearing reporting trips outside Washington.

Listening to news reports on the radio, I sped north to the blast site and spent the next four days covering the worst terrorist incident in American history. It had been a long time since I had talked to people who were not glib or media-savvy and whose words I could take at face value, and now I had a chance to witness such everyday folks trying their best to cope with disaster. I was very moved by the efforts of volunteers who had rescued survivors, given blood, and provided generous financial donations. The story of Rebecca Anderson, the nurse who paid the ultimate price for her altruism by dying from a wound sustained while trying to rescue survivors in the gutted building, was particularly touching. "Courage and competence, perseverance and grit—all have been on display," I wrote in an essay the following week in *U.S. News*. "Oklahoma City's story, of course, is a tragedy. But it also says something important about the American character: It's still incandescent."

Perspective is what Washington journalists desperately need, and you don't have to be near a tragedy on the scale of the Oklahoma City bombing to find it. The real America is easy to locate once you are outside the Beltway. Every so often, we should treat ourselves to a refresher course in our own country.

NOTES

1: WHITE HOUSE HORRORS

3 White House logistics had broken down completely: Administration officials later said the helicopter was diverted because of rain and fog. But at the time, White House staffers in the field were unable to locate it despite numerous frantic calls on their cellular phones.

5 "You can't have that kind of belligerent": Author's interview with Sheila Tate, March 5, 1995.

7 The presidency has always: Author's interview with Thomas Cronin, December 27, 1995.

9 The White House would have been well advised: Quoted in Bob Woodward, *The Agenda*. New York: Simon & Schuster, 1994, p. 101.

10 "At the pinnacle of their craft": Freedom Forum Media Studies Center, *Media Studies Journal*. Spring 1994, p. 163.

12 "As many people have observed": Author's interview with Brit Hume, April 12, 1995.

2: THE WAY IT WAS

15 In 1792, Washington: James Deakin, *Straight Stuff*. New York: Morrow, 1984, p. 45.

15 "From the complexion of some of our newspapers": John Tebbel and Sarah Miles Watts, *The Press and the Presidency, from George Washington to Ronald Reagan*. New York: Oxford University Press, 1985, pp. 12–18.

15 "If ever a nation was debauched": Ibid., p. 18.
16 By 1807, he wrote: Elizabeth Frost, ed., *The Bully Pulpit, Quotations from America's Presidents*. New York: Facts on File, 1988, pp. 190–192.
17 The crusty old hero of the War of 1812: Tebbel and Watts, op. cit., p. 79.
17 At one time, Jackson had fifty-seven: Carolyn Smith, *Presidential Press Conferences: A Critical Approach*. New York: Praeger, 1990, pp. 18–19. Also see Michael Nelson, "The Presidency A to Z," *Congressional Quarterly*, 1992, pp. 298–299.
17 "No President ever had a more supporting": Tebbel and Watts, op. cit., p. 88.
18 Lincoln sought favor with critical newspapers: Smith, op. cit., pp. 19–21. Also see Nelson, op. cit., p. 298.
18 "From the press point of view": Smith, op. cit., pp. 21–22.
18 "He had an excellent sense of timing": James E. Pollard, *The Presidents and the Press*. New York: Macmillan, 1947, pp. 389–390.
19 During the 1868 campaign: Ibid., pp. 434–435.
19 But when he was President: Ibid., pp. 440–441.
19 Despite the opposition of the *Sun:* Ibid., pp. 443–445.
20 "Without substantial or extensive press connections": Ibid., p. 452.
20 Lacking any riveting national issues: Tebbel and Watts, op. cit., pp. 261–266.
21 Cleveland brought an innovation: Ibid., pp. 270–271.
21 The forty-nine-year-old bachelor: Ibid., pp. 272–276.
22 Political scientist Michael Nelson points out: Nelson, op. cit., p. 301.
22 Like no President before him: Tebbel and Watts, op. cit., pp. 335–337.
23 But Teddy was extremely harsh: Smith, op. cit., pp. 23–25.
23 Woodrow Wilson was the first President: Nelson, op. cit., p. 299.
24 While Wilson was relaxing at his summer home: Tebbel and Watts, op. cit., p. 366.
24 At his first presidential press conference: James David Barber, *The Presidential Character: Predicting Performance in the White House*. Englewood Cliffs, N.J.: Prentice-Hall, 1985, p. 50.
24 After the Germans sank the *Lusitania:* Smith, op. cit., pp. 26–27.
24 At the end of his presidency: Tebbel and Watts, op. cit., pp. 390–391.
25 Harding turned out to be an innovator: Pollard, op. cit., pp. 697–712.
26 "As one shocking disclosure after another was bared": Ibid., p. 712.
26 "Hoover's rise coincided with an immense expansion": Barber, op. cit., pp. 58–59.
26 He said the Depression was such a massive crisis: Smith, op. cit., p. 30.

3: WORLD CRISES AND PRESIDENTIAL DOMINANCE

28 When he was upset by critical articles: Author's interview with Sarah McClendon, September 22, 1994.

29 "FDR used radio vividly": Hedrick Smith, *The Power Game*. New York: Ballantine, 1988, p. 394.

30 "The relationship between press and": Ibid., p. 28.

30 "Today the attitude of the press corps": Don Oberdorfer, "Lies and Videotape," *The Washington Post,* April 18, 1994, p. C1.

31 "It was Kennedy's show": Richard Reeves, *President Kennedy: Profile of Power*. New York: Touchstone/Simon & Schuster, 1993, pp. 278–279.

31 "He was shameless in exploiting": Ibid., pp. 279–280.

31–32 Not only did reporters bond with Kennedy: Ibid., pp. 315–316.

33 He once told David Gergen: Several author interviews with David Gergen, 1993–1994.

34 "They would persist in writing": James Deakin, *Straight Stuff*. New York: Morrow, 1984, p. 284.

34 In November 1969, Agnew delivered: Dom Bonafede, "One Man's Accuracy," *National Journal,* May 10, 1986, p. 1111.

34 He also condemned opponents: Tom Stuckey, "Spiro T. Agnew Lives Far From Spotlight 20 Years After Resigning," Associated Press dispatch, October 10, 1993.

35 It got so bad that just before: David S. Broder, *Behind The Front Page*. New York: Simon & Schuster, 1987, p. 174.

35 "I feel to this day": Author's interview with Jody Powell, April 4, 1995.

36 "Television, with its need for a simple": Author's interview with Brit Hume, April 12, 1995.

36 "Radio, and then television,": Cited in Smith, op. cit., p. 395.

37 "From 1960, when Eisenhower and Kennedy": Broder, op. cit., p. 175.

4: SECRETS OF THE GREAT COMMUNICATOR

40 "Reagan did well because": Author's interview with Bill Plante, March 1, 1995.

41 Journalist David Broder says Reagan's: David S. Broder, *Behind The Front Page*. New York: Simon & Schuster, 1987, p. 178.

43 "We'd spend a lot of time": Several author interviews with Richard Wirthlin, 1993–1994.

43 A primary purpose: Broder, op. cit., p. 180.

44 "The Reagan people knew": Author's interview with Andrea Mitchell, January 4, 1995.

45 "Reagan will be remembered for": Author's interview with Tim Russert, March 9, 1995.

50 The worst of the briefings: David Hoffman, "Speakes and the Press in the Dog Days of August," *The Washington Post,* August 15, 1982, p. A2.

50 At another briefing, in February 1983: United Press International, "Choice of Words Sparks Speakes," *The Washington Post,* February 26, 1983.

55 The system seemed foolproof: Author's interview with Bob Thompson, May 25, 1995.

5: THE 1988 CAMPAIGN

63 In 1980, Atwater ran the: Larry J. Sabato, *Feeding Frenzy: How Attack Journalism Has Transformed American Politics.* New York: Free Press/Macmillan, 1991, p. 161.

64 Fitzwater recalls that in 1985 and 1986: Author's interview with Marlin Fitzwater, January 3, 1995.

70 "The changes were not dissimilar": Jack W. Germond and Jules Witcover, *Whose Broad Stripes and Bright Stars? The Trivial Pursuit of the Presidency 1988.* New York: Warner, 1989, pp. 57–58.

71 In the end, of course, Hart's campaign: For a more extensive description of these incidents, see Germond and Witcover, op. cit., pp. 169–215.

72 In one memorable interview, he told me: Kenneth T. Walsh, "The Fragile Candidacy of a Front-runner," *U.S. News & World Report,* October 19, 1987, p. 22.

73 The Republican platform bashed Dukakis: Germond and Witcover, op. cit., p. 377.

74 Duberstein immediately called Kirk O'Donnell: Author's interview with Kenneth Duberstein, May 5, 1995.

6: THE BUSH YEARS

78 "There are not enough stories": Cited in Michael Duffy and Dan Goodgame, *Marching in Place.* New York: Simon & Schuster, 1992, pp. 45–46.

78 "It often seemed that some presidential scholar": Ibid., p. 46.

84 "The gung-ho postures": David Zurawik and Christina Stoehr, "The Windbags of War," *FineLine: The Newsletter on Journalism Ethics,* October 1990, p. 1.

84 "It was extraordinary": Author's interview with Brit Hume, April 12, 1995.

84 "Big-time media were getting résumés": Quoted in Bill Monroe, "How the Generals Outdid the Journalists," *Washington Journalism Review,* April 1991, p. 6.

85 "Consider the assumptions behind": Ibid.

86 "The media loved the story lines": Lewis H. Lapham, "Notebook: Trained Seals and Sitting Ducks," *Harper's Magazine,* May 1991, p. 10.

87 After Scowcroft's *tour d' horizon:* The interview was "on background," meaning that Scowcroft did not wish to be identified as the source of the information at the time. In October 1995, Scowcroft gave the author permission to identify him as the source.

96 But such scorn was mild: Duffy and Goodgame, op. cit., p. 126.

7: DAN QUAYLE

100 "the most blatant example of political vivisection": Quoted in Larry J. Sabato, *Feeding Frenzy: How Attack Journalism Has Transformed American Politics.* New York: Free Press/Macmillan, 1991, p. 156.

101 "Looking back, I realize": Dan Quayle, *Standing Firm.* New York: HarperCollins, 1994, p. 9.

101 At one point, Beckwith: Author's interview with David Beckwith, April 14, 1995.

102 Quayle and his supporters: Quayle, op. cit., p. 29.

105 "This is meant to convey": Cited in Paul Starobin, "A Generation of Vipers: Journalists and the New Cynicism," *Columbia Journalism Review,* March/April 1995, pp. 25–26.

105–106 He was also an early champion of: Quayle, op. cit., pp. 313–314.

107 In April 1989, only three months: Ibid., pp. 125–127.

108 On a trip to Chile: James Gerstenzang and David Lauter, "Quayle Set on Getting Last Laugh," *Los Angeles Times,* December 2, 1991, p. 1.

108 "The media sees itself as a debunker": Author's interview with William Kristol, March 21, 1995.

109 On May 19, 1992, three weeks: Rodney King was an African-American motorist who was stopped by Los Angeles police and beaten senseless as he lay on the ground. The beating was captured on videotape, broadcast repeatedly on local and national television, and shown at the trial of the police officers charged in the incident. The officers were acquitted, sparking riots in Los Angeles.

109 "The real ideological firestorm": Quayle, op. cit., p. 319.

109 Negative reaction to the speech: Andrew Rosenthal, "Quayle's Moment," *The New York Times Magazine,* July 5, 1992, p. 11.

111 NBC's Jay Leno, for example: Ibid.

111 "One story supporting the stereotype": Author's interview with William Kristol, March 21, 1995.

111 "It gave us a new appreciation": Author's interview with David Beckwith, April 14, 1995.

111 The Vice-President went on to: Ceci Connolly, "Quayle Starts Down the Road to a Refurbished Image," *Congressional Quarterly,* August 22, 1992, pp. 2517–2518.

111 A study by the Center for Media: Cited by Chet Lunner, "Quayle: 'Airhead Apparent' or Underrated Statesman?" Gannett News Service, August 11, 1992.

111 He followed advice from Baker and Teeter: Quayle, op. cit., p. 353.

8: THE 1992 CAMPAIGN

120 He said that the recession: David E. Rosenbaum, "On the Economy, Bush Tries to Keep Focus on the Future," *The New York Times,* September 13, 1992, section 4, p. 1.

121 James Carville had taken control: Ibid.
122 "That was an unrealistic expectation": Author's interview with Dee Dee Myers, May 10, 1995, with information drawn from other interviews with Myers, 1992–1995.
123 "I don't know what previous transitions": Ibid.

9: BATTLE STATIONS

128 "We were walled in": Author's interview with Helen Thomas, January 25, 1995.
128 Journalist David Maraniss points out: David Maraniss, *First in His Class*. New York: Simon & Schuster, 1995, p. 408. Maraniss reports that Clinton's concept of the perpetual campaign was developed after "endless" discussions with New York pollster and political strategist Dick Morris in 1982 and 1983, after Clinton was reelected Arkansas governor. "His entire strategy in governing the state," Morris told Maraniss, "was based on flanking the press through the paid media."
129 The day after his Inauguration: In a January 25, 1995, interview with the author, Helen Thomas recalled that a TV technician was setting up equipment at the senior-staff meeting, and he reported the President's remarks to his journalistic colleagues.
129 "When Clinton became President": Author's interview with Tim Russert, March 9, 1995.
130 He pointed the story out: McCurry had been a prominent adviser for three losing Democratic presidential candidates—Ohio senator John Glenn in 1984, former Arizona governor Bruce Babbitt in 1988, and Nebraska senator Bob Kerrey in 1992. McCurry also was chief spokesman for the Democratic National Committee. Shortly after Clinton took office, McCurry was named chief spokesman for the State Department. In early 1995, he was appointed White House press secretary by the President.
130 "There's a view that holds": Freedom Forum Media Studies Center, *Media Studies Journal*, Spring 1994, pp. 27–28.
133 "We got off to a rocky start": Author's interview with Dee Dee Myers, May 10, 1995.
134 "The simplest thing, the time of day": Author's interview with Helen Thomas, January 25, 1995.
135 "It was more than the new team's": Stephen Hess, "President Clinton and the White House Press Corps—Year One," *Media Studies Journal*, Spring 1994, pp. 3–4.
135 "The message here may be very simple": Frank Mankiewicz, "Can the Media Tame the Outsiders?" *Media Studies Journal*, Spring 1994, p. 19.
135 "So much of our problem was": Author's interview with George Stephanopoulos, April 7, 1995.
137 the body of deputy White House legal counsel: For a fuller discussion of the Vince Foster case, see Elizabeth Drew, *On the Edge: The*

Clinton Presidency. New York: Simon & Schuster, 1994, pp. 251–259.

138 And of course there was Whitewater: For a summary of the Whitewater issues and other character issues, see Drew, op. cit., pp. 376–393.

142 It was widely acknowledged: Ibid.

145 "That quest for balance": Kenneth T. Walsh, "America's First (Working) Couple," *U.S. News & World Report,* May 10, 1993, pp. 32–34.

146 "At that point," McQuillan recalls: Author's interview with Larry McQuillan, April 15, 1995.

146 "No amount of contact": *Media Studies Journal,* Spring 1994, pp. 163–175.

146–147 Bill Plante of CBS News adds: Ibid.

148 McLarty told friends that the drumbeat: Author's interview with Mack McLarty, December 15, 1994, and information drawn from at least a dozen interviews with McLarty from 1993–1994.

148 For a fuller account of the hiring of David Gergen, see Bob Woodward, *The Agenda.* New York: Simon & Schuster, 1994, pp. 202–214.

150 "Clinton admits he is still 'working through' ": Kenneth T. Walsh, "Clinton's Journey Inward," *U.S. News & World Report,* December 13, 1993, pp. 40–44.

155 Despite his frequent Washington-bashing: Begala later moved to Texas to become a consultant.

10: HILLARY

158–159 "The coverage often lacked seriousness": Bob Woodward, *The Agenda.* New York: Simon & Schuster, 1994, pp. 147–148.

159 "Hillary Clinton is the first First Lady": *Media Studies Journal,* Spring 1994, pp. 169–170.

159 Also in February 1994, Deborah Mathis: Ibid., p. 173.

160 "I don't think you can ever know": David Maraniss, *The Washington Post,* January 15, 1995, p. A26.

162 "Mrs. Clinton really came in hostile": Author's interview with Helen Thomas, January 25, 1995.

169 "Mrs. Clinton is full of surprises": Phyllis C. Richman, "Chewing the Fat with Mrs. Clinton," *The Washington Post,* February 17, 1995, pp. F1–4.

171 "Sometimes it's difficult": Author's interview with Hillary Rodham Clinton, February 15, 1995; excerpts were published in *U.S. News & World Report,* February 27, 1995.

11: A FAILED CHARM OFFENSIVE

176–177 "In Washington, White House special counsel": Ruth Marcus, "The White House Isn't Telling Us the Truth," *The Washington Post,* August 21, 1994.

177 "What Ms. Marcus fails to appreciate": Leon Panetta, letter to the editor of *The Washington Post,* August 31, 1994, p. A24.

12: MIDTERM: DISASTER

193 "the explosion of bad information about government": Author's interview with Paul Begala, February 28, 1995.

13: THE ARRIVAL OF MIKE MCCURRY AND THE NEWT FACTOR

198 "the level of complaints about": Author's interview with Michael McCurry, March 25, 1995.

204 "I am a genuine revolutionary": Dan Balz and Ruth Marcus, "Gingrich Calls Criticism 'Grotesque,' " *The Washington Post,* January 21, 1995, p. 1.

205 "People have begun to see": Author's interview with Brian Lamb, May 23, 1995.

205 "TV news criticism shifted": Press release from Center for Media and Public Affairs, Washington, D.C., February 22, 1995.

206 "In an odd way, Clinton's lifelong instinct": Kenneth T. Walsh, "Clinton's Many Faces," *U.S. News & World Report,* January 30, 1995, pp. 24–27.

14: STATE OF THE UNION

210–211 Opinion-makers generally panned: For examples, see the following: "The State of the President," *The New York Times,* January 25, 1995, p. 20; Robert A. Rankin, "New Image Looks a Lot Like Old One," *The Arizona Republic,* January 25, 1995, p. A1; "Clinton Returns to Themes on Which He Won in 1992," *The Washington Post,* January 25, 1995, p. A28; R. W. Apple, "State of the Union: News Analysis, A Deflated Presidency," *The New York Times,* January 25, 1995, p. 1; David S. Broder, "Squandered Opportunity," *The Washington Post,* January 26, 1995; "Clintessential," *Newsday,* January 26, 1995, p. A36.

211 "He is a man who likes to speak": "Clinton Returns to Themes on Which He Won in 1992," *The Washington Post,* January 25, 1995, p. A28.

212 "Newt's always able to handle": Kevin Merida, "Armey Insult Causes Furor in the House," *The Washington Post,* January 28, 1995, pp. A1–7.

215 "My recommendation that the governor not run": Ann Devroy, "Book Sheds Light on Clinton Past," *The Washington Post,* February 3, 1995, p. 1. Gary Hart, the former Democratic senator from Colorado, was forced to withdraw from the 1988 presidential race because of allegations about adultery that also raised questions about his credibility and judgment.

215 The second disclosure in the book: Clinton had withdrawn from

ROTC and received a high number in the draft lottery, meaning that he would not be drafted at all. Critics say he only enrolled in the ROTC program long enough to make sure he could avoid active military service. In the letter, Clinton said the only reason he had temporarily exposed himself to the draft was to "maintain my political viability within the system."

215 The same week that the *Post* published: Laurie Goodstein, "Differentiating Reputation, Character," *The Washington Post,* February 3, 1995, p. 1.

216 After all, Ronald Reagan had shown: Norman C. Thomas, Joseph A. Pika, and Richard A. Watson, *The Politics of the Presidency.* Washington, D.C.: CQ Press, a Division of Congressional Quarterly, Inc., 1994, p. 258.

216–217 John Kennedy had used the bully pulpit: Transcripts of President Kennedy's news conferences, the White House, April 11, 1962, and April 18, 1962.

217 and Theodore Roosevelt had used the prestige: Henry F. Graff, *The Presidents: A Reference History.* New York: Scribner's, 1984, pp. 404–405.

15: UPSWING

221 The real news was the extent: Kenneth T. Walsh, "Trying the Old 'Rope-a-Dope,' " *U.S. News & World Report,* March 13, 1995, p. 26. Clinton at this stage was particularly upset with three of his political advisers from 1992 whom he had retained as outside consultants: pollster Stan Greenberg, media adviser Mandy Grunwald, and political strategist Paul Begala. The President believed the trio had badly misread the voter mood in 1994. At their urging he had campaigned aggressively against the GOP "Contract with America," a plan hatched by Newt Gingrich that called for tax cuts, a balanced budget amendment to the Constitution, and other popular proposals. Clinton called the Contract a leap backward and a reprise of the wrongheaded policies of Ronald Reagan, but his approach fell flat. "He looked like he was fighting yesterday's war," admitted a White House adviser who had been a critic of the political team.

16: IN SEARCH OF A MESSAGE

228 "At some point, voters are entitled": Gloria Borger, "Sweet-talking Guy," *U.S. News & World Report,* October 9, 1995, p. 44.

231 *Newsweek's* Howard Fineman: Howard Fineman, "A Powell Scenario," *Newsweek,* September 25, 1995, p. 38–42; Jonathan Alter, "Why Powell's Race Matters," *Newsweek,* September 25, 1995, p. 43.

231 "As trust in government": John Walcott, "The Man to Watch," *U.S. News & World Report,* August 21, 1995, pp. 19–22.

231 "The general has become the nitroglycerin": Jeffrey H.

Birnbaum, "Can He Stay on the Pedestal?" *Time,* September 25, 1995, p. 32.

234 "In an interview": Author's interview with Mike McCurry, December 19, 1995.

17: THE MEDIA IN TRANSITION

236–237 "Of all evaluative references": Thomas E. Patterson, *Out of Order.* New York: Knopf, 1993, p. 19.

237 "News coverage has become a barrier": Ibid., p. 26.

237–238 "[Critics say] the journalists were not": James Deakin, *Straight Stuff.* New York: Morrow, 1984, p. 91.

238 In fact, much of the public had come to hate: Howard Kurtz, "Tuning out Traditional News," *The Washington Post,* May 15, 1995, p. A1.

238 Seventy-one percent of Americans: Stephen Budiansky, *U.S. News & World Report,* January 9, 1995, pp. 45–47.

239 "The problem is economic": Jack Farrell, in response to survey of White House correspondents conducted by the author in 1995.

240 "When I hear somebody say that": Author's interview with Brian Lamb, May 23, 1995.

240 "We [C-SPAN] might be one of the reasons": Ibid.

241 "The pressure has been on print reporters": Author's interview with Wolf Blitzer, May 17, 1995.

241 "You can be wrong as long as you're negative": Quoted in Stephen Budiansky, *U.S. News & World Report,* January 9, 1995, pp. 45–47.

241–242 "In the 1970s, most television commentary": Carl P. Leubsdorf, "Following Carter's Footsteps," *The Dallas Morning News,* June 10, 1993.

242 "everyone operates out of cynical self-interest": Quoted in Stephen Budiansky, *U.S. News & World Report,* January 9, 1995, pp. 45–47.

242 "a mean-spiritedness to American journalism": Ibid.

242 "They'll look you": Ibid.

243 A veteran White House correspondent says: Survey of White House correspondents conducted by the author in 1995.

243 "It happened during the Reagan administration": Author's interview with Bill Plante on March 1, 1995.

18: DOWNGRADING THE WHITE HOUSE BEAT

246 "All of us together": Eric Pianin and Kenneth J. Cooper, "Gingrich: 'Contract' Is Only a Start," *The Washington Post,* April 8, 1995, p. A1.

246 "I do not want a pile of vetoes": Ibid.

248 "White House correspondents" and "I'm thinking of starting": Quoted in Howard Kurtz, "The Snooze at 11: White House Correspondents Wait While Nothing Happens," *The Washington Post,* March 24, 1995, p. C1.

249 Times and technology, however, have changed: The press corps'

lack of commitment to the body watch was all the more remarkable because, with the attacks on the White House in 1994 and 1995, many reporters thought it was only a matter of time before someone made a direct attack on President Clinton himself. In the worst incident, a man sprayed the White House with bullets from an assault weapon, but no one was hurt. A few weeks later, a man was shot and killed by law-enforcement officers when he wielded a knife outside the White House on Pennsylvania Avenue. In May 1995, an armed man climbed over a fence and ventured on the south grounds. Both he and a Secret Service agent were shot and wounded.

249–250 "There's a trend that started": Author's interview with Brit Hume, April 12, 1995.

251–252 "Scratch any Democrat": Author's interview with Michael McCurry, March 25, 1995.

252 "I believe," says Jack Farrell: Response to survey of White House correspondents conducted by the author in 1995.

19: AT THE CORE OF THE PRESS CORPS

257 There are many myths and misunderstandings: During the first half of 1995, I surveyed the sixty-four reporters who are regulars at the White House—the journalists who consider their principal assignment the coverage of the presidency. I sent a detailed questionnaire to all sixty-four. Their employers included the television networks ABC, CBS, NBC, and CNN; the newspapers *The Dallas Morning News,* the *Los Angeles Times, The New York Times, USA Today,* and *The Washington Post;* the newspaper chains Copley, Cox, Hearts, Knight-Ridder, and Scripps Howard; and the magazines *Business Week, Newsweek, Time,* and *U.S. News & World Report.* I received nineteen written responses, and I interviewed an additional nine White House correspondents in person, bringing the total number of responses to twenty-eight.

259 This herd mentality is one of the most common complaints: Political scientist Stephen Hess also found considerable dissatisfaction with pack journalism when he surveyed the Washington press corps in 1981 for his study *The Washington Reporters,* for the Brookings Institution in Washington. The soul-searching within the press corps appears to have become more intense since then.

260 There have been many cultural changes: Timothy Crouse, *The Boys on The Bus.* New York: Ballantine/Random House, 1972, 1973.

260 "Now the road is filled with": Maureen Dowd, *Media Studies Journal,* Winter 1995, pp. 46–47.

265 "If one of the White House press-office": Author's interview with Helen Thomas, January 24, 1995.

266–267 "There is a definite style to the coverage": Author's interview with Brit Hume, April 12, 1995.

268 "I don't care what the food is like": Author's interview with Andrea Mitchell, January 4, 1995.

270 "Wolf justifies it by saying": Author's interview with Dee Dee Myers, May 10, 1995.

271 Myers says that there was no: Ibid.

271 Blitzer loves to tell about "the night I broke the story": Author's interview with Wolf Blitzer, May 17, 1995.

273 "The only thing that has changed is": Author's interview with Bill Plante, March 1, 1995.

275 "The reason you have to respect her": Author's interview with Dee Dee Myers, May 10, 1995.

275 "That makes the *Post* a feared publication": Author's interview with Marlin Fitzwater, May 25, 1995.

276 "A lot of journalists forget": Author's interview with Richard Benedetto, May 25, 1995.

278 "The less you know about something": Howard Kurtz, "Thinking Out Loud," *The Washington Post,* October 4, 1994, p. E1.

278 "I was a much more thoughtful person": Quoted in Ken Auletta, "Fee Speech," *The New Yorker,* September 12, 1994, p. 40.

20: WHAT'S WRONG WITH THE PRESS

281–282 A two-month study of front-page stories: Thomas B. Rosenstiel, "Reporters Putting Their Own Spin on News Events," *Los Angeles Times,* November 25, 1993, p. A1.

282 "The hard lead, the hard news": Author's interview with Michael McCurry, March 25, 1995.

282 A survey conducted by the [*AJR*]: "The Best in the Business," *American Journalism Review,* March 1995, p. 37. AJR mailed ballots to five thousand randomly selected readers; 20 percent replied.

282–283 My survey of White House correspondents: Survey conducted of sixty-four White House correspondents by the author in 1995.

283 The Center for Media and Public Affairs: Fred Barnes, "The Media on Clinton: How Tough?" *Forbes Media Critic,* Winter 1995, pp. 37–38.

284 "Reporting has been replaced": Ibid., p. 36.

284 "No show has done a better job": James Wolcott, "Mighty Mouths," *The New Yorker,* December 26, 1994–January 2, 1995, pp. 131–132.

284–285 "When we live with five hundred news channels": Author's interview with Mark Gearan, April 27, 1995.

285 "more often than not it focuses on": Kathleen Hall Jamieson made the comments during a panel discussion on CNBC, *Tim Russert: Meet the Media,* October 24, 1994, 8–9:30 P.M.

285–286 "There's been a tendency to move much more toward": Author's interview with George Stephanopoulos, April 7, 1995.

286 "great fun to read and selectively true": Paul Starobin, "A

Generation of Vipers," *Columbia Journalism Review*, March/April 1995, pp. 26–27.

287 CBS's Bill Plante said that during the Reagan administration: Author's interview with Bill Plante, March 1, 1995.

287–288 "I think the coverage reflects the nature of": Author's interview with Tim Russert, March 9, 1995.

289 "Decision-makers no longer have any room": Author's interview with Dee Dee Myers, May 10, 1995.

291 "[What's] driving so much of the adversarial relationship": Author's interview with Michael McCurry, March 25, 1995.

293 A survey taken for *U.S. News* in the spring of 1995: Survey taken for *U.S. News & World Report* by the Tarrance Group and Lake Research in the spring of 1995.

293 A survey taken by the Times Mirror Center: Howard Kurtz, "Study Suggests 'Cultural Divide' Separates the Press, the Public," *The Washington Post*, May 22, 1995, p. A6. The survey was conducted of 515 national and local journalists and two thousand other Americans in the spring of 1995.

295 "Journalists don't appreciate how mystifying": Joann Byrd, "Circle of Distrust," *The Washington Post*, November 27, 1994, p. C6.

297 In mid-May, an ABC News/*Washington Post* poll: Alicia C. Shepard, "A No-Win Situation," *American Journalism Review*, July/August 1994, p. 26.

21: BACKLASH

298 "People don't think the media tell the truth": Author's interview with Geoff Garin, April 4, 1995.

298 Newspaper reading is on a long, steady decline: Floris W. Wood, ed., *An American Profile—Opinions and Behavior, 1972–1989*. Detroit: Gale Research Inc., 1990, pp. 844–847.

299 "In American politics, there's a tendency": Quoted in Elizabeth Kolbert, "As Political Campaigns Turn Negative, the Press Is Given a Negative Rating," *The New York Times*, May 1, 1992, p. A18.

300 Jody Powell, a public-relations consultant: Author's interview with Jody Powell, April 4, 1995.

300 Libel laws could be weakened: Junda Woo, "Juries' Libel Awards are Soaring, with Several Topping $10 Million," *The Wall Street Journal*, August 26, 1992, p. B3.

301 By 1994, two years into Bill Clinton's presidency: Wood, op. cit., p. 680. Updated data provided by the National Opinion Research Center, University of Chicago.

301 This decline has paralleled: Ibid., p. 656. Updated data provided by the National Opinion Research Center, University of Chicago.

301 The depth of this negative mood: Richard Harwood, "Sad News from the Heartland," *The Washington Post*, October 15, 1994, p. A15.

302 "Journalists are now creating the coverage": Kathleen Hall Jamieson during discussion on CNBC, *Tim Russert: Meet the Media,* October 24, 1994, 8–9:30 P.M.

302 "We haven't managed to get in touch with": Joann Byrd, "Voters' Revolt," *The Washington Post,* October 23, 1994, p. C6.

303 One change that would help is for journalists: Alicia C. Shepard, "Should Journalists Take Big Bucks For Speeches?" *American Journalism Review,* May 1994, cover story. See also Ken Auletta, "Fee Speech," *The New Yorker,* September 12, 1994, p. 40.

303–304 "There was a day not far distant": Quoted in Jonathan Cohn, "Perrier in the Newsroom," *The American Prospect,* Spring 1995, pp. 15–18.

305 "Courage and competence": Kenneth T. Walsh, "The Soul and Character of America," *U.S. News & World Report,* May 8, 1995, pp. 10–11.

INDEX

military draft, avoidance of by
Clinton, 132, 189, 212, 215
minimum wage increase, 222-23
Mitchell, Andrea, 44, 45, 47, 142,
262, 283, 289
profile of, 267-69
Miyazawa, Kiichi, 97
Mogadishu, 153
Mondale, Walter, 69, 124, 263
Monkey Business, 71-72
Monroe, Bill, 85
Morris, Dick, 221-22, 226, 228
Morris, Gouverneur, 15
Mosbacher, Robert, 114, 119
MTV, Bill Clinton appearance on,
112, 130
Mudd, Roger, 303
Mullin, Dennis, 53
Murdoch, Rupert, 203-4
Murphy, Liz, 55
Murphy Brown, 109-10
Myers, Dee Dee, 5, 9, 122, 123, 127,
133-34, 140, 144, 182-83,
243, 250-51, 253, 254, 255,
256
on Ann Devroy, 275
on Brit Hume, 266
on giving news to Wolf Blitzer and
CNN, 270-71
lack of experience with press, 198
miscast as press secretary, 124
on the rush to judgment of the
media, 289
snubs press at Christmas parties, 194

NAFTA. *See* North American Free
Trade Agreement (NAFTA)
Nast, Thomas, 19
National Enquirer, 72
National Gazette, 15
National Intelligencer, 16
National Security Council, 44, 57
national-service program, 207
Naughton, Jim, 260

negativity and the media, problem of,
285-88
Nelson, Jack, 151
Nelson, Michael, 22
Nepal, 173
Neuman, Johanna, 55
New Deal, 245
New Republic, 105, 185, 270
"news management," by White
House, 31
newspaper reading, decline of, 298-99
newspapers, numbers of, 1810-1828,
17
Newsweek, 86, 223, 277, 278
erroneous story on Hillary's
commodities investments, 139
New York Daily News, 233-34
New York *Evening Post,* 17
New York *Sun,* 19
New York Times, 3, 29, 51, 86, 223,
257, 259
editorial on 1995 State of the Union
Address, 211
New York Times Magazine, Maureen
Dowd article criticizing
Clinton, 5
New York *Tribune,* 19
New York *World,* 19, 21, 23
Nicaragua, 42, 190
Nightline, 239
Nixon, Richard
antipathy against, 32
bypasses White House reporters,
32-34
death of, story on, 271-72
evaluation of, by media, 236
relationship with press corps and
"enemies list," 6
resignation, 34, 37
Nobel Peace Prize, 1906, T. Roosevelt,
217
No Ordinary Time, 166
North, Oliver, 302
North American Free Trade

KENNETH T. WALSH has covered the presidency for *U.S. News & World Report* since 1986. He is the winner of the two most prestigious awards for covering the White House, the Aldo Beckman Award and the Gerald R. Ford Prize, and is the former president of the White House Correspondents' Association. He is an adjunct professor of communication at the American University in Washington.

Mr. Walsh lives in Bethesda, Maryland, with his wife, Barclay.

ABOUT THE TYPE

This book was set in Sabon, a typeface designed by the well-known German typographer Jan Tschichold (1902–74). Sabon's design is based on the original letterforms of Claude Garamond and was created specifically to be used for three sources: foundry type for hand composition, Linotype, and Monotype. Tschichold named his typeface for the famous Frankfurt typefounder Jacques Sabon, who died in 1580.